£14.99

WITHDRAWN
from College LRC

BOURNEMOUTH & POOLE COLLEGE OF F.E.
250021894 V

# APPLIED TYPING AND INFORMATION PROCESSING
## Sixth Edition

Archie Drummond

Anne Coles-Mogford

Copyright © Stanley Thornes (Publishers) Ltd, 1994

All rights reserved. No part of this publication may be reproduced or transmitted in any form or by any means, electronic or mechanical, including photocopy, recording, or any information storage and retrieval system, without permission in writing from the publisher or under licence from the Copyright Licensing Agency Limited. Further details of such licences (for reprographic reproduction) may be obtained from the Copyright Licensing Agency Limited, of 90 Tottenham Court Road, London W1P 9HE.

First published in 1994 by:
Stanley Thornes (Publishers) Ltd
Ellenborough House
Wellington Street
CHELTENHAM
Glos. GL50 1YD
United Kingdom

**British Library Cataloguing in Publication Data**

Drummond, A. M.
 Applied Typing and Information
 Processing. – 6Rev.ed
 I. Title  II. Coles-Mogford, Anne
652.30076

ISBN 0 7487 1897 4

Typeset by Paston Press Ltd, Loddon, Norfolk.
Printed and bound in Great Britain at the University Press, Cambridge.

# INDEX

A4/A5 paper sizes, **197**
Abbreviations:
    longhand, 5, **165**
    punctuation, 75, **165**
    standard, 5, **165**
Accents, **166**
    acute, 17
    cedilla, **206**
    circumflex, **166**
    diaeresis, **206**
    tilde, 17, **166**
    umlaut, 17, 77, **166**
Access time, 122
Accuracy and speed passages (*see* Skill measurement)
Accuracy drills (*see* Drills)
Acronyms, **165**
Acute accent, 17
Additional copies, **172**
Addressee:
    alternative placement, 80, **171**
    name and address of, 18, **171**
Addressing envelopes and labels, **182**
    airmail, 17, **174**, **182**
    attention line, 17, **182**
    by hand, **170**, **183**
    care of (c/o), 17, **166**, **182**
    confidential, 17, **182**
    esquire, 17, **166**, **187**
    exercises, 17, 76
    forms of address, 17, **187**
        full punctuation, 75, **202**
        open punctuation, 17
    freepost, 17, **170**, **182**
    personal, 136, **170**, **182**
    postcode, 17, 76, **182**
    poste restante, 17, **182**
    PO Box No, 76, **170**, **182**
    private, 17, **182**
    punctuation, 76, **202**
    registered post, 76, **182**
    urgent, 17, **182**
Address, forms of, 17, 75, **187**
Adjacent key drills, 21
Agenda 10, 11, **167**
    Chairperson's, 12, 37, **175**
    public limited company, 11
Agreement, 111, **191**
Aid to centring, **168**
Airmail, 17, 76, **170**, **174**, **182**
Alignment scale, **167**
Align right margin, 53, 71–73, 76, **167**
Align typing on typed/printed line, 27–29, 92, **167**
Allocating space, 44–48, 67, 106, 153, 162, **167**
Amended print, 119, 122
Amendments to text, 10, **167**
Ampersand (&), **166**
Analysis into columns, 104, 128, 141, **213**
Annual General Meeting, 11, **195**
*Ante meridiem* (am), **166**
Aperture envelopes, **216**
Apostrophe, 55, 70, 74, 83, 119
Application, letter of, 61
Appointments itinerary, 61, **191**
Arabic numbers, **195**
Asterisk, 40, 46, 119, 121, 122, **206**
Attention line:
    envelopes, 17, **182**
    letters, 16, 18, 79, **170**
Attestation clause, 113, **192**
Automatic centring, **179**
Automatic paper insertion, **168**

Backing sheet, **168**
Balance sheets, 71, **183**

Bank paper (*see* Paper)
Bibliography, 123, **168**
Bills of Quantities, **168**
Blind copies, 81, **172**
Blocked display, 50–52, **179**, **180**, **189**
Blocked paragraphs, 2, **197**
    double spacing, 4, 31, **197**
Blocked tabulation, 56–58, 86–88, **209**
Boilerplate (*see* Document assembly)
Bold print, **168**
Bond paper (*see* Paper)
Borders, ornamental, 50, 51, **169**
Bottom margin, **168**, **193**
Brace (brackets), 41, **206**
Brief notes, 50, 82, 88, 108, 126, 134, 151, **169**
Bring forward reminders, 136, **169**
Brothers (Bros), **166**
Bullet mark 42, 108, 154, **169**
Business letters:
    additional copies, **172**
    address, forms of, **187**
    airmail, 17, **170**, **174**
    alternative placement of addressee, 80, **171**
    attention line, 16, 79, **170**
    blocked display, 16, 18
    body of letter, **171**
    by hand, 23, **170**
    carbon copies:
        additional, 16, **172**
        blind, 81, 136, **172**
    circular, 91, 92, 125, 143, **175–176**
        blocked, 91, 92
        deletion, 92
        semi-blocked, 125, 143
        tear-off, 92, 109
    column display, 71
    complimentary close:
        blocked, 15, **169**, **171**
        semi-blocked, 79, 80–81, **171**
    confidential:
        envelopes, 17, **182**
        letters, **170**
    continuation sheets:
        blocked, 18, 103, **173**
        semi-blocked, 81, **173**
    date:
        blocked, 15, 18, 20, 35, **170**
        semi-blocked, 79, 81, **170**
    designation, 17, 79, **171**
    display, **171**
        blocked, 16, 18, 103
        semi-blocked, 79, 81, 136
    enclosure, 15, 79, **171**
    envelopes, 17, 76, **182**
    folding, **173**
    form letters, 90, **186**
    forms of address, 17, **187**
    freepost, 17, **170**
    full punctuation:
        blocked, 92, 136, **170**, **202**
        semi-blocked, 81, **170**, **202**
    inset matter, **190**
        blocked, 18, 91
        semi-blocked, 79, 81, 130
    layout, **169**
    name and address of addressee, 16, **171**
        at foot of page, 80, **171**
    name of organization, 16, 79, **171**
    name of signatory, **171**
    open punctuation:
        blocked, 15–20, 35, 64, 81, **170**, **202**
        semi-blocked, 79, 80, **170**, **202**
    overseas, 19, 79, **174**
    personal, **170**
    poste restante, **170**

    postscript, 19, 79, 103, 148, **172**
    printed letterhead, 15, **170**
    private, **170**
    punctuation, **170**, **202**
    recorded delivery, **170**
    reference, 15, **170**
    registered mail, 77, **170**
    routeing copies, 16, **172**, **179**
    salutation, 15, 79, **171**
    semi-blocked:
        full punctuation, 81, **170**
        open punctuation, 79, **170**
    signatory, 15, 79, **171**
    signing, 136
    special delivery, **170**
    special marks, 15, 17, 79, **170**
    subject heading:
        blocked, 15, 16, 18, 35, 88, 91, 92, 103, 125, **171**
        semi-blocked, 79, 81, 136, **171**
    titled persons, **173**
    two-page letters:
        blocked, 18, 64, 103, **173**
        semi-blocked, 81, 82, **173**
    United Kingdom, letters to, **174**
    urgent, 15, **170**
Business reports, 133, **203**
By hand, 23, **170**


Camera-ready copy (CRC) (*see* Typing from print)
Carbon copies:
    letters, 15, 20, **172**
    additional, **172**
    blind, **172**
    photocopies, **198**
    routeing (distribution lists), 16, 77, 140, **172**, **179**
Carbon film, **174**
Cardinal numbers, **195**
Cards, 30, 62, 78, 135, **175**
    typing on, **175**
Care of, 17, **166**
Caret sign, **206**
Catchwords, 81, **175**
Cedilla, **206**
Cent, **206**
Centimetres (cm), 3, **166**
Centred display, 78, **179**
Centred headings, 106, **179**
Centred tabulation (*see* Tabulation)
Centring:
    automatic, **179**
    horizontal, **179**
    vertical, **179**
Centring key, 2
Chairperson's Agenda, 12, **175**
Chapter headings, 47, **175**, **188**
Charts:
    flow, 90–101, **184**
    organization:
        blocked, 95, 96, **196**
        centred, 97, 98, **196**
Checking work (*see* Proofreading)
Circular letters, **175**, **176**
    blocked, 91, 92, 125
    deletions, 92
    indented, 143
    tear-off portion, 92, 109
Circulation lists, 77, **179**
Circumflex, 67
Civil decorations:
    forms of address, **187**
    titled persons, **173**
Clean and uncreased work, **176**
Closed capitals, 2, **180**


**Key**
Page numbers in roman (upright) type—Exercises
**Page numbers in bold type**—Data Bank entries

iii

# Key

Page numbers in roman (upright) type—Exercises

business letters:
blocked, 16, 18, 171
semi-blocked, 79, 171
Display:
Disk, 179
Disk drive, 179
Diagrams (see Allocating space)
Diaeresis, 206
semi-blocked, 79, 172
blocked, 15, 172
Designation
spelling (see Drills)
others, 178
Deliberate errors:
Deletions, 92, 186, 187
Degrees, university, form of address, 17, 187
Degree sign, 3, 41, 84, 178, 206
Default margin, 193
Decimal tab key, 178
Decimal tabulation, 56, 79, 84, 116, 117, 178
Decimals, 178
Decimalized enumeration, 8, 133, 182
Dead keys, 178
Dates, general, 33
semi-blocked, 81, 170
blocked, 15, 170
Date, business letters:
Datalink, 122
Data Files, ix, 163, 178
Data Bank, ix, 165
Daisywheel (see Single-element machines)
single, 42, 88, 206
double, 206
Dagger:
Cursor, 178, 216
Curriculum vitae, 60, 177, 178
Currency codes, 208
Courtesy title, forms of address, 17, 187
Correction signs (see Proofreaders' marks)
Correction of errors, 177
Copy of a document, 176
Continuous stationery, 176
Continuous dots (see Leader dots)
reverse side, 173
other documents, 45, 47
memo, 24, 173
semi-blocked, 81, 173
blocked, 18, 173
business letters:
Continuation sheets
Consistency, x
letters, 170
envelopes, 17, 182
Confidential:
Computer terminology, 128
Composing from brief notes (see Brief notes)
semi-blocked, 79, 171
blocked, 15, 171
Complimentary close:
Compact disk, 122
Combination characters (see Special signs, symbols and marks)
Column totals, 61, 71, 90, 122
centred, 84, 211
vertical, 85–87, 104, 141, 212
blocked, 57, 68, 69, 149, 211
subdivided:
oblique, 88, 212
centred, 84, 87, 210
blocked, 57, 58, 210
multiple:
centred, 84, 88, 209
blocked, 56–58, 86–88, 209
Column headings:

centred, 78, 106, 179
effective display, 50, 51, 179, 180
layout:
horizontal, 189
vertical, 190
Distractions, 33
Distribution lists, 77, 140, 172, 179
Ditto marks, 136, 179
Divide into, 3, 206
Division of words, 4, 192
Division sign, 3, 206
Doctor, forms of address, 17, 187
Document presentation, x
Document assembly, 117
Dollar sign, 206
Dotted lines, 28, 187, 211
tabulation, 211
Double dagger, 206
Double-letter drill, 9
Double-page leaflet, 51–54, 65, 131, 139, 184, 185
Double spacing, 4
Double underscore, 71, 72, 215
Down reaches drill, 9
Draft copy, 42, 121, 180
Drills:
accuracy, 1, 9, 14, 21, 26, 39, 43, 49, 55, 59, 70, 74, 83, 89, 94, 110, 114, 118
adjacent keys, 21
apostrophe, 55, 70, 74, 83, 119
answers, 161
double-letter words, 9
down reaches, 9
figures, 1, 9, 14, 21, 26, 39, 43, 49, 55, 59, 70, 74, 83, 89, 94, 110, 114, 118
first and fourth fingers, 83
fluency, 14
home and bottom row, 43
home and third row, 39
letter combinations, 9
right- and left-hand, 49
second and third row, 70
shift key, 1
speed, 1, 9, 14, 21, 26, 39, 43, 49, 55, 59, 70, 74, 83, 89, 94, 110, 114, 118
spelling, 1, 9, 14, 21, 26, 39, 43, 49
answers, 161
subject and verb agreement, 89
answers, 161
symbols, 1, 9, 14, 21, 26, 39, 43, 55, 59, 70, 74, 83, 89, 94, 110, 114, 118
third and fourth rows, 74
up reaches, 14
Dropped heading, 47, 48, 175
Effective display, 50, 51, 180
Electronic dictionary (see Spelling)
Electronic typewriters, xi, 180
Elision, 136, 181
Ellipsis, 31, 47, 48, 68, 122, 181
Emboldened, 181
Emphasis, 50, 181
Employment, x
Enclosure, 15, 171
Endorsements, 113 (see also Legal documents)
Enumeration
arabic, 6, 7, 10, 11, 12, 13, 24, 41, 42, 45, 77, 111, 113, 119, 121, 181
decimalized, 8, 133, 182
roman, 7, 12, 28, 129, 142, 154, 181
Envelopes and labels:
addressing, 17, 76, 182
airmail, 17, 76, 174
attention line, 17, 182
by hand, 17, 183
care of (c/o), 17, 182
confidential, 17, 182
esquire, 17, 182
forms of address, 17, 187
freepost, 17, 170, 182
overseas, 77, 174
personal, 136, 182
postcode, 15, 76, 182
POP envelopes, 182
PO Box No, 76, 170, 182
poste restante, 17, 170, 182
private, 71, 182
punctuation:
full, 76, 202
open, 17, 76, 202
registered post, 76, 182
sizes, 182
special delivery, 17, 76, 182
special marks, 17, 76, 182
urgent, 17, 76, 182
window, 216
Equation sign, 40, 206
Ergonomics, 119
Erasing, 177
Errors, correction, 177
Esquire, 17, 166, 187
Examination hints, x
Exclamation mark, 206
Exempli gratia (eg), 166
Fair copy, 183
FAX (Facsimile), 55 (S/M 10)
Feet, 3, 206
Figure drills (see Drills)
Figures (see Numbers)
Figures and words, use of, 7, 217
Figures in columns, 71–73, 183, 195
Figures in continuous matter, 195
Financial statements:
A4 landscape, 73
Balance sheet:
horizontal, 71, 183
vertical, 72, 184
Income and Expenditure Account, 71, 183
Receipts and Payments Account, 146, 183
First and fourth finger drills, 83
Fit, 184
Floppy disk, 179
Flow charts, 99–101, 107, 111, 184
Fluency drill, 14
Flush right facility (see Word processor symbol and Aligned right margin)
Folded leaflets, 51–54, 65, 131, 139, 184, 185
Folders, 32
Folding:
leaflets, 184, 185
legal documents, 192
letters/memos, 113, 173
Footnotes, 40, 41, 42, 46, 47, 117, 119, 122, 133, 185
tabulation, 41, 57, 58, 86, 88, 185
Form layout, 27–29, 127, 186, 187
completion, 27–29, 36, 65, 127, 187
preparation, 27–29, 107, 150, 186
Form letters, 90, 109, 186
Forms of address, 17, 187
For the attention of, 17, 170, 182
Fractions:
sloping, 40, 187
underscore/underline, 187
vulgar, 40, 188
Freepost, 17, 170, 182
Full punctuation, 75, 76, 202
Gateway, 122
Golf ball head (see Single-element machines)
Gram(s) (g), 166
Grave accent, 187
Guide to document presentation, x

Half-space corrections, **188**
Handwritten brackets, 41
Hanging paragraphs, 77, **197**
Hard copy, **188**
Hard disk, **179**
Headings:
   centred, 106, **189**
   chapter, 47, **175**, **188**
   columns:
      blocked, 56–58, **209**
      centred, 84–88, **209**
   dropped, 47, **175**
   main:
      blocked, 1, 2, **189**
      centred, 78, 106, **189**
   oblique, 88, **212**
   paragraph:
      blocked, 2, 5, 23, 42, 119, **189**
      indented, 79, **189**
   shoulder, 2, 5, 7, 8, 18, 23, 24, 44,
      45, 60, 67, 81, 92, 121, 129, **189**
   side, 3, 13, 62, 64, 119, 122, **189**
   subdivided column:
      blocked, 57, 58, 69, 149, **212**
      centred, 84, **211**
   subheadings:
      blocked, 2–5, **189**
      centred, **189**
   subject (*see* Business letters)
   vertical, 85–87, 104, 141, **212**
Home and bottom row drill, 43
Home and third row drill, 39
Horizontal centring, 78, **179**
Horizontal display, **189**
Horizontal ruling, 56–58, 84–88, 141, 149, **209**
House style, **190**
Hyphen (minus sign), 3, **190**
Hyphen to replace 'to', **206** (*see also* Hyphen)

Identification code, 122
*Id est* (ie), **166**
Impact printers, **172**
Imperial measurements, 3, **165**
Inches, 3, **206**
Income and Expenditure Account, 71, **183**
Indented paragraph, 79–81, **197**
Ink ruling, **210**
Input, **190**
Inserting paper, **168**
Insertion mark (caret), **201**
Insert space, **201**
Inset matter, 18, 45, **190**
   business letters, 48, 81, 92, **190**
   other documents, 42, 48, **190**
Inside address (*see* Name and address of addressee)
Integrated Production Typing, 32
   Log Sheet 1, 34  2, 63  3, 102
        4, 124  5, 138  6, 147
   urgent documents, 33
Interliner, **190**
Internal telephone index, 76, **213–214**
International currency codes, **208**
Inter-office memoranda (*see* Memoranda)
Interruptions, 33, 63, 108, 126, 138, 147
Introduction, x
Invitations, 78, **191**
Italic (slanted), 40, 47, 121–123, 155, **191**
Itineraries, 62, **191**

Junior, 76, **187**
Justified right margin, 123, **191**

K equals one thousand, 25, 135, **195**, **196**
Keyboard (design and position), xi
Keyboard reviews (*see* Drills)
Kilogram(s) (kg), 3, **166**

Labels, addressing, 17, 76, **182**
Language arts:
   apostrophe, 55, 70, 74, 83
      answers, 161
   spelling (*see* Drills)
   subject and verb agreement, 89
      answers, 161
Laser printer, **198**
Last Will and Testament, 113, **191**
Layout, display, **179**, **180**
Layout of forms, 27–29, **186**, **187**
Leader dots (leader lines):
   forms, 27–29, **187**
   other documents, 76, **211**
   tabulation, 56, 58, 71, 72, 85, 87, 88, 141, 149, **211**
Leaflet, folded, 51–54, 65, 131, 139, **184**, **185**
Legal documents:
   Agreement, 111, **191**, **192**
   attestation clause, 113, **192**
   endorsement, **192**
   folding, **192**
   Will, 113, **191**, **192**
Letter combination drills, 9
Letter of application, 61
Letterheads, printed, 2, 15, **170**
Light pen, 122
Lighting, office, 120
Limited (Ltd), **166**
Line-end division of words, 4, **192**
Linespace selector, 4
Literary work, **193**
Litre sign, 3
Locating information (Data Files), **178**
Logo, **193**
Log Sheet, Typist's, 32, 34, 63, 102, 124, 138, 147
Longhand abbreviations, 5, **165**
Lower case, **201**

Mailable documents, 32
Main headings:
   blocked, 2, **189**
   centred, 78, **189**
Manuscript, 2
   two-page exercises, 45, **173**
Margins:
   aligned right, 53, 71–73, 76, **167**
   bottom, **168**, **193**
   centring on typing line (*see* Display)
   default (pre-set), **193**
   justified, 123, **191**
   reverse, **204**
   side, 6
   standard, 6, **193**
   temporary (*see* Inset matter)
   top, **168**, **193**
Measurements, typing, 3, **193–194**
Meetings, Notice of, 10, **195**
   Annual General Meeting, 11, **195**
Memoranda, **194**
   A5, 10, 22, 40, 108, 126, 134, 140
   A4, 23, 50, 68, 77, 140, 152
   A4 (two page), 24
   special marks, 22, 23, 108
Menu, 30, 65, 68, 77, 151
Messrs, **187**
Metric measurements, 3, **166**
MICR (Magnetic ink character reader), 122
Microwriter, 122
Military decorations, forms of address, **187**
Minus and plus signs, hyphen, 40, **192**, **206**
Minute sign, **206**
Minutes of Meetings, 13, **195**
Modification and rearrangement:
   other documents, 41, 42, 77, **195**
   tabulation, 58, 104, 131, 141, **195**

Money, sums of, **208**, **215**
Multiplication sign, 40, **206**

Name and address of addressee, 16, **171**
   at foot of page, 80, **171**
*Nota bene* (NB), 165
Notice of Meetings, 10, 11, **195**
Numbered items (*see* Enumeration)
Numbering of pages, 47, **196**
Numbers:
   arabic, **195**
   cardinal, **195**
   in columns, **195**
   in continuous matter, **195**
   ordinal, **195**
   roman numerals, **195**, **204**, **205**
   totals, **215**
   use of minus sign, 40, **194**, **206**
   use of plus sign, 40, **206**
Numerals, roman, **204**, **205**

Oblique (/), 88
Office environment, 119
Omission of words, 31, 47, **181**
Open punctuation, 75, 76, **202**
Optical character recognition (OCR), **183**
Ordinal numbers, **195**
Organization charts, **196**
   blocked, 95, 96, 98
   centred, 97, 98, 145
Ornamental borders, 50, 51, **169**
Overseas mail, 77, **174**

Page numbers, 47, **196**
Pagination, 47, **196**
Paper and paper sizes, **196**, **197**
Paragraph headings, **189**
   blocked, 2, 5, 8, 23, 42, 119, **189**
   indented, 79, **197**
   spacing, **189**, **197**
Paragraphing, **197**
   blocked, 2
   blocked (double spacing), 4
   hanging, 77
   indented, 79, 81, 143, **197**
Paragraph sign, **206**
Paragraphs, standard, 93, **207**
Parentheses (brackets), 41, **206**
Personal (special mark):
   envelopes, 23, 136, **182**
   letters, 80, **170**
   memo, 24
Personal letters, **197**
   blocked, 20, 61
   semi-blocked, 80
Photocopying, **172**, **198**
Pitch, **198**
Play, 115, **198**
Plus sign, 40, **206**
PO Box number, 76, **170**, **182**, **183**
Poetry, 116, 117, **198**, **199**
POP (Post office preferred) envelopes, **182**
Postcards, 30, 62, 102, 108, 135, **199**
Postcodes, 17, **182**
Poste restante, 17, **170**, **182**
*Post meridiem* (pm), **166**
Postscripts, 19, 79, 103, 148, **172**
Post town, **182**
Posture, xi
Posture chair, 119
Press release, 137, **199**
Pre-stored margins, **193**
Pre-transcription reading, 31
Print, typing from, 119–122, **215**
Printed forms, **186**, **187**
Printed heading, **170**
Printers, **172**, **198**, **200**
Printer's bracket, 68

**Key**
Page numbers in roman (upright) type—Exercises
**Page numbers in bold type**—Data Bank entries

v

# Key

Page numbers in roman (upright) type — Exercises

Private (special mark), 170, **182**
Production development, viii
Production target time (see Timing)
 production rate, **203**
Production typing (see Integrated Production Typing, viii, 32)
Productivity, viii
Programme, 53 (see also Folding leaflets)
Proofreaders' marks, **201**
Proofreading, **202**
 exercises, 31, 150–160
 keys, 161
Proportional spacing, **202**
Proxy form, 28
Public Limited Co (PLC), **166**
Public Limited Co Agenda, 11
Punctuation, 75, 76, **202**

Quotation marks, 31, 47, 48, 117, **203**

Ratchet release (interliner), **190**
Rate of production, **203** (see also Timing)
Rearrangement of:
 other documents, 42, 77, **195**
 tabular matter, 104, 128, 141, **195**
Recorded delivery:
 envelopes, **182**
 letters, **170**
Reference:
 blocked, 16, **170**
 semi-blocked, 79, **170**
Registered mail, 76, **170**
Registry Information Form, 29
Repetitive printing, **203**
Repetitive Strain Injury (RSI), xi, 4, 119
Reports, 133, **203**
Resource material, 33
Reverse side, typing on, **204**
Reviews (see Drills)
Ribbons, **204**
Right- and left-hand drills, 49
Right margin, aligned, 67, **167**
Right margin, justified, 123, **191**
Roman numerals, 195, **204, 205**
 blocked to left, 7, 12
 blocked to right, 28
enumerations, 7, 12, 28, 129, 142, 154, **181**
Routing copies, 172, **179**
RSVP, 78, **191**
Ruled lines, typing on, 27, **187**
Ruling, tabulation, 56–58, 84–88, 141, 149, 209
Run on, **201**
Salutation, 15, **170**
Second and third finger drills, 70
Seconds sign, **206**
Section sign, **206**
Semi-blocked letters (see Business letters)
Senior, **187**
Shift key drills, 1
Shoulder headings, 2, 7, 8, 18, 24, 44, 45, 60, 67, 81, 92, 121, 129, **189**
Side (standard) margins, 6, **193**
Side headings, 3, 13, 62, 122, **189**
Signatory, **171**
Signed letters, 136, **173**
Signs, symbols and marks, 40, **206**
Single-element machines, **205**
Sizes of paper, 196, **197**
Skill building, viii

Skill measurement, viii, 1
 one minute, 1, 39, 70
 two minutes, 9, 43, 74
 three minutes, 14, 49, 83
 four minutes, 21, 55, 89
 five minutes, 26, 59, 94, 110, 114, 118
 six minutes, 132
Sloping fractions, 40, **187**
Soft copy, **205**
Solutions and Resource Material, ix, 33
Space, allocating, 44, 45, 67, 153, **167**
Spaced capitals, 3, 7, **180**
Special delivery, **170**
Special marks:
 envelopes, 17, 76, **171**
 letters, 15, **170**
 memo, 22, 23, **170**
Special signs, symbols and marks, 40, **206**
Specialized typing, **207**
Speeches, 137, **207**
Speed and accuracy (see Skill measurement)
Speed drills (see Drills)
Spelling, **207** (see also Deliberate errors)
Spelling drills, 1, 9, 14, 21, 39, 43, 49
 answers, 161
Square brackets, 3, **206**
Square root, 40, **206**
Standard abbreviations, 6, **165**
Standard margins, 6, **193**
Standard paragraphs, 93, **207**
Standard sizes of paper, 196, **197**
Stationery requisition, 32
Subdivided headings, tabulation (see Tabulation)
Subheadings:
 blocked, 2, 3, 4, **189**
 centred, 106
Subject and verb agreement, 89
Subject heading (see Business letters and Memos)
Subscripts, 40, **207, 208**
Sums of money:
 in columns (Totals), 215
 in context, **208**
 international currency codes, **208**
Superfluous wording, 33
Superscripts, 40, 58, **208**
Symbol drills (see Drills)

Tabulation, **208–213**
A4 landscape paper, 73, 149
columns of figures, 71, 72, **212**
decimal, 56, 79, 84, 116, 117, **178**
footnotes, 57, 58, 69, 88, 149, **212**
headings:
 column:
  blocked, 56–58, 69, 86–88, 209
  centred, 84, 85, 87, **209**
 multiple-line:
  blocked, 57, 58, **210**
  centred, 84, 87, **210, 211**
 oblique, 88, **212**
 subdivided:
  blocked, 57, 58, 69, 149, **212**
  centred, 84, **211, 212**
 vertical, 85–87, 104, 128, 141, **212**
paper lengthwise, 149
leader dots, 56, 58, 71, 72, 85, 87, 88, **141, 211**
rearrangement of, 104, 128, 141, **213**
reference signs and footnotes, **212**
ruling, 56–58, 84–88, 141, 149, 209

Tailpiece, 51, **213**
Tear-off portion, 92, 109, **176**
Teleconferencing, 122
Telephone area code, **214**
Telephone index, 76, **213–214**
Text-editing instructions, 162
Text-editing machine, **214**
Theory and conventions (see Guide to document presentation and Mallable documents)
Third and fourth finger drills, 74
Thousand (equals K), **206**
Tilde accent, 17, **166**
Time (24-hour clock), **215**
Timed exercises (see Timing)
Timing, 32
Titled persons, **173**
To (use of hyphen), **206** (see also Hyphen)
Top margin, **193**
Totals, **215**
Travel itinerary, 61, **191**
Twenty-four-hour clock, **215**
Two-page exercises, 45, 171, 172, **196**
Typeface styles, **215**
Typing element (daisywheel), **205**
Typing from print, **215**
Typing reverse side (see Reverse side)
Typist's chair, 119
Typist's Log Sheet, 32, 34, 63, 102, 124, 138, 147

Umlaut, 17, **206**
Underscore/underline:
 double, 71, **215**
 emphasis, **180**
University degrees, 17, **187**
Up reaches drills, 14
Urgent:
 envelopes, 17, **182**
Integrated Production Typing, 33
 letters, 15, 79, **170**
 memos, 22, 108
Urgent typing, 33, 63, 108, 126, 138, 147
User-friendly, 122

Variable linespacer, **216**
Variables, 90, 109, **216** (see also Form letters)
Vertical Balance Sheet, 72, **184**
Vertical centring, **190**
Vertical column headings, 85–87, 104, 141, **212**
Vertical ruling, 56–58, 84–88, 141, 149, 209
Vertical spacing (see Rearrangement of tabular matter: saving space)
Videostream, 122
Visual display unit (VDU), xi, **216**
Voice commands, 122
Vulgar fractions, 40, **188**

Will, 113, **191**
Window envelopes, 148, **216**
Word division, 4, **192**
Word processing exercises, xi, 12, 16, 17, 19, 20, 41, 42, 46, 51, 54, 58, 60, 62, 71, 72, 79, 86
Word processing terms, 122
Word processor symbol, xi
Word processors, xi, **216**
Words and figures, 7, **217**
Workstation, x

# PREFACE

Advanced technology is making it practical for business people to work from their cars, from aeroplanes, from hotel rooms and, of course, from home.

They will have:

Their machines to transmit facsimile documents.
Their car telephones linked to their electronic offices.
Their personal computers sending messages around the world by satellite.
Their Qwerty keyboard and function keys with which to receive and despatch vast amounts of information.

Therefore, to meet the changes being brought about by the effect of technology on office work, you must not only have the confidence and ability to produce neatly typed and mailable transcripts, but must also develop proficiency in certain skills that will make you more employable and give you greater opportunity for promotion in the electronic office.

A new vocabulary has evolved with the development of electronic machines, and the efficient operator must be highly skilled in proofreading and editing for accuracy in word usage, spelling, punctuation and grammar. In addition, as a typist with an **intermediate** qualification, you should have had experience in:

1 Decision-making skills.
2 Setting priorities.
3 Working under pressure.
4 Following instructions (verbal and written).

Further, you should be aware of the capabilities of integrated information systems and have the ability to operate an electronic keyboard efficiently.

As an **advanced** typist, you should have a high degree of proficiency in typing, an understanding of a wide range of business documents, and be skilled in the presentation of clean, mailable copies without error and within a given time, together with the ability to deal adequately with the rearrangement and typing of tabulation, statistical and technical reports, forms, lists, etc.

The advanced typist seeking employment with responsibility or looking for promotion should have:

1 The ability to use materials and time economically and effectively.
2 The ingenuity to organize the workload and workstation for greater efficiency.
3 The confidence to manage the obligations of responsibility and authority.
4 The expertise to manipulate skilfully the keyboards and the various devices found on computers, word processors and electronic typewriters.
5 A clear understanding of the concepts and applications of the automated office.

*Applied Typing and Information Processing, Sixth Edition*, has been designed and planned to give you a high degree of success in meeting the objectives outlined above. It has been thoroughly revised and offers the intermediate and advanced typists a comprehensive and modern typewriting programme. The extensive Data Bank of theory and typing conventions has also been updated. This text will meet the needs of candidates for Stages II and III of any typewriting examination and for:

The LCCI Private Secretary's Certificate and Personal Executive Secretary's Diploma.
The RSA Teacher's Certificate in Office Studies.
The City and Guilds Further and Adult Education Teachers' Certificate.

While your aim, no doubt, is to gain an examiner's certificate, we have also kept well to the fore the needs of business, and many exercises are based on material, layout and standards required by an employer. However, we would mention that, while this textbook gives the best advice, layout and exercises that are possible after a great deal of research into office requirements and examiner's needs, you may find that your employer, or examiner, will ask you to display a document in a slightly different style from that given in the textbook. An employer and an examiner may, for a great variety of reasons, require certain matter to be set out in what could be considered an unusual style. But that is their prerogative! In such instances, follow the layout of a previously typed document or follow instructions. In business, you must conform to the wishes of your employer; in an examination you follow instructions. In both, you must be consistent in layout, spelling, punctuation, use of words and figures, etc.

*Applied Typing and Information Processing, Sixth Edition*, thus combines a realistic modern approach with the carefully planned unit structure of the previous editions. Each of the units is divided into two sections.

**Preface**

# Preface

## Skill building

In order to be able to carry out the various kinds of typing required in an office, or in an examination, you will have to improve your basic typing power, and this section provides a consistent review of the typing and machine techniques that will increase speed and improve accuracy. The **skill building** pages contain:

1. A review of the alphabet keys, figures, signs, symbols and marks.
  (a) When typing the **speed practice**, aim for speed and type at a rapid, controlled rate. Wherever possible, time yourself and work towards not more than two errors for each minute typed.
  (b) When typing the **accuracy practice**, aim for accuracy. Time yourself and set a standard of not more than one error for each minute typed.
  (c) Figures and symbols—practise diligently until you reach a level of speed and accuracy comparable with that in (b).

2. Intensive drills on:
  (a) Adjacent keys, down reaches, double letters, first and fourth fingers, fluency, home and bottom row, letter combinations, second and third row, shift key and up reaches.
  (b) **Spelling skills**   Before typing the drill, find the word misspelt; make a note of any words that cause you difficulty and type them at every available opportunity.
  (c) **Proofreading**   Because proofreading is such an important part of your training, we give greater emphasis and a greater variety of proofreading exercises on pages 156–160. We strongly recommend that these exercises be completed each time they are mentioned in the **skill building** pages.
  (d) **Language arts skills**   In addition to the drills on spelling and proofreading, there are a number of exercises providing a review of the **apostrophe** and **subject/verb agreement**. Frequently refer to and type these reviews.

3. **Skill measurement**   As only you or your tutor will know whether, at any given time, you should be practising for speed or accuracy, we have called the speed/accuracy material skill measurement, and a choice must be made as to whether the practice should aim at increasing speed or working for greater accuracy. There is a skill measurement chart in the **Solutions and Resource Material** on which you should record your progress. We believe that controlled but random and unselected vocabulary is the most effective way of building typing skill and, therefore, the difficulty of copy in the skill measurement exercises has been graded according to the syllabic intensity. Syllabic intensity is the average number of syllables per word contained in a passage and gives you an indication of the relative difficulty of the copy. In *Applied Typing and Information Processing, Sixth Edition*, you are presented with graded and controlled copy so that you build speed with accuracy and sustain your speed for gradually lengthening periods of time. For a further explanation see page 1.

## Productivity

Office productivity refers to the amount of work produced by each person employed in the office. You could work in a busy office, but it need not necessarily be a productive office, which is one where employees create complete, concise, error-free and appropriate information within a given time and at the lowest possible cost.

## Production development

Both speed and accuracy are components of production skill, and this section of each unit provides a thorough review of all machine and typing techniques and develops them to the higher levels required for fast and accurate production typing; also, it introduces (or revises) all the theory and conventions that you will need for instant decisions, in order that you may complete a particular task accurately and within a given time. In business, you must follow the house style preferred by your employer; in examinations, you should follow the layout and instructions—if neither are given, follow the typewriting conventions in this textbook. Candidates taking the advanced stage of any typing examination should be capable of using any style of display.

The course moves gradually from the very simple to the complex and you will have to:

Take decisions and make judgements—paper, margins, display, etc.
Follow oral and written instructions.
Abstract information and details from unorganized sources.
Copy information from previously completed tasks.
Compose correspondence from notes.

## Integrated Production Typing

Our objective here is to simulate typical office typing, and the tasks are preceded by a Typist's Log Sheet which gives the name of the organization, the originator's name and department, additional

v

directions for operators using word processors, text-editing electronic typewriters and correction only electronic typewriters. For further details about timing, folders, mailable documents, etc, please read pages 32 and 33.

### Information processing procedures

Although you may not have access to word processors, electronic typewriters, and computers with word processing capabilities, you should take every opportunity to familiarize yourself with the terminology. We have included information processing terminology throughout the text, and wherever we considered it appropriate we have mentioned information processing concepts and applications that would apply to the operations being practised. We hope these points will enable you to prepare more fully for the electronic office. Further, we have suggested certain tasks that may be used as **input**, and **text-editing changes** are listed separately.

### Data Files

These are on pages 163–164 and from the details listed under a **filename**, you have to select information to complete certain exercises (names, addresses, prices, standard paragraphs, etc).

### Data Bank

This section contains all the theory and typewriting conventions that have been acceptable practice over the years. As you work through the production development exercises, you will find frequent references to the Data Bank which starts on page 165. It is important that you turn to the page stated and read the appropriate section if you are unsure about how the particular exercise should be displayed.

### Solutions and Resource Material for Students and Tutors

This is a separate book which suggests possible answers to all exercises not displayed in *Applied Typing and Information Processing, Sixth Edition*; these examples give paper sizes used, margins and tab stops together with calculations for horizontal and vertical display where appropriate. When you have typed an exercise, compare it with the solution and note any differences, taking care to see that you have carried out all the instructions. It also contains letterhead paper, forms, etc, which may be duplicated and which will make your typing much more meaningful. In the sixth edition, there are a number of pages covering language arts skills—punctuation, subject and verb agreement, word comparisons, comparatives/superlatives, etc.

### Practical Typing Exercises, Book Two, Third Edition

Because of the wide variety of documents covered in *Applied Typing and Information Processing, Sixth Edition*, it has not always been possible to give, in this textbook, the additional exercises for which many tutors and students have asked. Therefore, the third edition of *Practical Typing Exercises, Book Two*, contains further examples of exercises introduced in *Applied Typing and Information Processing, Sixth Edition*. Also, users of word processors, electronic typewriters, and computers with word processing capabilities will find a number of exercises that may be used as input together with text-editing changes listed at the end of the book.

### Acknowledgements

We wish to express our gratitude to the following authors for their kind permission to use extracts from their writings:

Christopher Beddows: *Communication and the World of Work*
John Dossett-Davies: *Evans the Bridge, The Freedom to Travel*, and *Life's Rich Feast*
Bea Holmes and Jan Whitehead: *The Practical Secretary*
Kathleen Trotman: *Modern Secretarial Procedures*
Central Scotland Police, Community Safety Department, and Jim Butler of the Falkirk District Community Safety Panel who gave us the idea to include the articles on crime prevention.

Finally, we sincerely thank our colleagues for their valuable help and suggestions as well as for assisting with the copying of the manuscript work.

The pages that follow will give you a comprehensive and complete coverage of typewriting conventions and practice, together with sufficient information to help you to understand information processing terminology and techniques, and we hope that this will give you a sound basis on which to build your future. We see the electronic office as an absorbing and stimulating place in which to work—a place of changes and challenges—and if you are both flexible and receptive to change, and willing to adapt to new office equipment, your future would seem assured. We wish you well and hope that your expertise will bring you satisfaction and a rich reward.

Archie Drummond
Anne Coles-Mogford

**Preface**

# Introduction

To make sure you understand the objectives you have to aim for, you must read this introduction (and the preface) and refer to it from time to time.

## Guide to document presentation

Over the years, certain conventions with regard to display and layout of typewritten documents have become accepted practice. While examining bodies and employers do not now worry unduly about layout as long as the document is clean, attractive and correct (no typing, spelling, or grammatical errors), we do suggest that you use the 'theory'/conventions given in this textbook as a guide.

There is no one correct style of layout for any typed document. In a business letter, there is no reason why you should leave only one clear space between the different parts before the salutation; a short letter will look more attractive if you leave two or even three spaces, but be consistent! However, it would be ridiculous to turn up six single spaces between the parts. In any situation, where **specific instructions** are given, these must be followed precisely.

## Employment

Many employers will be adamant about how a particular document should be displayed, because a uniform style increases efficiency and reduces costs. If there are few variations in style, the mechanics of typing become automatic. Also, most electronic machines and word processors have preset margins which, if desired, need not be changed. The advantage of **uniformity** is obvious: a consistent style does not call attention to itself but enables the reader to concentrate on the meaning. Be consistent with spelling and the use of capitals. Do not type an abbreviation in one paragraph and then type the same abbreviation in full in the next paragraph. Also, be consistent in the use of words and figures, open and full punctuation, style of headings and enumeration.

If your employer does not indicate a house style, or give you a specific format, then you are more or less free to use your own initiative, but the nearer your layout and style are to what is considered appropriate display (mainly based on typewriting conventions) the more acceptable the finished document is likely to be.

## Examinations

Examiners are allowing greater latitude in the layout used by candidates, and this is to be welcomed. Certain examining bodies insist that candidates must attempt each task; otherwise, they fail the examination. This means that examination candidates should not be indecisive about formatting and typing documents, and, in the absence of specific instructions, must be able to complete the work with confidence. We suggest that the necessary self-assurance, theoretical knowledge and practice can be acquired only by following a particular course of training which offers the fundamentals, the necessary refinements, and speed plus accuracy to prepare the typist for an advanced examination and a responsible post. *Applied Typing and Information Processing, Sixth Edition*, offers the typist exactly this type of training.

## Language arts

In business today, and more so in the electronic office of tomorrow, typists must be proficient in the application of English language skills and have a comprehensive knowledge of modern business technology. Typists taking an advanced typewriting examination, or seeking a post of responsibility, should:

1. Have a good knowledge of words and their meanings.
2. Know how to spell correctly.
3. Know how to form plurals, compound words and possessives.
4. Know how to punctuate.

We all find difficulty in **spelling** certain words and, to help you overcome some of the more common spelling errors, we have included spelling drills in the skill building pages. When typing these words, pay particular attention to the sequence of letters and make a note of words that cause you difficulty. Also included are drills on the use of the **apostrophe** and **agreement** of subject and verb.

Word errors (spelling errors, typing errors, wrong use of the apostrophe, etc) are included in a number of exercises in this textbook. To help you, these word errors are circled and you must type the word(s) correctly. In the Integrated Production Typing, there are word errors that are **not** circled—you must find them and correct them. See also *Solutions and Resource Material* for simple explanations of use of words and grammar.

## Workstation

A workstation is defined as the place where an employee performs his/her office tasks, and the object of the modern workstation is to help the individual increase productivity. However, the most up-to-date workstation will not in itself increase your output if you do not have all your needs to hand and, at the same time, make good use of today's office aids, furnishings and machines.

Arranging your workstation carefully will not only help to increase your output; in addition, it will give you a more comfortable and pleasant workplace. Reserve the top of your desk for the materials you will use constantly. At all times you must have quick access to:

Note-pad, telephone message forms.

All types of stationery (bond paper for top copies, bank paper for carbon copies) including envelopes, labels and carbon paper.

Pens, pencils, rulers, correction paper/fluid/eraser, paper clips (a tray with built-in dividers is indispensable for these items).

Reference materials: dictionary, calendar, telephone directory, telephone index, office reference manual, pocked-sized calculator, etc.

Personal items should be kept at the back of a bottom drawer.

Items normally kept inside drawers, or on shelves, should be returned immediately after use.

Disks should be stored upright (not stacked) and **must** be returned to the disk file when no longer required and particularly at the end of the day; keep related disks together—perhaps a disk-file box for commercial software, another for current work, and yet another for seldom-used disks.

## *Posture*

An adjustable desk is preferable. The height of the working surface should be between 660–700 mm (26–30 inches) and should not reflect light. The surface must allow ample space for the VDU screen, keyboard and other accessories such as note-pad, stationery, reference materials, etc. The framework of the desk should have no sharp corners or edges. There should be adequate leg room underneath the work surface.

## *The keyboard*

Keyboard design and position may have adverse effects on the users.

1 The keyboard should be separate from the screen.
2 The front frame of the keyboard should be parallel with the front edge of the desk.
3 The keyboard should be positioned so that the letter J is opposite the centre of the body.
4 The body should be about a hand-span away from the edge of the desk.
5 Hands should not rest on the frame of the machine.
6 The forearms should be on the same slope as that of the keyboard—elbows slightly lower than the home keys.
7 Elbows should be close to the body.
8 Wrists should be flat.
9 The chair should be adjusted so that thighs are approximately horizontal, calves vertical, and feet squarely on the floor.

Repetitive motion studies are suggesting new keyboard designs and work patterns in order to protect wrists and hands against carpal tunnel syndrome and other problems.

## *Repetitive Strain Injury (RSI)*

Ever since our first publication in 1963, we have advocated and emphasized the need for correct posture at the keyboard. For many years RSI has been a common ailment in industrial jobs, but only recently have office workers, particularly word processor operators and typists, complained. This affliction can be minimized by correct positioning of the hands, correct stroking of the keys, suitable seating, reduction of tension and undue pressure, perfecting of typing techniques and rest periods away from the keyboard.

Employers who introduce equipment and furniture without planning how and where it will be used are letting themselves in for employee complaints that range from eye strain, blurred vision, pins and needles, numbness, headaches, backaches and wrist problems. When employees are not comfortable and happy in their work environment, absenteeism and workers' compensation claims increase while production drops.

## *VDU screen*

Wherever possible:

1 Position the body so that you are looking straight ahead at the VDU—avoid looking at the screen sideways.
2 Lean forward from the hips—do not bend your shoulders.
3 Eyes level with the top of the screen and between 16 and 30 inches from the screen.
4 Use adequate lighting and see that there is no glare on the screen from daylight or artificial light.

**NOTE** For details about posture, chair, etc, please see pages 119–120.

## *Electronic typewriters and word processors*

 This is the symbol that we will use to draw your attention to information and instructions for **electronic typewriters** and **word processors**. In business today, it is important that you understand how these machines may be employed to format more easily a great variety of documents.

The text-editing instructions are given on pages 162–163. In the top right corner of the hard copy, write the filename and keep all the hard copies in alphabetical order (according to the filename) in a folder. Text-edited copies of the word processing exercises are in the *Solutions and Resource Material* and may be duplicated for class use.

**Introduction** xi

## Words and figures

1 Use words instead of figures for:
    1.1 The number one on its own.*
    1.2 Figures at the beginning of a sentence.
2 Use figures in all other cases.

* If number one is part of a list of figures, it should be typed as a figure, eg 'Follow the instructions in 1, 2 and 3'.

**NOTE** These are the basic rules, but other methods may be used.

## Workstation

See page x.

# SKILL BUILDING

Type each line three times and, if time permits, complete your practice by typing each group once as it appears.

Margins:
12 pitch 22–82
10 pitch 12–72

### A  Keyboarding skills

1  Speed      We should like you to call on us at home one day quite soon.
2  Accuracy   Kay was amazed by the number of subjects that Max discussed.
3  Figures    Read pages 123 and 234, and sections 56, 67, 78, 89, and 90.
4  Symbols    He said, "Send Jean's cheque (£23.80) to J Franks & Co Ltd."

### B  Review shift key

5  Adam, Sally, David, Frank, Gregg, Harry, James, Kelly, Lynn.
6  Mary, Nancy, and Oliver are going to Penrith on Sunday next.
7  Queeny, Roger and Vera will visit Tom at Ullswater in March.

### C  Spelling skill—correct the one misspelt word in each line
           —see page 161 for answer

8   arguing ensuing debatable enforceable desireable serviceable.
9   accommadation manageable resourceful inconvenient necessary.
10  Lawrence Brown was a resourceful and ingeneous business man.

## Skill measurement

As only the student and/or teacher will know whether, at any given time, the student should be practising for speed or accuracy, we have called the speed/accuracy practice material *skill measurement*, and a choice must be made as to whether the practice should aim at increasing speed or working for greater accuracy.

We suggest that you begin by typing as much as possible of the first skill measurement passage below and establish your speed.

(a) If in the first timing you have not more than one error, your aim should be to increase by five words a minute the speed reached in the first typing. For example, if your present speed with not more than one error is 35 words a minute, your starting point for building speed should be 40 words a minute.

(b) If you have more than one error in the first timing, continue to practise the passage at the speed reached in the first timing until you can type it with not more than one error. As the length of timing increases by one minute in each of the next four units, you should continue to practise at the selected speed up to the end of unit 5.

At the beginning of units 6, 11, 16 and 21 endeavour to increase your speed by five words a minute. Each time the speed is increased, practise the one-minute timing until you reach the goal within the error tolerance, and then continue with the next four units at the same speed. Your ultimate goal should be a minimum of 80 words a minute with not more than four errors.

When you have selected your starting speed for the skill measurement exercises, type as much of the following passage as you can in one minute and continue with your practice until you can type within the accuracy standard indicated. On the special skill measurement chart, in the *Solutions and Resource Material*, record the number of words typed, number of minutes, and number of errors for the final typing.

### Skill measurement            One-minute timing            Not more than one error

S/M1  If the new shop is to be ready in June, there are a few jobs   12
      that must be done at once.  First, we must find a person who   24
      is able to make some effort to put this business on its feet   36
      again, and, further, I am sure that the person must be given   48
      a free hand as to how many people we should employ and what   60
      pay each will receive for full-time work.         (SI 1.19)   68

       1  |  2  |  3  |  4  |  5  |  6  |  7  |  8  |  9  | 10 | 11 | 12 |

**UNIT 1**                    *Skill building*

etc, after keying in. On certain word processors, the underline key will give a neater 'join' when ruling vertical and horizontal lines.

## Variable linespacer

You will find the variable linespacer (sometimes called cylinder release) on the left cylinder knob. By pressing in (or pulling out on some machines) the variable linespacer, you release the spacing mechanism, and the cylinder can be moved to any desired position.

It is used for:
Filling in form letters.
Typing on ruled lines.
Finding the correct alignment when paper has been reinserted to make a correction.

## Variables

Items that differ from one to another. See *Forms*, pages 186–187, *Form letters*, page 186, and *Standard paragraphs*, page 207.

## Vertical display

See *Display*, page 179.

## Visual display unit

A word processor has a visual display unit (sometimes referred to as a cathode-ray tube (CRT)). This is a screen, similar to a television screen, on which you can see what you have typed. While the typing is on the screen, alterations and amendments may be made. The typist moves the cursor (a moving marker which indicates to the typist the point at which the next character may be typed) across the screen to a mistake, the correction is typed over the mistake or the wrong character is erased by the correction key and the correct character is inserted.

The checked and corrected typing is transferred to the permanent memory by pressing a particular function key, and the print-out of the document on the screen takes place when the print key is pressed.

## Window/aperture envelopes

A great many organizations now use envelopes from which a panel has been cut out at the front; they are known as window/aperture envelopes. The object of the window envelopes is threefold:

1. It saves time in typing the name and address on both letter and envelope.
2. It avoids the possibility of error in copying the address on to the envelope.
3. It eliminates the almost impossible task of typing envelopes on certain printout machines where an envelope feeder is not fitted.

The name and address of the addressee must be typed so that, when the document is folded, the position of the address will coincide with the cut-out portion on the envelope. To help the typist, the position of the cut-out is shown on the headed paper by marks in the corners of a rectangle or by a ruled box. Window envelopes usually have a transparent cover over the cut-out part; aperture envelopes do not. Any special marks (for the attention of, urgent, etc) should be typed, in the box, two spaces above the name and address and must be visible when the folded sheet is placed in the envelope.

## Word processors

Throughout this textbook we have referred to **word processors** where we felt it appropriate, and we hope that the following brief notes will be of help.

The word processor consists of four basic components (referred to as a workstation):

1. QWERTY keyboard, plus function keys.
2. Disk drive.
3. Visual display unit (VDU) sometimes referred to as the screen.
4. Printer.

The keyboard has the same arrangement of keys (letters, figures, shift keys, space bar, etc) as the typewriter and, in addition, has function keys (command keys) for giving instructions. For example, if there is a function key marked 'centre', this key will be depressed to tell the system to centre a heading or line of type, etc. The keyboard may be part of the unit or a separate component that can be placed in the most agreeable position to suit the well-being of the operator.

Once an operator understands word processing concepts, and can identify the steps involved in **input** and **output**, he or she will have little difficulty in transferring from one make of word processor to another.

The most common storage medium used in word processing is the **floppy disk**. This disk is inserted into the **disk drive**, in much the same way that a cassette is inserted into a recorder. The **printer** is the device that produces the **hard copy** or **print-out**.

U/V/W     Data Bank     216

# PRODUCTION DEVELOPMENT

*See pages 188, 189*

## Main headings, Subheadings and Shoulder headings

1  Type the following exercise on A4 paper in single spacing. Margins: 12 pitch 22–82, 10 pitch 12–72.

*TYPIST – Leave one clear linespace, ie, turn up 2 single spaces, at points marked with a cross.*

A D V A N C E D   T E C H N O L O G Y

✗

Personal Computers

✗

It is obvious that both companies and individuals require personal computers with a performance specification, not only for today, but also for the future. As software becomes more sophisticated, so should the computer which runs it.

✗

QUALITY PERFORMANCE

✗

The most efficient computer will be able to handle the latest in computer software – word processing, spreadsheets, graphics, database, desktop publishing & accounting packages.

✗

PRINTER

✗

To get the maximum benefit from your computer, it is important to have a printer that is fast and versatile. Choose between a laser, bubble-jet, daisywheel or dot matrix.

*See page 189*

## Paragraph headings

2  Type the following exercise on A5 portrait paper in single spacing. Margins: 12 pitch 13–63, 10 pitch 6–56.

*TYPIST – Either type the paragraph headings in bold as shown, OR underline them.*

DESKTOP PUBLISHING

Print your own stationery

A very convenient and cost-effective method of producing leaflets, stationery, forms, etc, is to use a desktop publishing package.

**Letterhead stationery**  You can design and print the amount of letterhead paper you require, and make alterations to the logo as and when necessary.

*TYPIST: Leave 2 clear character spaces after ea. para. heading.*

**Variety**  With the vast variety of fonts available with a desktop publishing package, and by adding borders, tints, shadows, graphics, boxes and shapes, documents can be designed to suit every need.

---

**UNIT 1**    *Main headings, Subheadings, Shoulder headings, Paragraph headings*    **2**

typing—large typeface for main headings, pica typeface for subheadings, italic typeface to emphasize particular words, etc.

## Time

### 1 Twenty-four hour clock

As international travel has become more popular, we are all more aware of the 24-hour clock. It always consists of four figures with no full stops; for example:

0001 hours (one minute after midnight) 0700 hours (7.00 am) 1200 hours (noon) 1300 hours (1.00 pm) 1800 hours (6.00 pm) 2359 (11.59 pm). Midnight is always represented by the word 'midnight'.

### 2 am/pm and o'clock

Words or figures may be used with o'clock: one o'clock, 9 o'clock. Use **am** and **pm** with figures with no space between the two letters; see examples above. There is a full stop after each letter when using full punctuation, eg 4.00 p.m.

## Totals

When typing totals proceed as follows:

1  Type the underscore for the first line above the total. **Do not** turn up before typing this line.
2  Turn up twice and type the total.
3  Turn up once and type the line below the total.
4  Turn the cylinder up slightly by using the interliner lever and type the second line. Then return the interliner to its normal position.

**NOTE** The underscore in total must extend from the first figure to the last figure as in the example below.

```
                              £
                          1,643
                          2,456
Do not turn up →          1,021
Turn up two spaces →
                         £5,120
Turn up one space →      ======
```

## Typeface styles

See also *Pitch*, page 198.
In addition to the standard pica and elite, a wide selection of typefaces (styles and sizes) is available—italic, script, extra light or dark faces and a number of others.

International typefaces (German, French, Spanish, etc) are also available.

## Typing from print

Today, most firms keep on hand a wide variety of type sizes and styles for use in typing documents of all kinds and especially for preparing camera-ready copy (CRC). The increasing use of electronic keyboards and other sophisticated machines now available for desktop publishing, means that many organizations print their own circulars, leaflets and catalogues. When copying from print, make judicious use of the following in order to effect more eye-catching headings, subheadings, etc.

1  Where a word(s) is in italic print, underline the word when typing.
2  Where a word(s) needs to be emphasized, use bold face, underscore (not if you are already using the underscore for italic print) or closed capitals.
3  Main heading in spaced capitals three spaces between words with/without underscore/bold face.
4  Subheading in closed capitals with one or two spaces between words, with/without underscore/bold face.
5  Other subsidiary headings: Initial capital(s) and lower case letters with/without underscore/bold face.
6  Shoulder headings and paragraph headings with/without underscore/bold face.

Consider the relative value of the various headings before you start typing and place the emphasis accordingly. For the sake of clarity and smooth continuity, you must be economical in the use of any one form of emphasis; otherwise, the value of that method will be lost.

## Typing on reverse side of paper

See *Reverse side of paper*, page 204.

## Typist's Log Sheet

See page 32.

## Underscore/underline keys

The **underscore** key, to be found on all QWERTY keyboards, is included on the **word processor** keyboard but cannot be used for underscoring: it could be used for inserting horizontal lines. The **underline** key is the one used for underlining words and the method of automatic underlining varies from one machine to another. On some machines, when the correct function key is depressed, word(s) will be underlined as the text is keyed in; also, there is usually a facility for underlining a word, sentence,

## Side headings

*See page 189*

3 Type the following on A4 landscape paper in double spacing. Margins: 12 pitch 37–82, 10 pitch 27–72. Set a tab stop at 22(12) for start of side headings and the main heading and subheading.

C E L E B R A T I O N   S T A M P   1 9 9 2   *Turn up ½ a space*
                                                *∴ 2 spaces*

Completion of Single European Market

*Unspaced caps*

POSTAGE           In October 1992 the Royal Mail issued a
STAMP             special single market stamp to mark the
                  completion of the Single European Market.

DESIGN            The stamp depicted a yellow star on a
                  blue background and was designed by David
                  Hockney.

DENOMINATION      First-class stamp.

COMMUNITY         The star element was taken for the
FLAG              European Community flag which
                  features 12 stars – one for ea.
                  Member State.

## Measurements

*See pages 193, 194*

4 Type the following exercise on A4 paper in single spacing. Follow the layout given.

            MEASUREMENTS AND TEMPERATURE          *NB: Underscore the side headings*
            COMPARISONS   *(lc + u/score)*

            Metric and Imperial    To convert inches into centimetres
            Measurements           multiply by 2.540; feet to metres
                                   multiply by 0.3048, and miles to
                                   kilometres multiply by 1.609.  Often
                                   it is only necessary to make approx-
                                   imate conversions between metric and
                                   imperial measurements.  As a guide

                                   1" = 2.5 cm           1 lb = 0.4 kg
                                   1 l = 1.75 pints
                                   1 sq in = 6.5 cm$^2$

            Temperature            32 °F = 0 °C; 68 °F = 20 °C

            Sizes                  The sizing of clothes and shoes varies
                                   between Britain, USA and the Continent
                                   of Europe. The equivalent of a size 6 shoe
                                   in America is 7½, & on the Continent 39½.

UNIT 1 — See Practical Typing Exercises, Book Two, page 1, for further exercises on *Side headings, Measurements*

made to take them. The surname is usually typed first, in upper case letters, followed by the initial(s) and then the address, all on one line if possible. If two lines are needed, these must be in single spacing as the strip is usually not more than 6 mm ($\frac{1}{4}$ inch) in depth. In order to carry the eye from the end of the address to the telephone number, continuous dots may be inserted, leaving one clear space before the first dot and one clear space after the last dot.

**NOTE** Samples of an index, or alphabetical list, are given below in open and full punctuation. With open punctuation commas are not usually inserted, but extra spaces are left between the parts. In the examples below it will be seen that the right margin has been aligned.

## *Open punctuation*

BROWN   A J   46 Thomas Street   Leeds   LS2  9JT ................................................................... 0532  213756
FISHER   L   & Co Ltd   20 Clitton Road   Northampton   NN1  5BQ ................................................. 0604  686868

## *Full punctuation*

BROWN, A. J., 46 Thomas Street, Leeds. LS2  9JT ...................................................................... 0532  213756
FISHER, L., & Co. Ltd., 20 Clitton Road, Northampton. NN1  5BQ ............................................... 0604  686868

## *Change in telephone area codes*

On 16 April 1995 all area codes will change. The United Kingdom geographic codes will have a 1 inserted after the initial 0. For example, the Dundee code changes from 0382 to 01382; the London code 081 will be 0181, etc. Bristol, Leeds, Leicester, Nottingham and Sheffield will each receive entirely new codes to help meet the rapid growth in demand for telecom services in these cities.

All international dialling codes will change from the 010 prefix to 00. This will bring the United Kingdom into line with the rest of Europe, as required by EC legislation.

## *Text-editing machines (word processors, computers, electronic typewriters)*

Specialists who studied the work done by office typists found that a great deal of time was spent in retyping documents that had been slightly altered, or retyping documents that required only minor alterations in wording and layout. As a result of this research, text-editing machines were designed with storage and revision capabilities.

They are automated pieces of equipment (with QWERTY keyboards and function keys) on which the material is typed and recorded on some form of medium for playback or for correction; therefore, text editing refers to the revision of documents that have already been recorded. The machines use magnetic disk, floppy diskette, or hard disk as a recording media.

Some text-editing machines have a 'temporary' memory, which means that if the machine is turned off, the matter just typed will be lost. Other machines will retain matter for a certain period of time. The more complex machines can be instructed to transfer the typing to 'permanent' memory or external storage.

When using a text-editing machine, the correction of typing errors no longer causes difficulty. Most have a simple backspace-strikeover sequence (backspace and strike the correct character over the error) to correct an error. When revising or reformatting text, it is possible, on the more sophisticated machines, to move a page, paragraphs or sentences from one section of a document to another.

**We would like to emphasize that although the correction of errors is very simple on text-editing machines, it is still time-consuming, and accurate typing in the first instance is imperative.**

The type font (all the characters in a particular type style) may be a golf ball head or a daisywheel and the font may be changed at any time while typing on an electronic machine, thus enabling the typist to give emphasis or style to a particular piece of

# Division of words
## Blocked paragraphs – Double spacing

See pages **192**, **197**

5  Type the following paragraphs exactly as they appear and note where we suggest that the words may be divided. Use A4 paper. Margins: 12 pitch 22–82, 10 pitch 12–72.

```
          DISABLED DRIVERS

  Orange Badges  ← (Highlight)

  The new orange badge for disabled drivers includes a photo-
  graph, and it should be displayed loosely on the fascia, not
  stuck to the windscreen.

  All badge holders can now park for up to 3 hours, instead of
  2, on yellow lines.  Orange badge holders can no longer park
  in a cycle lane.

  There are 2 new groups who are now entitled to a badge auto-
  matically, those who have war pensioners' mobility supple-
  ment, and those who have a severe disability in their upper
  limbs and cannot turn a steering wheel.

  You can get an orange badge from the social services depart-
  ment.  To qualify, you must have considerable difficulty in
  walking due to a permanent and substantial disability.
```

6  Type the following exercise on A4 paper in double spacing. If you feel that the right margin will be unsightly, divide a word at an appropriate point. Margins: 12 pitch 22–82, 10 pitch 12–72. (These margins have not been used in the exercise below.)

```
  REPETITIVE STRAIN INJURY

  Prevention


  The most common work-related illness today is known as repetitive

  strain injury (RSI).  Almost 7 million keyboard operators could be

  at risk.  At the moment up to 200,000 people in the UK have RSI,
                                 (in the neck, back, arms, hands and/or fingers)
  which can cause severe pain.  The disability can last for months,

  even years, but may be alleviated by regular physiotherapy.


      Prevention is easier than cure.
```
Measures shd be taken to ensure th operators are correctly trained; th adjustable chairs + footrests are used, if nec; th the VDU screen is separate from the keyboard + a copyholder is provided; th regular breaks are taken; th light + temperature are suitable; th employers arrange, + pay for, eye tests + spectacles (if req'd).

A European Community Directive wh became law in '92, sets out the minimum health + safety requirements for VDU operators, & must be complied with.

---

**UNIT 1**   *Division of words, Blocked paragraphs – Double spacing*   **4**

The scale points for these lines must be marked in pencil and the following procedure should be adopted:

11.1 In the usual way, find the horizontal spaces required for the column items and the spaces between the columns. Rule the first horizontal line, but add one extra column, ie if the longest line in the column is three, and three spaces have been left between the columns, then add six extra spaces to the first horizontal line.

11.2 Find the number of vertical spaces required for the headings in the same way as for vertical headings (see 10 on page 212). Leave the required number of spaces and rule the second horizontal line in the usual way.

11.3 Along the second line, mark in pencil the scale points for the vertical lines between columns (which will also be the scale points for the **bottom** of the oblique lines), and set tab stops for the start of each column as usual.

11.4 Mark the scale points for the **top** of the oblique line as follows:

11.4.1 The top of the first oblique line should be marked at the same scale point as the second vertical line, the top of the second oblique line at the same scale point as the third vertical line, etc.

## 12 Rearrangement of tabular matter

12.1 It is often necessary to rearrange the matter. Before starting to type, it is essential that you make a rough plan of what has to be done.

12.2 When columns in tabulation are very wide, it is necessary to consider where space can be saved. The following hints will be of help to you in such cases.

12.2.1 If the longest lines of the columns are in the headings, additional lines may be taken for these, so as to reduce the width required for the columns.

12.2.2 If the longest lines are in the descriptive column, the length of these lines may be reduced by taking extra lines for lengthy items. If this is done, allowance must be made for these extra lines when calculating the number of vertical lines required.

12.2.3 As a last resort, you may have to leave one space only between vertically ruled columns or a minimum of two spaces between unruled columns.

12.2.4 A small typeface will save space, eg 15 pitch.

12.3 It is unwise to carry a table forward to a second page and would be done only in exceptional circumstances. To **save vertical space** consider one of the following:

12.3.1 Do not rule any horizontal lines except for totals of figure columns (if there are any) when you should underline immediately under the last line of figures in the column, turn up **one** and type the total, **do not** turn up before inserting the final underscore. Examination candidates should note that if they are instructed to rule lines, then they must.

12.3.2 Turn up once after the main/subheading and rule first horizontal. Turn up **once** after horizontal and type column headings.
Insert underscore **without** turning up after the last line of the column headings.
For intermediate lines and the final horizontal line at the end of the table, **do not turn up** before the line, but turn up once after.

12.3.3 Turn up once after main/subheadings and insert first horizontal. After first horizontal, turn up half a space and type column headings.
After last line of column headings turn up one-and-a-half spaces before typing second horizontal.
Turn up one-and-a-half spaces before typing the final horizontal.

**NOTE** Whatever method is used, it is essential to be consistent, ie, leave the same space after the horizontal and before the headings as there is after the headings and before the second horizontal, or before or after intermediate horizontals and before the final horizontal.

## *Tailpiece*

This is an illustration or ornamental motif at the end of a page, unit or chapter and is made up by combining characters, such as hyphen, colon, etc.

```
        : - : - : - : - : - :
          - : - : - : - : - 
            : - : - : - :
              - : - : -
                : - :
                  -
```

## *Telephone index*

It is usual to keep a list of names, addresses and telephone numbers that are frequently required. For this purpose, use may be made of the strip-indexing method whereby each name, address and telephone number are typed on a separate strip. The strips are inserted alphabetically in devices or frames specially

## Abbreviations

See page **165**

**7** Type the following exercise on A4 paper in double spacing. Margins: 12 pitch 22–82, 10 pitch 12–72. Retain the abbreviation EC.

### BRITAIN'S HISTORIC ACRE

**Hectares.** It will be necessary for farmers to measure their fields in hectares, ie, 2.471 acres, after 31 Dec 1994 when an EC Directive comes into force. This will bring Britain into line with the rest of the EC.

**Acres.** The acre (4 840 sq yd) has been used in Britain since Saxon times and is seen as part of Britain's heritage. It was defined by Edward I as the amount of land a yoke of oxen could plough in a day.

**Change.** It is possible that a number of older farmers particularly, will experience difficulties in coming to terms with the changeover, but it is thought that they will acknowledge that it is necessary.

**8** Type the following exercise on A5 portrait paper in single spacing. Margins: 12 pitch 13–63, 10 pitch 6–56.

### EUROPACK CO LTD

**Cat items 4042, 3026 & 1097**

The miscellaneous items I received from your organisation on Thursday of this week were not as shown in the advert on p21 of your company's catalogue.

I am returning them to you immediately at your expense, and at some inconvenience to myself, and should be glad if you would send me the correct items as soon as possible.

I believe that your business has published a new catalogue, and should be glad to receive this also when you forward the replacement goods.

**NOTE** When the Maastricht Treaty was implemented in November 1993, the words European Union (EU) were introduced; these will not replace EC but will be used to describe new areas of cooperation between members.

**UNIT 1** — *Abbreviations* — **5**

blank lines taken so far in typing the column headings is four. If the words 'Departure on' are typed on the line beneath '9 nights' '12 nights' and the words 'or between' typed on the line below that, they will be centred to the headings already typed.

6.9 With the alignment scale at the base of the words '9 nights' turn up one single space. From the left margin find the centre point of the longest line in the first column. From this point backspace once for every two letters and spaces in the line 'Departure on'. At scale point 27(18) type the words 'Departure on'. Turn up one single space.

6.10 Centre the next line 'or between' in the same way, and type it at scale point 28(19), then turn up two single spaces and type the horizontal line.

6.11 Turn up two single spaces and type the column items remembering to type units under units, tens under tens, etc. Centre the hyphen where there are no figures given.

6.12 Turn up one single space before inserting the last horizontal line and mark the points at which the vertical lines will be placed.

## 7 Subdivided column headings—blocked style

If you use blocked-style tabulation, then it is not necessary to centre subdivided headings vertically or horizontally. Starting points for headings will be the left margin and the tab stops for each column. Each column heading will start on the same horizontal line which will be the starting point for the deepest heading.

## 8 Columns of figures

In columns of figures, care must be taken to see that units are typed under units, tens under tens, etc. When figures are in thousands and above, you may leave a space between hundreds and thousands, thousands and millions or you may put in a comma, eg 1,326,978; 793,220; or 1 326 978; 793 220.

## 9 Reference signs and footnotes

Tabular work frequently has footnotes to explain some references to the figures or details in the table. The same points apply to these footnotes and their corresponding reference signs in the body of the tables as those already explained for manuscript work, ie the footnotes are typed underneath the table in single spacing with double spacing between each. The reference sign in the body is typed immediately after the item to which it refers and is always a superscript. In the footnote, the sign may be typed either on the same line or as a superscript, and one space is left after the sign and before the start of the typing.

It should be noted that when you use the asterisk on the keyboard (not a combination character of x and hyphen) then the sign will be a superscript and any other footnote signs used in the same exercise must be superscripts. Usually there is no ruled line before a footnote in tabulation. With word processors it is usually impossible to type a dagger/double dagger—instead, use two/three asterisks, or any other sign on the keyboard.

## 10 Vertical column headings

Headings to the columns may be typed vertically, either for emphasis or because of lack of space.

To find the number of linespaces to be left between the first and second horizontal lines to allow for the vertical headings, count the number of character spaces in the longest line of the heading and add three extra character spaces (one before and one after the longest line, and one for the second horizontal line). If you are using 12 pitch, divide this number by two to find how many spaces to leave for the headings. For example: longest line contains 11 characters $+3 = 14 \div 2 = 7$. Type the first horizontal line, turn up seven single spaces and type the second horizontal line. If you are using 10 pitch, the calculation is more complicated, and we suggest that you type the longest heading on a piece of paper and measure, with a ruler, the space occupied.

Complete the tabulation and rule before reinserting the paper into the typewriter lengthways. Type the vertical headings. It is usual for all headings to start at the point fixed for the longest heading, even if the tabulation is typed in the centred style of display. The headings will be centred between the two vertical lines.

If the headings are typed downwards, they can be typed first with each letter of the heading typed one under the other and the ruling completed in the usual way.

## 11 Oblique column headings

Headings to the columns may be typed obliquely, usually for greater emphasis.

To type oblique headings it will be necessary to insert the paper into the typewriter diagonally, as the headings must be typed parallel to the oblique lines and centred between the two. Rule the table and, when the paper is reinserted, type the headings, the oblique lines being aligned with the alignment scale.

## Standard margins

*See page 193*

**NOTE**  In business, and in most examinations, you will have to decide on the margin settings; therefore, in many exercises we will not give you margins either in 12 or 10 pitch. Use the following short table as a guide.

| | | | |
|---|---|---|---|
| A5 portrait paper | Typing line 50 spaces | 12 pitch 13–63 | 10 pitch  6–56 |
| A4 and A5 landscape paper | Typing line 60 spaces | 12 pitch 22–82 | 10 pitch 12–72 |
| | Typing line 70 spaces | 12 pitch 18–88 | 10 pitch  6–76* |
| | Typing line 80 spaces | 12 pitch 13–93 | 10 pitch – not suitable |
| Memoranda | | 12 pitch 13–90 | 10 pitch 11–75 |

*Use only in exceptional circumstances.

## Enumeration

*See page 181*

**9**  Type the following exercise on A4 paper using suitable margins.

C O U N C I L    T A X

<u>Find out more</u>

*TYPIST: Please replace the word 'regional' with the word 'local' throughout the exercise.*

The Council Tax replaced the community charge or "poll tax" on 1 April 1993.

1  The Council Tax is a regional tax set by regional councils to help pay for regional services.

2  There is one bill per dwelling, whether it is a house, bungalow, flat, maisonette, mobile home or houseboat, and whether it is owned or rented.

3  The bill is based on the relative value of your property to others in your regional area.

4  Your home is placed on a valuation list in one of 8 Council Tax **valuation bands** as follows - *[Highlight "valuation bands"]*

  A  up to £40 000
  B  over £40 000 and up to £52 000
  C  over £52 000 and up to £68 000
  D  over £68 000 and up to £88 000
  E  over £88 000 and up to £120 000
  F  over £120 000 and up to £160 000
  G  over £160 000 and up to £320 000
  H  over £320 000

5  Council Tax Benefit of up to 100% is available for people resp for Council Tax bills who are on income support, or low incomes.

6  The Council Tax bill is payable by the owner/occupier(s) or tenant(s), including Council tenants.

---

**UNIT 1**    *Standard margins, Enumeration*    **6**

first line of the deepest heading just typed. From this point turn up one and a half spaces and start typing the next deepest heading. Use the same method as in 4.2.6 and 4.2.7.

4.2.12 Continue with other column headings in the same way.

## 5 Leader dots (leader lines)

Leader dots (full stops) are used to guide the eye along lines from one column to another. There are four methods of grouping which may be used, viz.

5.1 One dot three spaces .   .   .   .   .
5.2 Two dots three spaces ..   ..   ..   ..
5.3 Three dots two spaces ...   ...   ...   ...
5.4 Continuous dots ..................
5.5 Continuous dots are the simplest and are recommended unless you receive instructions to the contrary. Type leader dots lightly and evenly. When using continuous leader dots in a tabulated statement, move carriage/carrier to first tab stop and backspace one for each space between the columns **plus one**. At that point type last leader dot. Leave one space after the last typed character and then complete the leader dots.
5.6 If any item in the column takes more than one line, the leader dots should be typed only on the last line of the item.
5.7 When using grouped dots (5.2 for example) care must be taken to see that the groups of dots come underneath one another in all lines. To ensure this, you should adopt the following procedure: bring the carriage/carrier to the first tab stop set for the second column; backspace once for every space between first and second columns plus an extra two spaces. At this point set a tab stop. Backspace five from the tab stop just set, and set another tab stop. Continue in this way until you have reached the last word of the shortest line in the particulars column. Bring carriage/carrier back to margin and type first line, and using tab bar/key insert leader dots as and when required.

## 6 Subdivided column headings—centred style

Tabular statements may have subdivided columns. A column heading may be further divided into two or three separate items which are displayed beneath the main column heading as three separate columns. The example overleaf is exercise 3, on page 84, and the steps explained below will give you an idea of how to proceed. Paper used is A5 landscape.

6.1 Set left and right margins and tab stops.
6.2 Centre and type main heading.
6.3 Type first horizontal line, turn up two single spaces.
6.4 Move carriage/carrier to tab stop 47(38), and tap in one space for every two characters and spaces in the longest items in the two columns beneath '9 nights', ie Twin Single, and half the number of spaces between the two columns. This will bring you to the centre point, ie 53(44). From this point backspace once for every two characters and spaces in the heading '9 nights'. At this point 49(40) type the heading. It will then be centred over the two columns beneath.
6.5 Move to tab stop 63(54), and tap in one space for every two characters and spaces in the longest items in the two columns beneath '12 nights', ie 1,025 Single, and half the number of spaces between the two columns. This will bring you to the centre point, ie 69(60). From this point backspace once for every two characters and spaces in the heading '12 nights'. At this point 65(56) type the heading. It will then be centred over the two columns beneath.
6.6 Turn up once and type the horizontal line. Mark the top of the vertical lines, and keep a note of the scale points. Turn up twice.
6.7 Type each of the words 'Twin' and 'Single' at the tab stops.
6.8 The two lines of the heading in the first column 'Departure on or between' must be centred vertically. The number of lines of typing and

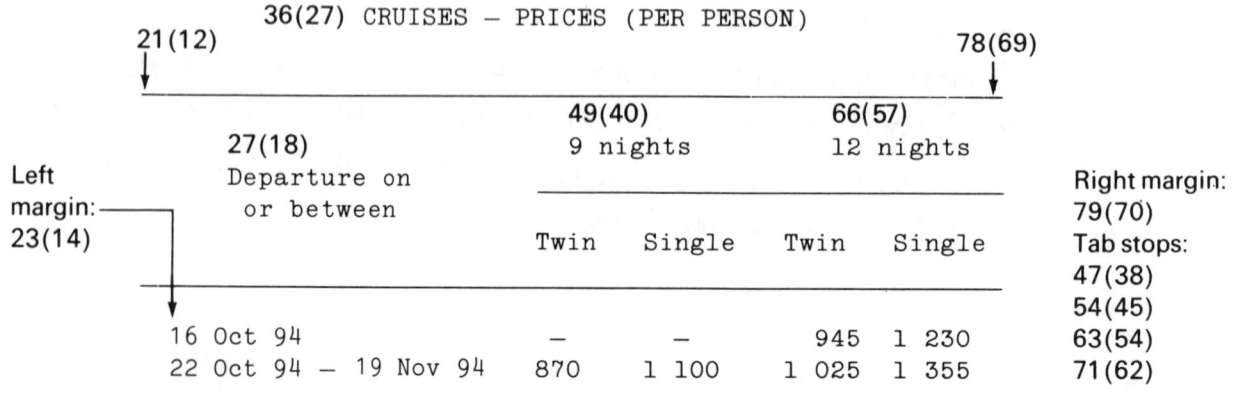

T    Data Bank    211

**10** Type the following exercise on A5 portrait paper. Although the exercise is in single spacing here, use double spacing and suitable margins.

F O O D   H Y G I E N E   *TYPIST – Emphasize paragraph headings, please.*

Shopping

1 WELL LIT, CLEAN AND ORGANIZED SHOP

   (a) **Staff** should not handle prepared food with bare hands. Look for cleanliness and helpfulness.

   (b) **Check** that no out-of-date food is on sale. There should be no damaged packs left on display. Note carefully the 'sell by' & the 'best before' dates on the package.

**11** Type the following exercise on A4 paper with suitable margins. Use the same spacing as shown in the text below.

*TYPIST – Please insert main heading from Ex 10.*

At Home

I 'SELL BY' DATE

   Make sure you do not eat food beyond the recommended 'sell by' date.

   i   Get the shopping home as quickly as possible.

   ii  Put chilled and frozen food straight into the refrigerator or freezer. Delay will mean that their temperature changes.

   iii Make sure that raw foods, like poultry and meat, do not come into contact with cooked foods.

II PERSONAL HYGIENE

   i   When handling foods it is important

       (a) to make sure that your hands are clean, and that you wash your hands between handling raw & cooked foods;

       (b) to cover any cut you might have with a clean, waterproof dressing.

   ii  Do not smoke while preparing food.

III THAWING FROZEN FOOD

   Read, and follow carefully, the thawing and cooking instructions on frozen foods. It is particularly important th meat & poultry are completely thawed before cooking.

UNIT 1    See Practical Typing Exercises, Book Two, pages 2–3, for further exercises on
***Enumeration***

3.3 If both horizontal and vertical lines are required, rule these (a) either by underscore, in which case the paper has to be removed from the machine after the table has been typed, and reinserted sideways for the ruling of the vertical lines; or (b) by ink; or (c) a combination of the two, eg horizontals by underscore, verticals by ink. See that the ink ruling is the same colour as the underscore line.

3.4 The vertical lines between the columns must be ruled exactly in the middle of each blank space. It is therefore advisable to leave an odd number of spaces between the columns—one for the vertical ruling and an equal number on either side of the ruling. The points on the scale at which the vertical lines are to be ruled should be marked by light pencil marks at the top **and** bottom of the columns.

3.5 To find the point at which to mark the vertical line, proceed as follows: (It is assumed that you have left either three, five or seven spaces between columns.) (a) Move to tab stop following first vertical line. (b) If you have left three spaces between columns, backspace two and make a pencil mark; if you have left five spaces between, backspace three; if seven spaces between, backspace four.

3.6 Move to second and other columns and repeat 3.5.

    **NOTE**  Do not extend the vertical lines above or below the horizontals—see that they meet precisely.

3.7 **Ink**  If horizontal and vertical lines are to be ruled in ink, follow the same procedures as for ruling by underscore, but in this case the beginning and end of each horizontal line must be marked in pencil, as well as the vertical lines. When the table has been completed, remove paper from machine and, with a fine nib, rule lines carefully and neatly to scale points marked. It is essential that vertical and horizontal lines meet exactly.

3.8 If you wish to make a very clear distinction between sections of a table, the horizontal and vertical lines can be emphasized by double or thicker ruled lines. With electronic keyboards, the **bold** function key may be used.

## 4 *Multiple-line headings*

Where column headings consist of more than one line or are of unequal depth, they are always typed in single spacing. They are never underscored in a **ruled** table.

4.1 **Blocked style**

 4.1.1 Set margins and tab stops.

 4.1.2 All column headings start on the second single space after the main or subheading. However, if the table is ruled, then the column headings will start on the second single space after the first horizontal line.

 4.1.3 The heading over the first column is typed at the left margin.

 4.1.4 Headings in other columns start at the tab stop set for the beginning of the longest line in the column. Each line in any one heading will start at the same scale point. The £ sign is usually typed above the first figure of the £'s.

4.2 **Centred style**

Each line of a column heading is centred horizontally within the space allocated for the longest line in that column/heading. The whole of the heading in any one column is centred vertically in the space allocated for the deepest heading.

When typing multiple-line headings, proceed as follows:

 4.2.1 Turn up two single spaces after the main/subheading or, if a ruled table, turn up two single spaces after the first horizontal line.

 4.2.2 Type the deepest heading first.

 4.2.3 Move carriage/carrier to tab stop set for column with deepest heading.

 4.2.4 If the longest line is the column itself, then all lines in the column heading are centred on the longest line in the column.

 4.2.5 If the longest line is the column heading, then that line is typed at the tab stop and all other lines in the heading centred on it.

 4.2.6 Find the centre point by tapping once for each two spaces/characters in the longest line. Make a note of this point.

 4.2.7 Backspace one for each two characters/ spaces in the line to be centred. Type the line at the point reached.

 4.2.8 In this way centre and type all lines in the heading.

 4.2.9 Move to the next deepest heading.

 4.2.10 Count the number of lines in this heading and subtract the number from the number of lines in the deepest heading just typed. Divide the result by two, eg:

| | |
|---|---|
| Deepest heading 5 lines | |
| Next deepest | <u>2</u> |
| Difference | 3 |
| Divide by two | $1\frac{1}{2}$—turn up one and a half spaces from first line of deepest heading. |

 4.2.11 Turn the cylinder towards you so that the alignment scale is at the base of the

T  Data Bank  210

**DATA FILES** You will notice that, while typing exercise 12 below, you are asked to refer to the Data Files for additional information. Throughout the book you will find other exercises where facts or additional information will need to be checked with, or extracted from, the Data Files which are on pages **163–164**.

## Decimal enumeration

See page **182**

12  Type the following on A4 paper using suitable margins.

M E E T I N G S

It is said that executives may spend up to 50% of their time attending formal or informal meetings or conferences.  This means that a large part of a secretary's working time will be spent on the administrative details required for the smooth and efficient running of these meetings.

1   BEFORE THE MEETING

    1.1   Seven to 14 days before the meeting, the secretary should send out a notice of the meeting.

    1.2   Book the room for the meeting.

    1.3   Prepare the agenda in consultation with the chairperson.

        1.3.1   Send out the agenda.

2   DURING THE MEETING

    2.1   Prepare the room for the meeting.

        2.1.1   Ensure that water is available for members and/or speakers.

        2.1.2   Prepare the attendance register for signature, together with any other relevant documents.

    2.2   Attend the meeting.

        2.2.1   Take notes of the proceedings.

        2.2.2   Read apologies for absence.

*[TYPIST: Item 2.2.3 is in the Data Files (filename MTG) on page 164. Please type it here.]*

3   AFTER THE MTG

    3.1   Prepare draft minutes.

        3.1.1   Read & check w chairperson.

        3.1.2   Send out minutes.

        3.1.3   Deal w any correspondence arising from the minutes.

---

**UNIT 1**   See Practical Typing Exercises, Book Two, page 4, for further exercises on *Decimal enumeration*

## 1 Main headings and columns without headings

1.1 Clear margin stops and all previous tab stops.
1.2 Insert paper with left edge at 0.
1.3 Calculate number of vertical lines in exercise and subtract this number from number of vertical lines on paper being used. Divide answer by two and add one to this figure: turn up this number from top edge of paper. Example using A5 landscape paper:

| | | |
|---|---|---|
| Number of vertical lines in A5 landscape paper | 35 | |
| Less number of lines in exercise to be typed, say | 22 | |
| Divide by two | $13 \div 2 = 6$ | (ignore |
| Plus one | 1 | fractions) |
| Turn up | 7 | |

1.4 Bring carriage to horizontal centre point of paper.
1.5 If **centred** style is being used, from centre point of paper backspace once for every two characters and spaces in the main heading and type heading at point reached. Turn up two single spaces.
1.6 Mark the longest line in each column. From the centre of the paper backspace once for every two characters and spaces in the longest line of each column, carrying any odd letter to the next column.
1.7 Backspace once for every two spaces to be left between the columns, including any odd number left over in step 1.6.
1.8 Set margin stop at point reached.
1.9 From left margin, tap space bar once for each letter and space in the longest line of the first column, and once for each blank space between the first and second columns. Set tab stop at point reached for start of second column.
1.10 From the first tab stop, again tap space bar once for each character and space in the longest item of the second column, and once for each blank space between second and third columns. Set tab stop at point reached for start of third column.
1.11 Continue in the same way for any additional columns.

**NOTES** (a) If **blocked** style is being used, follow items 1.6–1.11 and type main heading at left margin.
(b) The number of spaces left between columns depends on the total width of the table. A minimum of three and a maximum of seven are recommended.

## 2 Column headings

2.1 **Blocked** Set margins and tab stops. Turn up two single spaces after the main/subheading or, if a ruled table, turn up two single spaces after the first horizontal line. The heading over the first column is typed at the left margin. Headings in the other columns start at the tab stop set for the beginning of the longest line of each column (could be heading or column item). The £ sign is usually typed above the first figure of the £'s.

The column **items** are typed at the tab stops set for the start of the longest item. With figures, remember to type units under units and tens under tens, etc.

2.2 **Centred** Set margins and tab stops. If the **column heading** is **longer** than the column items and if there is only one line in the heading, type it at the left margin or at the tab stop set. If there is more than one line in a column heading, see instructions under **multiple-line** column headings.

Before typing the **column items**, clear tab stop already set, find centre point of column by tapping space bar once for every two characters and spaces in the heading (this will give you the centre point of the heading) then backspace one for every two characters and spaces in the longest column item. Set a tab stop at point reached. If the column items are words, this scale point will give you the starting point for each item in the column. If the column items are figures, units must be typed under units and tens under tens.

Where the **column heading** is **shorter** than the **longest item** in the column, find the centre point of the longest column item by tapping space bar once for every two characters and spaces in that item. From the point reached, backspace once for every two characters and spaces in the heading. At this point type the heading. If there is more than one line in a column heading, see instructions under **multiple-line** headings.

## 3 Ruling

**NOTE** To save vertical and horizontal spacing, see page 213.

Tabulated statements are sometimes made more effective and clearer by ruling horizontal and/or vertical lines. Although it is assumed that you have already learnt how to rule up tabulated work, the following notes will serve as a reminder.

3.1 If horizontal lines only are ruled, use the underscore and let the lines project two spaces beyond the margins on either side.
3.2 Always turn up one single space before a horizontal underscore and two single spaces after.

# SKILL BUILDING

Type each line three times and, if time permits, complete your practice by typing each group once as it appears.

Margins:
12 pitch 22–82
10 pitch 12–72

### A  Keyboarding skills

1 Speed    It was good of you to write such a kind letter to my family.
2 Accuracy My four bracelets were exquisitely set with gold and silver.
3 Figures  w2e3 we23 e3r4 er34 r4t5 rt45 t5y6 ty56 u7i8 ui78 i8o9 io89.
4 Symbols  Give Clarke & Co 24 lengths of wood 6' 6" × 3' 1 7/8" × 2½".

### B  Improve control of down reaches

5 av pave cave save have crave shave avail avert averse travel
6 nk bank tank sank lank dank hank yank rank prank frank drank
7 May's bank savings will be spent on travelling to Sri Lanka.
8 Frank drank from the tank by the cave where we lost our way.

### C  Improve control of double-letter words

9  referred exceeded committed surpassed compelling regrettable
10 occurred possible efficient beginning appearance irrelevance
11 Mr Gibbs referred to my speech as irrelevant and immaterial.
12 That committee had some compelling reasons for choosing her.

### D  Practise common letter combinations

13 th they that this thank their month thought through nothing.
14 he when them hear other where heard neither reached weather.
15 Neither one of them reached the peak because of bad weather.
16 Last month we thought that we would hear from their adviser.

### E  Spelling skills—correct the one misspelt word in each line
—see page 161 for answer

17 achieve conceit benefited occurring livelihood advertisement
18 through delayed seperated developed unequalled organizations
19 She benefitted from the delay which occurred when we arrived.
20 At approximately 2015 hours the 2 company's arranged to buy.

**Skill measurement**          Two-minute timing          Not more than two errors

S/M2  Yes, they should call here to see the goods which I spoke to      12
      you about last Monday.  I do not send stock out on approval.      24
      I shall be very pleased to do business with you and to allow      36
      you monthly credit of £10,000.  In the late autumn I hope to      48
      offer some first-class quality goods, and in the meantime, I      60
      can let you have the best value in woollens, with a special       72
      line in sweaters.  I am sorry that I am unable to suggest a       84
      reliable house for socks: this is part of the trade in which      96
      I have not done business, and it would not be fair of me to      108
      pass an opinion on the firms whose names you mention in your     120
      letter.  I have always kept my prices low, and will write to     132
      you when next I have some special offers.          (SI 1.23)     140

       1  |  2  |  3  |  4  |  5  |  6  |  7  |  8  |  9  |  10  |  11  |  12  |

**UNIT 2**                          *Skill building*

2 If your typewriter does not have half spacing, proceed as follows:
  2.1 Release cylinder from linespacing mechanism by means of the interliner lever.
  2.2 Turn cylinder forward about half a linespace.
  2.3 Type subscript(s).
  2.4 Return interliner to normal position.
  2.5 See that cylinder returns to original typing line.

## Sums of money in columns

See *Totals*, page 215.

## Sums of money in context

1 If the sum comprises only pounds, type as follows: £5, £10 or £5.00, £10.00.
2 If only pence, type: 10p, 7p.

**NOTE** **No** space between figures and letter p, and no full stop after p (unless, of course, it ends a sentence).

3 With mixed amounts, ie sums comprising pounds and pence, the decimal point and the £ symbol should always be used, but **not** the abbreviation p.

**Example**
£70.05. The £ sign and p should **never** appear together.

4 If the sum contains a decimal point but no whole pounds, a nought should be typed after the £ symbol and before the point. Example: £0.97.
5 Thousands may be represented by a capital K, eg £20,000 = £20K.

## Sums of money — International currency codes

| | |
|---|---|
| Australian Dollar | AUD |
| Austrian Schilling | ATS |
| Belgian Franc | BEF |
| Canadian Dollar | CAD |
| Chad (CFA) Franc | XAF |
| Cyprus Pound | CYP |
| Danish Krone | DKK |
| European Currency Units | XEU |
| Finnish Markka | FIM |
| French Franc | FRF |
| German Mark | DEM |
| Greek Drachma | GRD |
| Hong Kong Dollar | HKD |
| Indian Rupee | INR |
| Irish Punt | IEP |
| Italian Lire | ITL |
| Japanese Yen | JPY |
| Kuwaiti Dinar | KWD |
| Luxemburg Franc | LUF |
| Malaysian Ringgit | MYR |
| Maltese Pound | MTP |
| Netherlands — Dutch Guilder | DKK |
| New Zealand Dollar | NZD |
| Norwegian Krone | NOK |
| Portuguese Escudo | PTE |
| Saudi Riyal | SAR |
| Singapore Dollar | SGD |
| South African Rand | ZAR |
| Spanish Peseta | ESB |
| Swedish Krona | SEK |
| Swiss Franc | CHF |
| United Arab Emirates Dirham | AED |
| United Kingdom Pound | GBP |
| United States Dollar | USD |

## Superscripts — superior (raised) characters

Some characters have to be typed above the normal typing line, such as degrees (small o), mathematical formulae and raised reference marks. These are called superscripts.

1 If your typewriter has half linespacing, proceed as follows:
  1.1 Turn cylinder back half a space.
  1.2 Type superscript(s).
  1.3 Return cylinder to original typing line.
2 If your typewriter does not have half linespacing, proceed as follows:
  2.1 Release from linespacing mechanism by means of the interliner lever.
  2.2 Turn cylinder back about half a linespace.
  2.3 Type superscript(s).
  2.4 Return cylinder to normal position.
  2.5 See that cylinder returns to original typing line.

## Tabulation

There are many kinds of statements and records that the typist may have to set out in tabulated form.

As you gain experience in the different forms of display, you should be able to look at a script and decide what margins are suitable. With tabulation, it is often possible to study a table and decide on a left margin. In other cases, all that will be necessary is to type out the longest line in each column, or tap out the longest line of each column (together with the spaces between columns) and see whether the table will fit in with the margins already set (within a document you are already typing) or whether a 25 mm (1 inch) left margin would be adequate.

In other situations, it will give a better result if you use the backspacing method for the horizontal centring and adopt the following procedure.

S/T   *Data Bank*   208

# PRODUCTION DEVELOPMENT

See pages **195**
**167**

## Notices of Meetings and Agendas—Incorporating amendments to text

1 Type a copy of the following Agenda on A4 paper. Margins: 12 pitch 22–82, 10 pitch 12–72.

*(TYPIST: Please change times throughout the UNIT to 24-hr clock.)*

VOLUNTARY CARERS' ASSOCIATION - NOTOWN BRANCH

A meeting of the Committee of the Voluntary Carer's Association is to be held in the Community Hall, Notown, at 7.30 pm on Tuesday *(Insert 1st Tues of next mth)*

A G E N D A

1 Apologies for absence

3 Matters arising, not dealt with ~~arising~~ elsewhere on the agenda

2 Minutes of last meeting

4 Correspondence, including branch circulars

5 Newsletter

6 Future programme:

*(Leave one clear space)*
    (a) Talk by Dr Dilys Falkland. Arrangements to be made for venue, etc
    (b) Details to be discussed with reference to visit to
*(Insert details from Data Files (filename AGENDA, Section A) p 163)*

7 Any other business

8 Date of next mtg

Camilla Foster-Crawford
Secretary

*(Today's date)*

2 Type the following on a printed memo form. Use suitable margins.

To    All Directors and Heads of Sections    Ref    PV/ADT

From    Maisie Trigg, Company Secretary    Date    *(Today's)*

NOTICE OF MEETING

A meeting of Directors and Heads of Sections will be held in Room B20 on the 6th floor on *(insert date - 2 wks from today)* at 10.00 am.

AGENDA

*(Take agenda from Data Files (filename AGENDA, Section B) p. 163.)*

**UNIT 2**    *Notice of Meetings and Agendas—Incorporating amendments to text*    **10**

## Specialized typing

Technical and legal work—specifications, articles of agreement, wills, plays, etc—are specialized documents and layout often varies from one office to another.

Management will supply the typist with copies of previous documents and these should be followed precisely. In offices today, the skeleton forms of much of this specialized work are held on disks and the typist can locate quite easily any one particular document on the disk, type in the information applicable to a client, and then have the document automatically typed out.

One or two examples of these documents are given in this book. Follow the layout or instructions given.

## Speeches

The amount of time spent on preparing and typing a speech will depend on a number of factors such as:
1. The degree of formality.
2. The nature of the topic.
3. The speaker's knowledge of the topic.
4. The length of the speech.
5. The amount of research necessary to verify data such as names, dates, historic facts, statistics, quotations, etc.
6. Whether a copy, or summary, is required as a press release.
7. Whether the speaker requires:
   7.1 Notes—essential points only (usually typed on postcards).
   7.2 Quotations and statistics only.
   7.3 The speech typed in full.

If the speech will be read verbatim, use pica typeface (or a larger typeface if you have one available) and double/treble spacing. No doubt the speaker will tell you what points, or headings, he wishes to emphasize and upper case/emboldening/underlining should be employed to highlight these objectives.

Perhaps the speaker may have a number of asides, jokes, quotations, etc, that she/he may, or may not, use, and it would be preferable to type these separately so that they may be utilized as and when appropriate or, perhaps, not at all, depending on the audience and their reactions.

Some speakers are very particular about using notations for 'stage directions', pauses, jesticulations, etc, and, where this is the case, leave wide side margins for reminders. In addition, speakers often wish to enhance their speech by audio-visual materials, overhead transparencies, etc, and the point of presentation should be indicated in the margin(s).

When typing a speech in full, the suggestions given for *Reports*, pages 203–204, will be helpful.

## Spelling

Your word processor may have an inbuilt memory for checking the spelling of many common words (a kind of electronic dictionary). The word processor scans the document, checking against all the words in its dictionary, and when it finds a mistake, the cursor moves to the word. However, it does not recognize the difference between **practise** and **practice**; **to**, **two**, or **too**; etc. With modern sophisticated word processors, the correct spelling automatically replaces the incorrect spelling.

See also *Deliberate errors*, page 178, and *Abbreviations*, pages 165–166.

## Square brackets

See *Special signs, symbols and marks*, page 206.

## Standard margins

See *Margins*, page 193, and also page 6.

## Standard paragraphs

Many organizations assemble a file of standard paragraphs covering routine replies to enquiries. The originator then indicates on the enquiry letter the numbers, or codes, of the standard paragraphs to be typed in reply, together with variable information where necessary. The typist copies the paragraphs in the sequence indicated by the originator; thus no time is needed for creative composition or dictation. With certain electronic typewriters, and word processors, the standard paragraphs are coded and stored, then retrieved and automatically inserted as and where required.

See also *Forms (Automation)*, page 187.

## Subscripts—inferior (lowered) characters

Subscripts are characters that have to be typed below the normal typing line as in chemical formulae.

1. If your typewriter has half linespacing, proceed as follows:
   1.1 Turn cylinder forward (away from you) half a space.
   1.2 Type subscript(s).
   1.3 Return cylinder to original typing line.

## Notices of Meetings and Agendas of limited and public limited companies

See page **195**

3 Type the following Notice of Annual General Meeting and list of items to be discussed for a Public Limited Company on A4 paper with margins of 12 pitch 18–88. With 10 pitch and margins of 11–75 line-endings will be different.

ABC plc

NOTICE OF MEETING

NOTICE IS HEREBY GIVEN that the fortieth ANNUAL GENERAL MEETING of ABC plc will be held in the Forefield Room, Grange Buildings, Oxford Street, London, WC1A 1DF, on Tuesday 1 March 1994 at 12 noon. (TYPIST - Don't forget to change time to 24-hr clock.)

Routine business

1  To receive and, if thought fit, adopt the directors' report for the year ended 31 December 1993.

2  To declare a final dividend on the ordinary shares of the Company.

3  To elect the directors.

4  To reappoint the auditor.

OTHER BUSINESS (lc & u/sc)

5  To consider and, if thought fit, pass a Special Resolution that the powers conferred on the Directors in the Articles of Association be renewed until the next AGM. (In full)

6  To consider and, if thought fit, pass as a Special Resolution that the share premium account be and is hereby cancelled.

By Order of the Board (CAPS)

B S Chawla

Secretary

London
18 February 1994

NOTES  A member entitled to attend and vote at the Meeting may appoint a proxy or proxies to attend and, on a poll, to vote instead of him/her. A proxy need not be a member of the Company. A form of proxy is attached for use by the holders of ordinary shares.

Copies of service contracts of directors with the Company will be available for inspection at the registered office during the usual business hours from the date of this notice until the date of the AGM, and also at the place of the meeting for at least 15 minutes prior to the meeting. (In full)

---

**UNIT 2**  See Practical Typing Exercises, Book Two, pages 5–8, for further exercises on *Notices of Meetings and Agendas of limited and public limited companies*

## Special signs, symbols and marks

A variety of words (sign, symbol, mark) is used when referring to the characters on this page. One speaks of punctuation marks, the brace symbol and the £ sign. The word symbol is employed mainly for mathematical and scientific formulae and in computer terminology.

| | | |
|---|---|---:|
| Degree | Small o, raised half a space. | 6° |
| Feet | Apostrophe typed after the figure(s). | 8' |
| Inches | Double quotation marks typed immediately after figure(s). | 7" |
| Minus | To show subtraction—hyphen with space either side. | 6 - 4 = 2 |
| Minutes | Apostrophe typed immediately after figure(s). | 10' |
| Multiplication | Small x with a space either side. | 4 x 5 |
| Seconds | Double quotation marks typed immediately after figure(s). | 9" |
| To | Hyphen. | 21-25 |

### Constructing special signs, symbols and marks

Some characters, not provided on the keyboard, can be typed by combining two characters, ie by typing one character, backspacing and then typing the second character, or by typing one character and then the second immediately afterwards. In a few cases the interliner must be used to allow the characters to be raised or lowered.

| | | |
|---|---|---:|
| Asterisk | Small x and hyphen. | ✶ |
| Brace | Continuous brackets typed one underneath the other. | ( ) ( ) ( ) |
| Caret | Underscore and oblique. | ∠ |
| Cedilla | Small c and comma. | ç |
| Cent | Small or capital C and oblique. | ¢ ¢ |
| Dagger | Capital I and hyphen. | ‡ |
| Diaresis | Quotation marks. | naïve ï |
| Divide into | Right bracket and underscore on line above. | ) |
| Division | Hyphen, backspace and type colon. | ÷ |
| Dollar | Capital S, backspace and type oblique. | $ |
| Double dagger | Capital I raised half a space, backspace and type another capital I slightly below; or capital I and equation sign. | ‡ |
| Equation | Two hyphens—one slightly above the other. | = |
| Exclamation | Apostrophe, backspace and type full stop. | ! |
| Paragraph | Small c and lowered capital I. | ¶ |
| Plus | Hyphen and lowered apostrophe. | + |
| Section | Two capital S's or two small s's. | § § |
| Square brackets | Oblique and underscore. | [ ] |
| Square root | Small v and oblique, followed by underscore on line above. | √ |
| Thousand | Capital K | £20,000 = £20K |
| Umlaut | Quotation marks. | ü |

On word processors many of the above characters are provided. It is difficult to type the division or plus as combined characters. Where this is the case, it would be wise to insert these in matching-colour ink.

When the **asterisk** has to be typed in the body of the text, it is typed as a superscript (raised character). Before typing the combination asterisk, turn the cylinder one half space towards you, type small x, backspace and type hyphen; then turn back to normal typing line. Where the asterisk is already fitted, **do not** lower the paper before typing, as the sign on the typeface is already raised.

To type a **square bracket** take the following steps:

Left bracket
(a) Type oblique sign.
(b) Backspace one and type underscore.
(c) Turn cylinder back one full linespace and type underscore.
(d) Turn cylinder up one full linespace, backspace once and continue with typing up to the right bracket.

Right bracket
(a) Type oblique sign.
(b) Backspace one and type underscore.
(c) Turn cylinder back one full linespace and type underscore.
(d) Turn cylinder up one single space, tap space bar once, and continue typing.

# Chairperson's Agenda

*See page 175*

4  Type the following Chairperson's Agenda on A4 paper. Margins: 12 pitch 13–93, 10 pitch 11–75. Tab stops at 53(43), 56(46).

    NOTOWN MUSEUM ASSOCIATION     *[Remember to change the time to 24-hr clock.]*

The ANNUAL GENERAL MEETING of the NOTOWN MUSEUM ASSOCIATION is to be held in the Corn Exchange, Notown, at 8.00 pm on Wednesday 6 April 1994.

A G E N D A                      N O T E S *[Unspaced caps]*

1   Apologies                      1

2   Minutes of the last Annual      2     *[Replace the word Chairman with Chairperson, throughout]*
    General Meeting held on
    2 April 1993.

3   Matters arising. The following    3
    points may arise.

    (i)     plaques on historic         (i)
            buildings in the town

    (ii)    items held in store for    (ii)
            future exhibitions

    (iii)   new building for museum    (iii)

4   The Secretary to give his        4
    annual report.                               *[Please take item 6 from Data Files (filename AGENDA, Section C) p 163.]*

5   Chairman's annual report.       5

~~6~~ 7   Election of:                   ~~6~~ 7

    (i)     Chairman                   (i)

    (ii)    Secretary                 (ii)

    (iii)   Treasurer.               (iii)

~~7~~ 8   AOB *[In full]*                    8

~~8~~ 9   Chairman to declare the       9
    meeting closed.

---

**1**   Key in document 4 (filename AGENDA) for 12-pitch print-out. When you have completed this task, save under filename AGENDA, and print an original only. Recall the document and follow the instructions for text editing on page 162.

**NOTE**   Text-edited copies of the exercises prepared on word processors are given in the *Solutions and Resource Material* and may be used instead of referring to the text-editing instructions on pages 162–163 of the book.

---

**UNIT 2**                              ***Chairperson's Agenda***                          **12**

**NOTE** I can be placed *only* before V or X;
X can be placed *only* before L or C;
C can be placed *only* before D or M.

5 To express numbers other than those in point 4, take the unit of five symbol immediately *below* and *add* to it the remaining symbols by putting these *after* the unit or five symbol.

**Examples**
6 = *5* + 1 = VI
7 = *5* + 2 = VII
8 = *5* + 3 = VIII
14 = *10* + 4 = XIV
15 = *10* + 5 = XV
16 = *10* + 6 = XVI
17 = *10* + 7 = XVII
18 = *10* + 8 = XVIII

60 = *50* + 10 = LX
70 = *50* + 20 = LXX
80 = *50* + 30 = LXXX
600 = *500* + 100 = DC
700 = *500* + 200 = DCC
800 = *500* + 300 = DCCC

6 A horizontal line drawn over the unit symbol means that the unit is multiplied by 1000.

**Example**
$\overline{M}$ = 1000 × 1000 = 1,000,000

7 To convert arabic figures into roman numerals, take each figure in turn.

**Example**
To convert 467, proceed as follows:
400 = 500 − 100 = CD; 60 = 50 + 10 = LX;
7 = 5 + 2 = VII; 467 = CDLXVII

8 Used as follows:
For monarchs, form and class numbers, chapters, preface pages, tables or paragraphs. Sometimes to express the year, enumerations, subsections, etc.

## Single-element machines

All electronic keyboards are fitted with single-element heads. These typewriters have no movable carriage, which also means that the cylinder is static, and there are no type bars. Instead, they have a printing head attached to a carrier that moves across the page from left to right, stroke by stroke. When you wish to return the carrier to the left margin, you press the return key as you would with the ordinary electric typewriter, or use the automatic return.

The printing element may be a golf ball head (seldom used today) which whirls and tilts to make an impression on the paper, or it may be a daisywheel which is a rapidly spinning disk of flexible arms, and on the tip of each arm there is a typeface character. The required character stops at the printing point and is struck by a small hammer which impinges the image on the paper.

See also ***Electronic typewriters***, pages 180–181, and laser printer under ***Pitch***, page 198.

## Soft copy

This is the text displayed on the screen of a VDU.

# Minutes

*See page 195*

5  Type a copy of the following Minutes on A4 paper.

VOLUNTARY CARERS' ASSOCIATION - NOTOWN BRANCH

MINUTES of a committee meeting of the Voluntary Carers' Association, Notown Branch, held in the (insert place, date & time from the Agenda on page 10.)

**Inset 5 spaces:**

PRESENT

Professor Isobel Coltham (In the Chair)
(Insert Sec's name from the Agenda on page 10.)
Miss Esme Jenner
Mrs Edna Harrop
Mr John Hugh
Miss Diana Greenshields
Dr Daniel Nash

1  APOLOGIES FOR ABSENCE      Mrs Liz Rushbridge, Mr Guy & Mrs Val Paige.

2  MINUTES OF LAST MEETING    The minutes had already been circulated and were taken as read.

3  MATTERS ARISING            There were no matters arising.

4  CORRESPONDENCE INCLUDING   A letter had been received from the
   BRANCH CIRCULARS           local home for the elderly asking for a volunteer to take one of the residents to visit her daughter on a reg basis. Esme Jenner & John Hugh both agreed to help out between them & said they wd contact the home & the resident concerned.

   Branch Circular 602119/H
   A circular had bn rec'd from the Head Office of the Assoc wh stated th all Branch Annual Reports shd be sent to HO not later than the last day of Mar. *(In full)*

5  NEWSLETTER                 Dr Nash said th the newsletter hd bn delayed because of unforeseen circs.

6  FUTURE PROGRAMME           (a) It was agreed th the talk by Dr Dilys Falkland be given in the Community Hall @ 7.30 pm on (insert date for a Wed 2 wks after the date given on the Agenda). Edna Harrop agreed to circulate members asap.
                              (b) A discussion was held abt a visit to Millfield Home for the Elderly. All present said they wished to participate.

**CAPS:**
7  Any other business         There was no further business.
8  Date of next mtg           The next mtg was arranged for (insert last Friday of next mth).

Chairman ......
Date ........

UNIT 2    See Practical Typing Exercises, Book Two, page 9, for further exercises on *Minutes*    13

The style you follow will be determined by your employer's preference. Many business firms provide typists with a typing manual and the instructions contained therein must be followed closely. Number every page of a report uniformly.

## Spacing

If you are typing a draft, type this word in capital letters at the top left margin of the first page and use double or treble spacing with wide margins—38 mm ($1\frac{1}{2}$ inches) × 25 mm (1 inch). The final typing should be single spacing with appropriate spacing between headings, paragraphs, etc.

## Quotations

When preparing a business report, an executive may wish to quote excerpts from other sources. Brief quotations run in with text matter that introduces them. These are enclosed in quotation marks. Longer quotations, say more than four lines, should be started on a new line and preferably indented from the left margin (or both margins). Quotation marks are put at the beginning of each paragraph and at the **end** of the last paragraph. Permission to use a quotation should be requested from the copyright owner.

## Reverse side of paper (typing on)

If the continuation sheet is typed on the reverse side of the paper, the margins are also reversed, eg if the first page was typed with margins of elite 19–88, pica 11–76, typing on the reverse side would be with margins of 13–83 and 6–73.

If you use equal left and right margins, this will save altering the settings when using the reverse side.

## Ribbons

### 1 Film ribbons

The more expensive the ribbon the better the finished product will look and the easier it will be to make a correction.

**Single-strike** correctable carbon film ribbon can be used once only, but it gives a top-quality finish. Excellent for typing offset-litho masters.

**Multi-strike** film ribbon can be used once only, but it lasts approximately four times longer than the single-strike ribbon because the points at which the characters strike the ribbon overlap each other. The appearance of the typescript is not so perfect as that produced by the single-strike carbon film ribbon.

### 2 Correction ribbons

A correction ribbon is used for correcting typing errors. It may be the bottom half of the carbon ribbon or it may be completely separate on additional spools. To correct a typing error, switch to the correction ribbon, type the same error (the correction ribbon will 'lift' the impression from the paper). Switch to normal ribbon and type correct letter(s).

See also Laser print under **Pitch**, page 198.

### 3 Fitting a new ribbon

The manufacturer always supplies a handbook with a new typewriter and complete instructions will be given on how to change the ribbon. Before removing the old ribbon, look very carefully at how it is threaded.

**Cartridge ribbon** This ribbon is enclosed in a cartridge which clips on to spindles, and it is not necessary to handle the ribbon when threading it through the ribbon guides.

## Roman numerals

1  Units:   I (1)   X (10)   C (100)   M (1000)
   Fives:   V (5)   L (50)   D (500)

2  The four *unit* symbols can be repeated to express two or three units of the *same* symbol.

**Examples**

| 1 = I | 2 = II | 3 = III |
|---|---|---|
| 10 = X | 20 = XX | 30 = XXX |
| 100 = C | 200 = CC | 300 = CCC |
| 1000 = M | 2000 = MM | 3000 = MMM |

3  The symbol I may be used or repeated (up to III) *after* any of the above units or fives, in which case it *adds* to the symbol in front.

**Examples**

| I = 1 | VI = 6 | XI = 11 | LI = 51 |
|---|---|---|---|
| II = 2 | VII = 7 | XII = 12 | LII = 52 |
| III = 3 | VIII = 8 | XIII = 13 | LIII = 53 |

| CI = 101 | DI = 501 | MI = 1001 |
|---|---|---|
| CII = 102 | DII = 502 | MII = 1002 |
| CIII = 103 | DIII = 503 | MIII = 1003 |

4  To express 4, 9, 40, 400 and 900, take the symbol immediately *above* and put the appropriate unit symbol *in front*, which means that *it is subtracted* from the higher symbol.

```
 4 =    5 −    1 = IV
40 =   50 −   10 = XL
400 = 500 −  100 = CD
 9 =   10 −    1 = IX
90 =  100 −   10 = XC
900 = 1000 − 100 = CM.
```

# SKILL BUILDING

Type each line three times and, if time permits, complete your practice by typing each group once as it appears.

Margins:
12 pitch 22–82
10 pitch 12–72

### A  Keyboarding skills

1 Speed     The boy who told this story is now better and at home again.
2 Accuracy  Max quoted for one dozen jars of good apple juice and cakes.
3 Figures   0181 472 8835, 0121 345 6789, 0123 987 6657, 0124 236 1941/2
4 Symbols   Add 25% to the £500 sent in by B Murray & Son (contractors).

### B  Improve fluency

5 Did you buy all the tea and pay the boy the sum you now owe?
6 The man saw the lad was not yet fit for the job you got him.
7 Few can now say why she and her son did not get off the bus.

### C  Improve control of up reaches

8  ar bar car far jar mar par star argue hearts shares targets.
9  pl plan plot plea plum plus plight explain explode displace.
10 The star of the play had planned to buy shares on Wednesday.

### D  Spelling skill—correct the one misspelt word in each line
          —see page 161 for answer

11 debited ceiling leisure monoplies appointment opportunities
12 surveys shelves stimuli noticeable unecessary miscellaneous
13 The company debited the account for the micellaneous items.
14 My survey showed that we had benefitted from the information.

15  To develop your proofreading skills, turn to page 156, exercise 1.

### Skill measurement          Three-minute timing          Not more than three errors

S/M3  All of you will be glad to hear that we now have a scheme for    12
      refunding to staff that part of their expenses for travelling    24
      long distances to work.  Some details of local conditions and    36
      of the grades of staff will help you to understand our query.    48

      We are faced with a sharp division between town-based staff,     60
      who would pay fares of between £6 and £9 a week, and members     72
      of staff living in the 'country' who are paying between £10      84
      and £17 a week.                                                  87

      There are about 500 people on the office staff — four-fifths     99
      live within the city boundary (a radius of some 4 miles) and    111
      the rest live at distances varying from 6 to 12 miles.  Some    123
      time ago a plan was thought up for paying travelling costs      135
      on a mileage basis to all employees who travel a distance of    147
      more than 4 miles from the city centre; however, the scheme     159
      was not a success.  It is hoped that the new plan which was     170
      put into operation last week will prove to be fairer.  The      182
      scheme ensures that no one in this group pays more than £9      194
      a week to get to and from her/his work.            (SI 1.27)    201

        1 | 2 | 3 | 4 | 5 | 6 | 7 | 8 | 9 | 10 | 11 | 12 |

| UNIT 3 | Skill building | 14 |

3.3 Punctuation is never inserted after a heading, or at the end of a line in displayed work (notice, menu, etc) unless the last word is abbreviated and full punctuation is being used.

3.4 **Never** put full stops in the 24-hour clock; eg 1830 hours.

3.5 The 12-hour clock requires a full stop even when using open punctuation; eg 2.45 pm.

3.6 Full stops are always inserted within decimal enumerations; 2.4.1 for example.

## *Quotation marks*

Used when typing direct speech; eg Tom said, 'I must catch the 8.30 train this evening.' Quotation marks are usually placed after the comma, question mark and exclamation mark, eg 'Will I see you tomorrow?' The full stop is placed inside the final quotation mark unless the sentence ends with a title in quotation marks or a single word quotation. For example, 'I will see you at the meeting.' June bought me a copy of 'The Times'.

When two or more paragraphs are quoted, the quotation marks are placed at the **beginning of each paragraph** and at the **end of the last paragraph** only.

These are seldom used in **poetry** except when a line of poetry runs on with the prose. If they are inserted, they are placed at the beginning of the first verse and at the end of the last verse.

With **ellipsis** there is a space after the initial quotation mark and before the first dot, and a space after the third dot and before the final quotation mark.

## *Rate of production*

In business, time represents money, and your employer will expect you to complete your typing as quickly as possible; obviously, all documents must be mailable, ie error free. When training, it is important for you to know whether your speed, accuracy and typing techniques are equal to that demanded by an examining body/employer. Certain examining bodies require candidates to attempt all questions; therefore, we have suggested the approximate number of minutes you should spend on each task so that you complete the Integrated Production Typing in $2\frac{1}{2}$ hours. See also *Integrated Production Typing*, pages 32–33.

## *Rearrangement of material*

See *Modification and rearrangement of material*, page 195.

## *Repetitive printing*

This is the printing of more than one original hard copy by means of a word processing or microcomputer printer. A typed original has more personal appeal than a duplicated letter; therefore, repetitive printing is ideal for sending identical letters/documents to several people.

## *Reports*

A business report may be a simple inter-office memorandum about the background of a would-be customer, or it may run into hundreds of pages and be as formal as a comparison of the relative merits of several proposed sites for a new factory, complete with facts and figures presented in tabular form. The formal report may be drafted and rewritten several times.

The aim of any report is to provide information and, while an executive would prepare the report, it is usual for the typist to be responsible for the layout and for the details of style.

Whether short or long, the report is usually divided into sections and subsections and, when it contains a great deal of statistical information, it is easier to understand the information if it is arranged as a table.

The formal report will have a **title** and there may be a cover page and a title page. Then follow the various sections of the report.

1 **Terms of reference**—why and for whom the report has been prepared.
2 **Procedure**—the method used to collect the information.
3 **Findings**—the results of the investigation—should be clearly set out with enumerated headings and subheadings.
4 **Conclusions**—a summary and analysis of the findings.
5 **Recommendations**—what action should, or should not, be taken; these should be individually numbered.

### *Headings*

Most formal reports contain headings that introduce each main division or subdivision. Co-ordinate headings should be typed exactly alike throughout the report.

### *Style*

Consistency in style is also essential. For example, if at the beginning of a report business titles are typed in capitals, then they should not be typed in lower case later on. Or, if a term is abbreviated, it should be abbreviated throughout.

# PRODUCTION DEVELOPMENT

See pages **169**
170
171

***Fully-blocked business letters (open punctuation) —
Special mark, Subject heading and Enclosure***

1 Type the following letter from Europack Co Ltd on A4 headed paper. (See *Solutions and Resource Material*.) Margins: 12 pitch 22–82, 10 pitch 12–72. Take an original and one copy.

---

**EUROPACK Co Ltd**    *Fifth Floor*
*Enterprise House*
*56/60 Lonsdale Road*
*Caterham*
*Surrey*
*CR3 8SY*

Telephone: (0883) 46412    Facsimile: (0883) 13025

---

ORT/FL

3 March 1994

URGENT

Mr G T Poulton
Tranter Hall Associates
12 Carlton Street
SOUTHAMPTON
Hants
SO1 2EX

Dear Mr Poulton

RELOCATION OF OFFICES

I am writing to let you know that we have now moved to Enterprise House - 3 months ahead of schedule. The building is in a prominent position with plenty of car parking.

When you come to see me this Wednesday, 9 March, would you please go to the fifth floor of Enterprise House, Room 35. The receptionist at the main entrance will direct you. I am enclosing a map which clearly shows our new location.

I look forward to seeing you on Wednesday.

Yours sincerely



OWEN R TROMANS
Planning Operations Manager

Enc

---

**UNIT 3**  See Practical Typing Exercises, Book Two, pages 10–11, for further exercises on
***Fully-blocked business letters (open punctuation) —
Special mark, Subject heading, Enclosure***

## Proofreading

Proofreading is not easy. Our eyes have a way of passing over the line of typescript and seeing what the mind thinks is there, and not what the fingers actually put there. Moreover, the time devoted to proofreading appears to be non-productive and the typist may feel that his or her time would be better used in getting on with another job. Yet proof-reading is the sole responsibility of the typist.

We cannot stress too strongly the necessity of reading through your typescript and making any alterations before removing the document from the typewriter.

There are several common types of errors for which you should look:

1. Word substitution: FROM for FORM, IS for IT, AS for IS, IN for ON, YOU for YOUR.
2. Transposition of letters: r and t, v and b, i and e— and substitutions that are difficult to detect: n for m, d for s, u for y, or vice versa.
3. Omission of a line, or lines, which does not outwardly affect the meaning. Check finished work with original.
4. Wrong choice of words when there are two or more words of similar sound, such as plain, plane; all ready, already; advice, advise.
5. Inconsistencies.
6. Names, addresses and figures need special attention.

## Proportional spacing

With proportional spacing, the characters do not all take up the same amount of space. As in printing, each character is given its natural width. For example, an n is wider than an i, an m is wider than an n and a capital M is wider than a lower-case m. The characters are not measured in spaces but in terms of units. One of the outstanding features of proportional spacing is that the typed copy appears to be printed rather than typed.

## Punctuation

### 1 Open

Many organizations are now using open punctuation in a variety of documents. This is particularly so in business letters. Note the following when using open punctuation:

1.1 Grammatical punctuation must still be used.
1.2 Where an abbreviation ends in a full stop, the full stop is omitted and replaced by a space. Example: Mrs (space) A (space) W (space) Gurney, senior partners in Messrs Gurney & Asquith, will discuss the change of trading name to W R Holt & Co Ltd, etc, when she calls tomorrow.
1.3 Where abbreviations consist of two or more letters with full stops after each letter, the full stops are omitted and no space is left between the letters, but one space is left after the group of letters; eg John R Jamieson   Esq  MBE  MP.
1.4 When typing a **business letter** with open punctuation, **no** punctuation at all is inserted in the reference, date, name and address of addressee, or salutation; nor following the complimentary close and any wording below. Similarly, when addressing an **envelope** in open punctuation, **no** punctuation is inserted; eg

OPEN

John R Jamieson   Esq  MBE  MP
97 Stirling Road
STAFFORD
ST17 1JP

FULL

John R. Jamieson, Esq., M.B.E., M.P.,
97 Stirling Road,
STAFFORD.
ST17 1JP

1.5 In continuous matter, where the name and address 'run on', the parts are separated by commas, or an extra space.
1.6 Full stops are omitted after figures used in enumerated items.

### 2 Full

Full stops are inserted after abbreviations as follows:
2.1 Mrs. (space) A. (space) W. (space) Gurney, senior partner in Messrs. Gurney & Asquith, will discuss the change of trading name to W. R. Holt & Co. Ltd., etc., when she calls tomorrow.
2.2 John R. Jamieson, Esq., M.B.E., M.P.

### 3 Notes

3.1 Certain abbreviations and acronyms may be typed without full stops even when using full punctuation. Here are a few examples: VAT, NATO, PAYE, UK, USA, RSA, LCCI, BBC, etc.
3.2 No punctuation is inserted in abbreviations used for metric measurements even when using full punctuation unless it is the end of a sentence; eg A4 paper measures 210 × 297 mm. Full stops should be inserted in imperial measurements when typing with full punctuation; eg Messrs. J. R. Smith & Co. asked for six doors each measuring 6 ft. 4 in. × 3 ft. 5 in.

P  Data Bank  202

# Fully-blocked business letters (open punctuation) — Attention line, Displayed matter, Routeing additional copies

See pages 169
170
172

2   Type the following fully-blocked letter from Europack Co Ltd on A4 letterhead paper. (See *Solutions and Resource Material*.) Margins: 12 pitch 20–85, 10 pitch 11–76. Take an original and two copies; mark one for Miss Julie Swainston and the other for the file.

```
Our ref   BH/CE                                           10 March 1994
                                                  (NOTE   The date may be
Your ref  WCDC/2615/RP                            typed so that it ends at
                                                      the right margin.)

FOR THE ATTENTION OF MS JAN PHIPPS

West End Craft and Design Centre
Lower Cwm
BUILTH WELLS
Powys
LD2 3SG

Dear Sirs

LATEST FABRIC DESIGNS

We are pleased to announce the launch of our latest fabrics in a
variety of colours and patterns, at competitive prices.  The designs
feature the following wild flowers -

cowslip    bluebell   cyclamen         poppy
primrose   violet     forget-me-not    foxglove

all depicted on a range of background colours.

Please find enclosed our new comprehensive leaflet, price list and
current order form for your use.

Our 50-page colour catalogue is now available showing beautiful designs in a variety of settings.

Yours faithfully
EUROPACK CO LTD



Barrie Howse
Sales Department

Encs

cc   Miss Julie Swainston
     File
```

**2** Key in document 2 (filename FAB) for 15-pitch print-out. Use the 'flush right' tab stop for the date. When you have completed this task, save under filename FAB, and print an original and two copies. Recall the document and follow the instructions for text editing on page 162.

---

**UNIT 3**   See Practical Typing Exercises, Book Two, pages 12–13, for further exercises on
*Fully-blocked business letters — Attention line, Displayed matter, Routeing copies*

# Proofreaders' marks

When amendmends have to be made in typewritten or handwritten work of which a fair copy is to be typed, these may be indicated in the original copy by proofreaders' marks. To avoid confusion, the mark may also be placed in the margin against the line in which the correction is to be made. The Royal Society of Arts use only the stet signs, ie ✓ , in the margin, but other examining bodies may use any or all of the examples that follow.

| Mark which may be in margin | | Meaning | Mark in text | | |
|---|---|---|---|---|---|
| lc | | Lower case—small letter(s). | — / | | Under letter(s) to be altered or struck through letter(s). |
| uc or CAPS | | Upper case—capital letter(s). | = / | | Under letter(s) to be altered or struck through letter(s). |
| | ⨍ | Delete—take out. | / | | Through letter(s) or word(s). |
| NP or | // | New paragraph. | // or ⌐ | | Placed before the first word of a new paragraph. |
| Stet or | ✓ | Let it stand, ie, type the word(s) that has been crossed out and has a dotted or broken line underneath. | - - - - | | Under word(s) struck out. |
| Run on | | No new paragraph required. Carry straight on. | ⤴ | | |
| | ⋀ | Caret—insert letter, word(s) omitted. | ⋀ | | Placed where the omission occurs. |
| | ⌒ | Close up—less space. | ⌒ | | Between letters or words. |
| | trs | Transpose, ie change order of words or letters as marked. | ⟲ ⟳ | | Between letters or words, sometimes numbered. |
| | # | Insert space. | ⋀ | | |
| | // | Straighten margin. | | | |
| ital. | | Italic | — | | (Underscore) |
| | ⊙ | Insert full stop. | | | |
| | ;/ | Insert semi-colon. | | | |
| | :/ | Insert colon. | | | |
| | ,/ | Insert comma. | | | |
| | ⟋ | Insert apostrophe. | | | |
| | H | Insert hyphen. | | | |
| | \|–\| | Insert dash. | ⎫ | | |
| | " " | Insert quotation marks. | ⎬ ⋀ | | |
| | # | Insert space. | | | |
| | ⋀ | Insert words. | ⎭ | | |
| | (⋀ )⋀ | Insert brackets. | | | |

(Pontypool) If a word is not clear in the text, it may have been written in the margin in capitals. The word should be typed in lower case, or as indicated in the original script.

Double underscore underneath words usually means that such words are to be typed in unspaced capitals. Treble underscore means that such words are to be typed in spaced capitals (one space between each letter, and three spaces between words).

**P**          **Data Bank**          201

## Addressing envelopes and labels—Forms of address

*See pages 182, 183, 187*

3   Type each of the following addresses on envelopes. Mark the first envelope 'FOR THE ATTENTION OF MISS BERYL GODDARD' and the second and fourth envelopes AIRMAIL.

   Group Life Assurance Co Ltd   89 Holden Road   BOURNEMOUTH   BH8 8XH

   Ms Barbara Binford   333 Carrillo Street   Apartment 5   SANTA BARBARA   California 800404   USA

   Mr & Mrs S W Britton   Poste Restante   The Post Office   West Bridgford   NOTTINGHAM   NG2 5FR

   Mme P Sené   10 Boulevard Dalez   76600 LE HAVRE   Normandy   FRANCE

   J Singh Esq   Managing Director   Eagle Equipment Plc   Loushers Lane   WARRINGTON   Cheshire   WA4 6RG

4   Type each of the following addresses on a label. Mark the first label 'CONFIDENTIAL' and the second 'URGENT'.

   Dr P Madden   The Health Centre   Corner House   HALESOWEN   West Midland   B62 9JQ

   The Manager   Alexandra Hotel   Canterbury Road   South Willesborough   ASHFORD   Kent   TN24 0BP

   Mrs Margaret Linklater   c/o Mr P Branson   20 Henderson Lane   DOUGLAS   Isle of Man

   Mr Ray Dunbar   Field Marketing Manager   Trifreight Limited   Victoria Street   NEWTON STEWART   Wigtownshire   Scotland   DG8 6GD

   Herrn Heinz Schmüde   Kapellenstrasse 2   WIESBADEN 6200   Hesse   ~~WEST~~ GERMANY   (Mark AIRMAIL)

5   Type the first three addresses that follow on envelopes and the remaining four on labels. Where necessary mark for AIRMAIL.

   Miss Shirley Lowes OBE MAMP   26 Tanners Drive   Blakelands   Milton Keynes   MK14 5BU   (Please mark BY HAND)

   Rev T R Prevost   2 Ocean View Rd   Bude   Cornwall   EX23 8NW   (Please mark PRIVATE)

   Global Office Systems   FREEPOST   246 Main Rd   Brereton   Rugeley   Staffs   WS15 2BE

   Speedwrite Employment Agency   10 Runton St   Cromer   Norfolk   NR27 9AR   (Please mark FOR THE ATTENTION OF JOHN REA-WALKER)

   R Dyson Esq   R Dyson & Sons Ltd   17 King Edward Rd   Heaton Moor   Stockport   Cheshire   SK4 3BS

   Señor Pedro Quijote   Carret del Lago   BEJAR   Salamanca   SPAIN

   Sir Joseph MacNee   Rock House   Causeway Rd   Antrim   N Ireland   BT41 4AR

Store these addresses under filename FORM for later use.

**UNIT 3**   See Practical Typing Exercises, Book Two, page 14, for further exercises on *Addressing envelopes and labels—Forms of address*

3   Wide margins—seldom less than: left 38 mm (1½ inches) right 25 mm (1 inch).
4   The subject heading should be short and factual.
5   Double spacing for body of the release
6   Leave two clear spaces between paragraphs (turn up three singles).
7   First paragraph is normally blocked; other paragraphs indented. The indentation is often just two spaces as seen in newspaper columns and printed matter.*
8   On second and subsequent sheets type heading at the right-hand side about 25 mm (1 inch) from the top; at the bottom of each page type the word MORE or CONTINUED in the usual place at the right margin.
9   The word (END) is typed, usually in brackets, at the end of the final paragraph.
10  Do not underscore any wording (for emphasis) as to the printer this means use italic.

* The release display should follow, as far as possible, standard newspaper conventions, rather than typewriting conventions.

## Pre-transcription reading

See page 31.

## Printer

An output device that produces hard copy on paper.

## Print-out

The hard copy of a document from a word processing system.

## Programme

See **Folded leaflets**, pages 184–185.

# Fully-blocked business letters — Continuation sheets, Postscripts

See pages 172, 173

**6** Type the following two-page letter from EUROPACK Co Ltd on A4 letterhead paper and take an original and two copies, one for Mary O'Shea and the other for the file. Mark the letter PERSONAL.

Ref AT/(Insert yr initials here, please)

Insert today's date

Mr Ralph S Parker
6 Marston Lane
BEDFORD
MK41 2AC

(TYPIST — Please type shoulder headings in lc underlined, & address an envelope of suitable size to Mr Parker.)

Dear Mr Parker

FLAT 2a  BEECHWOOD LANE

I am writing to let you know that the tenants, Dr and Mrs D Smythe-Johnson, have now vacated your flat. The keys may be collected from our offices in Lonsdale Road, if req'd. Generally speaking, the flat has been left in a very clean and tidy condition, other than some damp stains on the one wall in the second bedroom.

[NP] As we consider the flat has been well maintained we propose to release Dr and Mrs Smythe-Johnson's deposit in full. I trust this will be satisfactory to you.

EXPANSION OF SERVICES

On another matter, I wish to inform you that, as part of our current programme of expanding the breadth of service we offer to our customers [stet clients], we have recently appointed 3 new directors. /trs

(Inset 51mm (2") from left margin)

NIGEL P BLOUNT BSc DipTP MRTPI FRICS
    Planning and Development Consultancy

MARTIN F GRANT BSc FRICS
    Professional Services

Myra T Bradley BSc FRICS    Rent Reviews, Lease Renewals and Valuations  (TYPIST — Please display as above.)

All 3 directors have a wealth of experience in the profession and will offer services to our clients, not only in Surrey, but throughout the United Kingdom.

UNIT 3  *Fully-blocked business letters — Continuation sheets, Postscripts*    18

## 1 Positioning

The longest line of the verse should be centred on the page or typing line.

## 2 Spacing

Single linespacing, double between verses.

2.1 If alternate lines rhyme, these usually begin at the same scale point (unless they are of irregular length, when they are centred). The first line and all lines rhyming with it are typed at the margin, while the second and all lines rhyming with it are indented two spaces from the start of the first, third, etc, lines. (Short lines may be indented more than two spaces.)

2.2 In blank verse (ie where no lines rhyme) all lines start at margin.

2.3 When lines are of approximately equal length, and when successive lines rhyme, these start at the margin, ie there is no indentation.

2.4 If all lines rhyme, these all start at the margin.

## 3 Capitalization

Each line starts with a capital letter.

## 4 Poet's name

The last letter of the poet's surname ends at the same scale point as the last letter of the longest line.

## 5 Quotation marks

These are seldom used in poetry except when a line of poetry runs on with the prose. If they are inserted, they are placed at the beginning of the first verse, and at the end of the last verse.

## 6 Refrain

Typed at least five spaces to the right of the start of the verse(s).

## Postcards

Many firms send postcards (A6—[148 mm × 105 mm] [$5\frac{7}{8}$ inches × $4\frac{1}{8}$ inches]) in acknowledgement of letters and orders. These formal acknowledgements are typed like memos with no salutation and no complimentary close.

Note the following points:

1 Type firm's name and address, starting four spaces from top of card.
2 Use margins of five spaces on either side.
3 Use single spacing with double between paragraphs. Paragraphs may be indented or blocked.
4 After typing address, turn up two single spaces and at left margin insert the reference. On the same line, backspace from right margin and type date.
5 Turn up two single spaces and type body.
6 Type recipient's name and address on reverse side, parallel to the longest edge.
7 On some word processors it is difficult to type on a postcard or postcard-size paper.

## Postscripts

See *Business letters, 4.13*, page 172.

## Press releases (publicity releases)

Every business firm seeks favourable publicity. One way that a business gets coverage in newspapers and other media is by issuing press releases, sometimes called publicity releases, to news services. Announcements to the media about new products, executive promotions, new showrooms, mergers, etc, are common examples.

Many organizations have their own 'house' style; however, the following is considered to be acceptable:

1 Plain bond paper—type on one side only; very often special paper is used.

2 Headings such as:

NEWS RELEASE          JOHNSTONE & TARRANT PLC
                      30 Warwick Lane
                      EDINBURGH   EH14 1BY

   LOGO               Release: Immediate—10 December 1993

                      For further information contact:
                      Marjory Dolphin
                      Director of Public Relations
                      Telephone: 031–442 2736

**NEW SHOWROOMS IN BIRMINGHAM**

2

(Insert date here)

Mr Ralph S Parker

THE HALLMARK OF PROPERTY SERVICE

I enclose a copy of our new brochure The H—— of P—— S——, which I hope will illustrate our commitment to offer a comprehensive range of property services with an emphasis on personal attention to all our clients. If you would like a further copy, or copies, please let me know.

WINTER FROST PROTECTION

We would advise you that as your property is currently vacant all measures should be taken to ensure that it is protected from frost or water damage. In this respect we would suggest that appropriate and necessary steps are taken by draining down the central heating system, along with hot and cold water systems, asap.

NP

If you wish us to arrange the supervision of these tasks, we would of course be happy to do so at a cost of £35.00.

Yrs sinc

ANNABELLE TURNER
Deputy General Manager

PS  I will write to you again as soon as a new tenant for your flat is found.

---

**3** Key in document 6 (filename RENT) for 10-pitch print-out. When you have completed this task, save under filename RENT, and print an original and two copies. Recall the document and follow the instruction for text editing on page 162.

**UNIT 3** See Practical Typing Exercises, Book Two, pages 15–16, for further exercises on
*Fully-blocked business letters — Continuation sheets, Postscripts*

19

## Photocopying

Because of their versatility and speed, photocopiers are now replacing duplicators. They can reduce or enlarge copy, and the more sophisticated models have collating facilities which enable lengthy documents to be photocopied and the pages automatically collated and stapled; also, some photocopiers will print in colour.

It is now fairly common practice to use the photocopier instead of taking a carbon copy(ies) or in place of taking extra originals through the word processor or electronic typewriter. When sending out a business letter to a customer, always send the original.

Photocopiers cost money—time, maintenance, electricity, better-quality paper and other supplies—therefore, only make copies that are absolutely necessary and do not 'run off' a few more just in case they might be needed!

If you are typing an original only on a manual or electric typewriter, then not taking a carbon copy does save time as any corrections are more easily made.

## Pitch

This refers to the spacing of the typewriter and the space taken up by a typewritten character. The most common sizes are 10 and 12 pitch—10 pitch = 10 characters to the inch; 12 pitch = 12 characters to the inch. Originally, a typewriter was either 10 pitch (pica typeface) or 12 pitch (elite typeface), but with electric typewriters using golf ball heads, we moved on to machines with dual pitch, which meant that by fitting the appropriate head and by the movement of a lever, you could type in 10 **or** 12 pitch. Most electronic typewriters have 10, 12 and 15 pitch; however, on the more sophisticated machines there is a greater variety of pitches including proportional spacing (PS).

Daisywheels are now available in a great many typefaces and pitches which include technical, chemical, mathematical and optical character recognition elements.

The **laser printer** offers a great variety of typefaces and is a popular non-impact printer which varies in size from desktop to large floor models. Using focused light to create images on paper, lasers print high-quality characters extremely fast.

## Plays

Although the layout of plays may vary according to individual preference, the following points are generally acceptable and will be a guide to you. In a typewriting examination you should follow the general layout and instructions given.

1. Size of paper: A4.
2. Binding margin of 38 mm (1½ inches).
3. **Introductory pages**
   These are not usually numbered. The arrangement is as follows:

   First page—Title page: Title and type of play and author's name usually in capitals. May be centred vertically and horizontally in typing line, taking into account the binding margin, ie elite 19–94 (centre point 56), pica 16–77 (centre point 46).

   Second page—Synopsis of acts and scenery: Acts and numbers of acts in capitals. May be centred vertically and horizontally in typing line as on first page above.

   Third page—List of characters: Typed in capitals. If cast is included, characters are in lower case and cast in capitals. Type in double spacing and centre vertically and horizontally in typing line as in first page. Sometimes list of costumes is included on this page.

4. **Start of play. Page 1**
   4.1 Dropped head for act and act number, ie leave 51 mm (2 inches) at top of paper. May be centred in typing line, ie margins elite 19–94 (centre point 56), pica 16–77 (centre point 46).
   4.2 Turn up two single spaces and type the name of the play etc, as in 4.1.
   4.3 Margins for body of play—left 76 mm (3 inches), right 13 mm (½ inch).
   4.4 Names of characters: In capitals, starting 38 mm (1½ inches) from left edge of paper; set tab stop here and use margin release when typing names of characters.
   4.5 Scene directions: Block at left margin.
   4.6 Speeches: Block at left margin.
   4.7 Unspoken words are underscored.
   4.8 Numbering of pages: Pages numbered consecutively at top right side, leaving 13 mm (½ inch) at top of page. Turn up two single spaces after number before starting to type. Number may be just page, eg 2, or –2–. It may include the act and scene number, eg 1–1–2 = Act 1, Scene 1, page 2.

## Poetry

The following points are a guide to the typing of poems:

## Personal letters — Fully-blocked (open punctuation)

See page 197

**7** Type the following formal personal letter on plain A4 bond paper. Take one carbon copy on bank paper and type an envelope to Sir Joseph MacNee. Locate and correct the three circled errors.

```
41 Craig Street
Co Antrim
N Ireland
BT39 5PT

4 April 1994

Sir Joseph MacNee
```

TYPIST: You will find the address on page 17. Please type it here.

Dear Sir Joseph

HISTORICAL SOCIETY

On behalf of the above Society I am writing to ask if you wd be willing to accept the position of President. For the past 10 yrs the position has bn held by Dr Maureen Phillips. No doubt you hv heard th, sadly, Dr Philips died at the end of last yr. She was an excellent President with a great deal of knowledge & expertise. I give below a breif outline of our next 3 mtgs. The lectures are held in the Buffet Room in the Guildhall, High St.

27 April         Annual General Mtg
(7.30 pm)        Followed by slides of local historical interest

25 May           "Roman Highways"
(7.30 pm)        Speaker: Daniel T Montague

30 June          Local visit

TYPIST — Insert details from Data Files (filename HIST), page 164.

We know th you hv many demands on yr time, but our members wd be delighted if you were able to except.

Yrs sinc

NINA PEEL
Hon Sec

**4** Key in document 7 (filename HIST) for 12-pitch print-out. When you have completed this task, save under filename HIST, and print an original and one copy. Retrieve the document and follow the instructions for text editing on page 162.

**UNIT 3** See Practical Typing Exercises, Book Two, page 17, for further exercises on
*Personal letters — Fully blocked (open punctuation)*

## Paper sizes — reference table

| Paper | Size (Inches) | Size (Millimetres) | Horizontal spacing: Number of horizontal spaces Pitch 10 | Pitch 12 | Pitch 15 | Horizontal spacing: Centre point of paper Pitch 10 | Pitch 12 | Pitch 15 | Vertical spacing: Total number of single line spaces |
|---|---|---|---|---|---|---|---|---|---|
| **International** | | | | | | | | | |
| A4 portrait | $8\frac{1}{4} \times 11\frac{3}{4}$ | 210 × 297 | 82 | 100 | 124 | 41 | 50 | 62 | 70 |
| A4 landscape | $11\frac{3}{4} \times 8\frac{1}{4}$ | 297 × 210 | 117 | 141 | 176 | 58 | 70 | 88 | 50 |
| A5 portrait | $5\frac{7}{8} \times 8\frac{1}{4}$ | 148 × 210 | 59 | 70 | 88 | 29 | 35 | 44 | 50 |
| A5 landscape | $8\frac{1}{4} \times 5\frac{7}{8}$ | 210 × 148 | 82 | 100 | 124 | 41 | 50 | 62 | 35 |
| A6 postcard | $5\frac{7}{8} \times 4\frac{1}{8}$ | 148 × 105 | 59 | 70 | 88 | 29 | 35 | 44 | 25 |
| $\frac{2}{3}$ A4 portrait | $8\frac{1}{4} \times 7\frac{4}{5}$ | 210 × 198 | 82 | 100 | 124 | 41 | 50 | 62 | 47 |

## Paragraphing

### 1 Styles

There are three different styles of paragraph layout:

1.1 **Indented** The first line usually starts on the sixth space to the right of the second and subsequent lines of the paragraph. You should indent at least five clear spaces before starting to type the first line of the paragraph.
1.2 **Blocked** or **flush** All lines start at the same point on the scale.
1.3 **Hanging** The second and subsequent lines of the paragraph are typed two spaces to the right of the first line.

### 2 Spacing between paragraphs

2.1 **All** paragraphs typed in **single** spacing have **one** clear space between each paragraph, ie turn up two singles between each paragraph.
2.2 **Indented** and **hanging** paragraphs typed in **double** spacing have **one** clear space between paragraphs, ie turn up one double between each paragraph. In other words, the whole exercise is typed in double spacing.
2.3 When **blocked** paragraphs are typed in double spacing, leave two or three clear spaces between each paragraph, ie turn up three single or two double spaces between each paragraph. A minimum of two clear spaces must be left between paragraphs typed in double spacing.

## Personal letters

### 1 Personal business letters

Used when writing to an unknown person or firm about a personal business matter. The layout is similar to that of a business letter. If your home address is not printed on your stationery, type it about 13 mm ($\frac{1}{2}$ inch) from the top at the left margin, or centred on page, or in such a way that the last line ends flush with the right-hand margin. Date in usual place. Name and address of addressee may be typed in usual place or two spaces below your name at the left margin.

### 2 Formal personal letters

Used when writing to someone older than yourself or to whom you owe respect. Layout as for personal business letter. Salutation is formal, eg Dear Miss Brown, Dear Mrs Taylor, Dear Mr Emery.

### 3 Personal letters

Used when writing to a personal friend. Your address and date as in a personal business letter. No name and address of addressee. Salutation is informal, eg Dear Mary, Dear Arthur, Dear Uncle George.

**NOTE** It is now fairly common practice not to use courtesy titles when writing to personal friends; therefore, when addressing an envelope to your close friend Anne Crawford or John Taylor, you would not use Ms, Mrs, Miss or Mr. We suggest that you exercise great care so as not to offend the more mature or pedantic person!

# SKILL BUILDING

Type each line three times and, if time permits, complete your practice by typing each group once as it appears.

Margins:
12 pitch 22–82
10 pitch 12–72

### A  Keyboarding skills

1 Speed     The accounts and my full report were sent to you last month.
2 Accuracy  Marjory and Zena expected to visit Mrs Cameron by aeroplane.
3 Figures   He ordered 24 roses, 36 daffodils, 50 conifers and 78 cacti.
4 Symbols   Send 9 @ £5 and 10 @ £12.  Ask for 12% discount on the £190.

### B  Improve control of adjacent keys

5 er here jeer were mere merge there ferry newer finer powers.
6 ui suit Muir ruin quid fruit juice guilt build fluid tuition
7 There is the new suite that Ms Quinn ordered from Muirheads.
8 Many of the fruit farmers will agree eventually to a merger.

### C  Spelling skills—correct the one misspelt word in each line
—see page 161 for answer

9  wholly reducible debateable journeying courageous resourceful
10 dyeing catalogue recommend committees experience temporarilly
11 We recommend the goods advertised in that catelogue and feel
   that the comittee should purchase all the office furniture.

### D  Skill measurement      Four-minute timing      Not more than four errors

S/M4 We understand that you will be leaving this country shortly    12
     to take a job overseas, and we thought that your friends and   24
     family might like an up-to-date photograph of you before you   36
     leave.  We can supply large prints, and we should be pleased   48
     to arrange a sitting at short notice when convenient to you.   60

     May we also mention that we offer a service for business men   72
     which is both efficient and complete in every way.  We will    84
     be pleased to show you numerous pictures which show clearly    96
     the eye-catching style presented by our photographers.  We    107
     enclose a list of firms that employ us and for whom we have   119
     produced many advertisements for industrial magazines.        130

     Transfer Travel, our branch in High Street, can help you in   142
     a number of ways to solve your travel and transport queries.  154
     In these days when time seems to be the most important com-   166
     modity of all, you can depend on Transfer Travel to deal      177
     with all your arrangements.  Just telephone Sean Gallagher    189
     and he will use both his own and his staff's time in dealing  200
     with the hundred and one irritating little things that crop   212
     up, but which are so easily overcome by the expert who has    224
     made the whole subject his own intimate profession.  Should   236
     you wish to do business with a country with which you are     247
     not in touch, our agents will be pleased to help you with     259
     advice and contacts.                              (SI 1.34)   264

     1 | 2 | 3 | 4 | 5 | 6 | 7 | 8 | 9 | 10 | 11 | 12 |

5.2 Certain examining bodies prefer a comma, rather than a space, when using full punctuation.

5.3 Always **be consistent** when typing figures, eg type 20 000 not 20 thousand; type 300 not 3 hundred.
EXCEPTION   It is acceptable to type £3,000,000 or £3m or £3 million, but it would seem preferable always to use figures.

5.4 Thousand(s) may be represented by K, eg 24K equals 24,000.

## *Organization charts*

An organization chart shows the various departments in a business (in a large establishment it could be details of the structure of one department or even a section of a department) and sets out lines of communication, delegation and authority.

By studying an organization chart, one can see the responsibilities of each department and to whom each department is responsible. Usually, but not necessarily, top management is at the head of the chart and the connecting lines lead downwards to lower management.

The layout and style of organization charts vary considerably, and each one should be studied and planned before typing starts. A chart may be blocked at the left margin or centred, typed on A5 or A4 paper, and the linespacing can vary from chart to chart. The lines may be ruled by underscore, by ink, or a combination of both, provided that the ink is the same colour as the underscore lines. It is usual to leave three clear character spaces between separate items.

The organization chart shown on page 95, exercise 1, has been blocked and is a simple form of display. When typing exercise 2, which also is in blocked style, it will be necessary to backspace from the centre point of the paper for the longest lines in each of the items, ie Accountant   Manager Home Sales Manager   Production   Research, plus half the number of spaces to be left between each, and set the left margin at the point reached. Tab stops should then be set in the usual way for the start of each column: Sales Director starting at the second tab stop and Technical Director at the fourth tab stop. It is usual to return once before, and twice after, a horizontal line but more, or less, space may be left.

Exercise 5 on page 97, is a simple form of the centred style. Exercise 6 is also centred, but is a little more complicated. Centre BOARD OF DIRECTORS and Managing Director in the usual way; then backspace (one for every two characters and spaces) from the centre point for the **last** line, allowing three spaces between each group of items. Set a left margin and the tab stops for this line. It is sometimes easier to insert the typed horizontal line after you have typed the items beneath it; therefore:

1  Type Company Secretary at the left margin.
2  Indent to second tab stop and tap in one for every two characters and spaces in Home Sales and Export Sales plus the number of spaces between them.
3  From this point, backspace one for every two characters and spaces in Sales Director and then type the words.
4  Indent to the fourth tab stop and centre Technical Director over Production and Research.
5  Turn back two single spaces and type the horizontal line so that it starts at the centre point of Company Secretary and ends at the centre point of Technical Director.
6  Turn up five single spaces and type the last line.
7  Type the horizontal lines above it, centring the lines as in the copy.
8  Carefully insert the short vertical lines in ink.

## *Output*

The production of soft or printed copies in an information processing system.

## *Pagination*

This means the numbering of pages. The first page is not usually numbered, second and subsequent pages are numbered 13 mm ($\frac{1}{2}$ inch) (turn up four single linespaces) from the top edge of the paper, in arabic figures. The number may be blocked at the left or right margin or centred on the typing line. Some business houses prefer to have the pages numbered at the bottom.

On a **word processor**, a document can be separated automatically into pages containing the number of lines required. The page number will appear automatically at the top or bottom of the printed page according to the operator's instructions.

## *Paper*

Different qualities and weights of typing paper are available: plain bond, letterhead, bank, duplicating, etc. Most businesses use a good quality bond for their letterheads (except for airmail letters, when a light-weight paper is used) and a similar quality of plain bond paper for continuation sheets and top copies of documents.

Carbon copies are normally typed on a thin paper known as bank (flimsy); it is also available in a variety of weights and qualities. Many organizations prefer an inexpensive coloured paper for carbon copies.

# PRODUCTION DEVELOPMENT

## A5 memoranda and special marks

See page **194**

1  Type the following on a memo form with printed headings (copy in *Solutions and Resource Manual*). Use margins of 12 pitch 13–90, 10 pitch 11–75.

**MEMORANDUM**

TO    Robin Towson

FROM  Molly Dunoon

DATE  14 April 1994

HIGH-PERFORMANCE COPIER

*(Can you look into this, please?)*

# We need to give some thought to acquiring a new, reliable, high-performance copier. I have read articles describing machines with a 2000 sheet capacity that have sorting, stapling and electronic editing facilities as well as a menu card reader which should simplify the programming of complicated jobs. Apparently, it is necessary to mark the card once only, and when you repeat a job you simply insert the card - the rest is automatic.

MD/PT

2  Type the following on a memo form with printed headings. Take an original and two copies—one for the file and one for Molly Dunoon. Use suitable margins. Type an envelope to Ian Cobb. Type the same subject heading as in exercise 1.

URGENT                 **MEMORANDUM**

TO  Ian Cobb  Reprographics      DATE  15 April 1994

FROM  Robin Towson  Assistant Office Manager    REF  RT/Cop.1/*[Yr initials]*

*I shd be glad if you wd let me know asap the ~~copying~~ applications you wd require from such a copier, eg, copies per minute, colour copies, touch button control, etc.*

*We are in the process of purchasing a new copier to complement those already in use in yr dept.*

3  Type the following on a memo form with printed headings. Use suitable margins. Locate and correct the two circled errors.

MEMORANDUM  [DUNOON]

TO  *Molly Dunoon*

FROM  *Robin Towson*

DATE  *28 April '94*

*backgrounds – + it (conects) directly to a PC! Well worth the money!*

*I am enclosing full details of the copier I feel would best suit our needs. You will note that the machine I suggest not only has the features you outlined in your memo of (insert date here from Ex1), but also has the facility of 5 (colors), zoom, ~~reverse~~ merge*

UNIT 4    See Practical Typing Exercises, Book Two, page 18, for further exercises on
**A5 memoranda and special marks**    **22**

## Minutes of a Meeting

Details of any decisions or resolutions, or business discussed at a Meeting, are recorded and preserved. These are known as Minutes. Each Minute is numbered as this facilitates indexing. The order in which the Minutes are typed always follows the order in which the items appeared on the Agenda.

1. Description of Meeting, including time, date and place.
2. Names of those present—Chairperson's name appearing first, followed by the names of the officers/members.
3. Apologies received.
4. Reading of Minutes of last Meeting.
5. Matters arising.
6. Correspondence.
7. Reports of officers.
8. General business discussed—with details of any resolutions taken.
9. Any other business.
10. Place, date and time of next Meeting.
11. Place for Chairperson's signature.
12. Date on which Minutes are signed.

The Minutes may be typed with shoulder headings or side headings in blocked or indented style with either full or open punctuation.

## Modification and rearrangement of material

In an office, your employer may give you specific or general instructions about altering the layout of a document, and these instructions should be followed very carefully.

If in an examination you are directed to modify or alter the layout of an exercise, these instructions **must** be followed; otherwise marks will be lost. Before starting to type, thoroughly read through the task and mark the script clearly in ink where any alterations have to be made. For example, if items have to be rearranged in date order, write 1, 2, 3, 4, etc, against the items in the order in which they should be typed. Time spent in preparation will lead to greater accuracy and speed in typing.

## Notice of Annual General Meeting and Agenda of limited and public limited companies

Usually typed in blocked style with open or full punctuation. The wording is more formal than that used in other Notices and Agendas. In addition to the Notice and Agenda, certain other information (where applicable) is given about: voting rights, proxy votes and forms, directors' service contracts, directors' shares and debenture interests, etc.

## Notice of Meetings

For formal Meetings, such as general Meetings, extraordinary general Meetings, and committee Meetings, written Notices are sent to those entitled to attend. The Notice which is prepared by the secretary should contain details of the date, place and time of Meeting. The salutation and complimentary close may be omitted. They may be typed in centred or blocked style with open or full punctuation.

## Numbers

### 1 Cardinal numbers

These are arabic numbers—1, 2, 3, etc.

1.1 The figure 1 is expressed either by the lower-case l or by the figure 1 if this is provided on the typewriter, but these must not be mixed, ie the same key must be used for figure 1 throughout an exercise. **Never** use capital I for the cardinal number 1.

### 2 Ordinal numbers

Denote order or sequence, eg 1st, 2nd or first, second.

2.1 These are not abbreviations and must not, therefore, be followed by a full stop.
2.2 Words or figures may be used: follow the script and be consistent—either words or figures.

### 3 Roman numerals

These are formed from seven symbols known as units and fives, viz:

3.1 Units    I (1)    X (10)    C (100)    M (1,000)
3.2 Fives            V (5)     L (50)     D (500)

### 4 Figures in columns

4.1 Units under units, tens under tens, etc.
4.2 Thousands, etc, may be indicated by a comma or space—be consistent.

### 5 Figures in continuous matter

5.1 In general, thousands and millions may be indicated by a comma or space.*

---

\* Because certain member countries of the EC use the comma to represent the decimal point, it would seem wise to omit the comma from amounts of four or more figures in order to avoid confusion. Perhaps the Community will decide on a uniform method for all members. Operators should note that, at present, certain examining bodies have set rules. When the Maastricht Treaty was implemented in November 1993, the words European Union (EU) were introduced. These will not replace EC, but will be used to describe new areas of cooperation between members.

## A4 memoranda with display

**4** Type the following memo on A4 paper with suitably printed headings (copy in *Solutions and Resource Material*). Please mark BY HAND. Take an original and one copy. Locate and correct the circled errors.

**MEMORANDUM**

FROM Frederick Dalby, Facility Manager  
TO Sheena Sutherland, Purchasing  
DATE 2 May 1994  
REF FD/NB(28)/(your initials)

### Estimate (sp caps)

As you know our spacious, state of the art, new building with its attractive glass-fronted façade wl accommodate the marketing, sales, accounts & administrative staff.

### Accommodation

The bldg wl accommodate 250 staff, mainly in open-plan areas, but there wl be individual offices for first & second line managers.

### Conferencing Facilities

Conference & presentation rooms wl be provided with the main conference facility accommodating over 100 personnel.

### Equipment & Furniture

We shl retain one hundred of our existing workstations, but they wl need some refurbishment, & we shl also require 150 additional system workstations. The restaurant wl seat 140 people.

Would you please let me hv a rough estimate on the following lines asap.

*(Double spacing)*

| Refurbished | Cost | Additional Workstations | Cost |
|---|---|---|---|
| Sales | | | |
| A/cs | | | |
| Administration | | | |
| Marketing | | | |
| **Total** | | | |

*Typist — shoulder headings in unspaced caps — not underscored*

UNIT 4 — See Practical Typing Exercises, Book Two, page 19, for further exercises on **A4 memoranda with display** — 23

3 When the signs for feet and inches are used, no space is left between the figures and the sign, but one space is left after the sign, eg 2 ft 3in = 2' (space) 3".

4 Full stops are **never** used in abbreviations of metric measurements (except at the end of a sentence) and they should not be used in ft (foot/feet), in (inch/inches), etc, when typing with open punctuation. However, when **full punctuation** is being used, the full stop must be inserted in imperial measurements, eg 3 ft. 4 in. × 6 ft. 9 in. Do not mix the signs (' and ") with the abbreviations (ft and in).

5 The letter 'x' (lower case) is used for the word 'by'. Example: 210 mm × 297 mm (space before and after the 'x'.

6 At line ends **never** separate the figure(s) from the symbol.

7 Most symbols are small letters, but there are a few in upper case such as C and M which stand for Celsius and mega. Certain keyboards (teleprinters, for example) have upper case letters only, and when using such machines, the unit should be typed in full, eg 15 METRES.

8 As is may cause confusion, the symbols l (lower case L) for litre(s) and t (lower case T) for tonne(s) should not be used—better to write the words in full. If, for some reason, the abbreviation for litre is essential, then insert it in ink or type it using a suitable script style and use a looped 'el', ie $\ell$.

## Memorandum

The memorandum (usually referred to as 'memo') is one of the most convenient ways of sending messages from one person to another in the same firm, or from the head office to a branch office or agent. A memo may be typed on any of the usual sizes of paper, and firms have the headings printed and the paper cut to the size required. The layout of the headings varies.

It is quite common practice to set the left margin to coincide with the beginning of the printed headings, provided it is not less than 25 mm (1 inch). It is preferable not to have the right margin wider than the left margin. The insertions are typed two spaces after the end of the printed headings. It is important that this space is consistent after each heading.

### Other points to remember

1 No salutation or complimentary close.
2 **Body** Usually in single spacing with double between paragraphs. Blocked or indented paragraphs must be used consistently.
3 Some firms have the writer's name or initials typed two single spaces after the last line of the body of the memo.

4 If there are printed dotted lines after the printed headings, the insertions must be typed slightly above these, so that the 'long' letters are not touching the dotted lines. If there are no lines, the insertions will be aligned with the printed headings. The variable linespacer will be used in both cases to make sure that the alignment is correct.

5 **Continuation sheets** Always use **plain paper** of the same size, colour and quality as the first page; turn up four single spaces from the top and type the page number, date and the name of the addressee. If blocked paragraphs are used, these details are typed at the left margin in single or double spacing in the following order: page number, date, name of addressee. If indented paragraphs are used, the name of the addressee is typed at the left margin, the page number is centred in the typing line, and the date ends at the right margin. The memo is continued on the third single space below the continuation sheet details. If a continuation sheet is needed, the memo must be so arranged that the matter on the continuation sheet extends at least to a second line. Do not divide a word from one page to the next. The word CONTINUED or PTO may be used in memos. A catchword, ie the typing of the first word of the text appearing on a continuation sheet, is sometimes placed at the foot of the preceding page. The number of the next page must not be used as a catchword.

6 Memos are not, as a rule, signed by the author—sometimes they are initialled.

7 The notation for directing carbon copies is the same as for business letters.

### NOTES

(a) A great many organizations no longer use courtesy titles for personal names in memoranda—follow house style or instructions.

(b) A printed memorandum heading may be stored on the word processor disk and recalled as and when required: the variables and the message are easily inserted.

## Minus and plus signs

These are placed close to the figure to show a minus or plus quantity, eg −78, +22. However, when used to show subtraction or addition, the dash (space either side) and the + sign with a space on either side are used, eg 218 − 118 + 50 = 150. The following is an example of the two uses of the minus sign:

20 − 10 = 10; 10 − 20 = −10.

# A4 memoranda with continuation sheet

See page **194**

5  Type the following two-page memo on suitably headed paper. A sheet of plain bond paper should be used for the continuation sheet. Address an envelope to Sylvia Anderson, Staff Room, and mark the memo and the envelope PERSONAL. Locate and correct the circled errors.

PERSONAL

## MEMORANDUM

**FROM**   David Such   Headmaster          **REF**   DS/tpi

**TO**   Sylvia Anderson                    **DATE**   (Tomorrow's)

Governing Body  ← (Caps - not underlined)

I understand that Jack Whittacker in Group 2a, of which you are Tutor, has said that his mother is interested in becoming a member of the Governing Body of this School.

Would you please see Mrs Whittacker and give her the following information. If she is still interested ask her to get in touch with me.

A   Qualifications of Governors

Governing (Bodys) are made up of a variety of people who generally live and work in the area. Almost anyone over the age of 21 years is eligible to be a Governor. Formal qualifications (is) not necessary.

B   (Committment)

(a)   One meeting per term plus additional meetings such as school visits and training sessions.

(b)   Time off work may need to be taken.

(c)   No payment is made to Governors.

C   Duties

(a)   What is taught in school, a responsibility Governors share the Head and the local authority.

(b)   Appointing staff.

(c)   The school budget.

(d)   The conduct of the school.

(d)   Keeping the buildings in good order.

Continued/

UNIT 4         A4 memoranda with continuation sheet         24

## Literary work

For the typing of reports, short stories, scripts for books, theses, etc, the following will be a guide:

1. A4 paper is generally used.
2. Linespacing will depend upon the matter to be typed. Follow instructions or house style.
3. Margins may be equal all round—preferably 25 mm (1 inch). However, if you have to leave a binding or stitching margin, it would be preferable to leave 38 mm ($1\frac{1}{2}$ inches) on the left and 25 mm (1 inch) on the right. To ensure uniform top and bottom margins on each sheet, either:
   - 3.1 Put a light pencil mark 25 mm (1 inch) from the top and at least 25 mm (1 inch) from the bottom edge of the paper before inserting into the machine; or
   - 3.2 Rule a heavy line on a backing sheet (which is usually wider than the typing paper) across the complete width of the sheet 25 mm (1 inch) from the top, and at a point at least 25 mm (1 inch) from the bottom.
   See also *Margins*, opposite.
4. **Pagination**—the numbering of pages. The first page is not usually numbered; second and subsequent pages are numbered in arabic figures 13 mm ($\frac{1}{2}$ inch) (turn up four linespaces) from the top edge of the paper. The number may be blocked at the left or right margin or centred on the typing line. Some offices prefer to have the pages numbered at the bottom.
   Some **word processors** have the facility to perform this function automatically—others require special instructions.
   In lengthy reports, it may be necessary to date and name each page as well as number it, resulting in text appearing at both the top and bottom of a page. This procedure is referred to as inserting **headers** and **footers**.
5. Chapter headings—See *Headings*, pages 188–189.
6. Catchword—See *Catchword*, page 175.
7. The typist is expected to correct errors in spelling, grammar or punctuation, should these occur in the original draft. Where a word can be spelt in two ways, the same spelling **must** be adopted throughout the document.
8. In any piece of work it is essential that the layout for chapter headings, use of capitals, numbering, etc, is consistent. In fact, it is a good plan only to vary your style where this would improve the layout or where you are instructed to use a particular form of display.
9. **Reverse of paper** If a continuation sheet is typed on the reverse of the paper and the margins used are not equal, the margin settings should also be preserved.

## Locating information

See *Data Files*, pages 163–164, 178.

## Log sheets

See page 32.

## Logo

Symbol or trademark of an organization.

## Margins

In business, or in an examination, you are seldom given margin settings, and, therefore, you must get accustomed to choosing the most suitable margins for the length of the document and the type of display. On page 6 of this textbook, we have set out our suggestions for standard left and right margins; however, in unusual circumstances you may use margins of 13 mm ($\frac{1}{2}$ inch) on either side. Also, it can detract from the display if the right margin is wider than the left. Top and bottom margins should be 25 mm (1 inch), but here, again, in order to set out a long document on one page, 13 mm ($\frac{1}{2}$ inch) at top and bottom would be acceptable.

If you are given specific measurements (inches/millimetres) for margins—say 1 inch on the left and $\frac{1}{2}$ inch on the right—then it is better to measure and mark the paper in pencil, before inserting it into the machine and setting the margins.

To save the operator's time, **word processors** have pre-set (default) margin settings, tab settings, page length, etc, which may be changed to suit the layout required for a particular document. When any of these default settings are not appropriate for a particular exercise in this textbook, we suggest that you may wish to change the setting(s) by following the instructions given in the manufacturer's handbook.

## Measurements

In typing measurements, the following points should be noted:
1. One space is left after the number(s) and before the unit of measurement. Example: 148 (space) mm; $8\frac{1}{2}$ (space) in; 2.5 (space) cm.
2. Do not add an 's' to the symbol to form the plural—symbols are the same in the plural as they are in the singular, eg 20 metres = 20 m; 14 inches = 14 in.

2

(Tomorrow's date)

Sylvia Anderson

D   Types of Governor

uc/  (a)   Parent governors elected by the parents.

(b)   Co-opted Governors appointed collectively by the other members of the Governing Body.

(c)   Local education authority Governors appointed by Councillors.

(d)   Teacher Governors elected by the teachers.

TYPIST: Please take items (e), (f) & (g) from the Data Files, (filename GOV) on page 163, & type here.

E   Aims of Governing Body

(a)   To help to secure the best poss education for the children of the school.

(b)   To support the interests & protect the particular character of the school.

(c)   To promote good communications within the school & with parents & the wider community.

Double spacing here → (To support Governors, the local education authority runs comprehensive training programmes, including introductory courses for new Governors [stet] & sessions on specific topics such as the National Curriculum, finances & health education.

BLOCK AT LEFT MARGIN

TYPIST — Apparently it is Jack Whittaker's father, not his mother, who is interested in becoming a Governor. Please change the wording accordingly.

UNIT 4   See Practical Typing Exercises, Book Two, pages 20–21, for further exercises on
**A4 memoranda with continuation sheet**                                       25

## Linespacing

Usually typed in double spacing.

## Attestation clause

The section of a legal document where the witness(es) sign(s) to testify that he/she (they) has(have) witnessed a particular signature or signatures. The name, address and occupation of each witness is included.

The person(s) witnessing the signature need not necessarily know the contents of the document. The attestation clause starts at the left margin, is typed in single spacing and may be bracketed as follows:

```
SIGNED by the said JOHN BERK )
in the presence of:           )   Signature
(Name of Witness)             )
(Address and occupation) etc  )
```

## Folding

A4 documents are folded into two lengthways or into four horizontally.

**To fold into two lengthways**   Place the sheet or sheets face upwards on the table, and turn left edge over to meet right edge.

**To fold into four**   Place the sheets face upwards on the table, turn bottom edges to meet top, crease flat, then take folded edge, turn upwards and crease again.

## Endorsement

When the document is folded, the endorsement is typed on the uppermost side, with the open edges to the right and the fold to the left. The details contain the following information in the order given — date, names of parties, name and description of document, name and address of solicitor.

In a modern legal office, the skeleton form is recorded on the storage media for a word processor. When required, the skeleton form is retrieved and the variables are inserted.

## Line-end division

### 1 General

1.1  If possible, avoid dividing a word at the end of a line.
1.2  If it is necessary to do so in order to avoid an unsightly right-hand margin, you should not divide on more than two consecutive lines.
1.3  Divide according to syllables *provided that the pronunciation of the word is not thereby changed.*
1.4  Wherever possible, let the portion of the word left at the end of the line indicate what the word is.

### 2 Specific

**Divide**

2.1  After a prefix and before a suffix. Examples: inter-sect, absorp-tion.
2.2  *Before* the repeated consonant if the final consonant is doubled (to apply spelling rule). Example: shop-ping.
2.3  *After* the repeated consonant if the root word ends in a double consonant. Example: miss-ing.
2.4  Between the two consonants (usually) when a consonant is doubled medially. Example: bag-gage.
2.5  After a single-letter syllable in the *middle* of a word. Example: manu-script.
2.6  Between two *different* consecutive consonants in the *middle* of a word. Example: desig-nation.
2.7  After the first of three consecutive consonants in the *middle*. Example: magis-trate.
2.8  At the original point of junction in compound words and words already hypenated. Example: fisher-man, pre-eminent.
2.9  Between two separately sounded vowels. Example: radi-ator.

**Do not divide**

2.10  Words of one syllable or their plurals. Examples: course, courses.
2.11  After one or before two letters only. Examples: again, aided.
2.12  Proper names. Example: Wilson.
2.13  Sums of money, sets of figures, or contracted words. Examples: £14.32, isn't, 123,456,789.
2.14  At a point which alters the pronunciation. Examples: prod-uct (*not* pro-duct), kin-dred, (*not* kind-red).
2.15  The last word of a paragraph or a page.
2.16  Foreign words — unless you know the language and where to divide.

**NOTE**   With many electronic keyboards/word processors it is not necessary to press the return key at the end of each line to move the cursor down to the beginning of the next line. If the last word does not fit on the line, the system automatically brings the word down to the next line. This is known as wraparound or wordwrap. However, it will be necessary to press the return key for extra linespacing and after short lines, headings, etc.

It may also be possible for your machine to hyphenate a word at the end of the line, but, as the machine does not know the rules for hyphenation, it will insert the hyphen after the last character on the line, whatever it may be.

# SKILL BUILDING

Type each line three times and, if time permits, complete your practice by typing each group once as it appears.

Margins:
12 pitch 22–82
10 pitch 12–72

### A  Keyboarding skills

1 Speed      Bob said that he would like to see you on Monday at 12 noon.
2 Accuracy   Jacob and Kate require extra power for their valuable yacht.
3 Figures    Account Nos: 88/2345, 88/5678, 88/6789, 88/7890, 88/8908/09.
4 Symbols    Window (Ref 2/SA): 4' 3" h × 5' 9" w or 4' 6¼" h × 7' 10" w.

5  To develop proofreading skills, turn to page 156, exercise 2.

### Skill measurement         Five-minute timing          Not more than five errors

S/M5  Proofreading is a skill and like any skill it must be prac-     12
      tised.  If you are to become efficient at spotting errors       24
      of all kinds, it is necessary to undergo training in the art    36
      of proofreading.  To be effective a proofreader needs to be     48
      able to spell and punctuate correctly, and to know the basic    60
      rules of grammar, as well as acceptable typewriting display     71
      and layout.                                                     73

      It is not a question of just reading through a completed        85
      piece of typescript in case a typing error may have been        96
      overlooked; it is often necessary to ask the help of a col-    108
      league to read through the copy to make certain that figures   120
      are correct, that nothing has been omitted, or that unread-    131
      able handwriting has been deciphered correctly.                141

      It may be that you are an audio typist and that you have to    153
      listen to a recording on a transcribing machine.  You will     165
      need to take great care when proofreading, and, in order to    177
      check certain details, it may be necessary for you to play     189
      part of the recording again.                                   193

      If the transcription is from shorthand notes, it is a good     205
      plan to check the transcript very closely with the notes to    217
      make certain that nothing has been omitted.  Keep one finger   229
      following the shorthand notes with a finger of the other       240
      hand following each word on the typed copy.  Take particular   252
      care with words that sound alike but are spelt differently —   264
      homophones, eg, check and cheque; aloud and allowed.  If you   276
      have any doubt as to which spelling is required, check the     287
      meaning of the word in a dictionary.                           294

      If you are proofreading from a VDU, it may be helpful to use   306
      the cursor to guide the eye across the screen, and to vary     318
      the density of the brightness on the screen.                   326

      Make sure that you have used the correct stationery, typed     338
      accurately any labels or envelopes required, and attached      349
      any enclosure before the documents are placed for signature.   361
                                                        (SI 1.41)

      1 | 2 | 3 | 4 | 5 | 6 | 7 | 8 | 9 | 10 | 11 | 12 |

UNIT 5                          *Skill building*                               **26**

## Invitations

It is customary to use formal wording when sending out invitations to weddings, coming-of-age parties, etc. The invitations are written in the third person with a blank space left for the insertion of names of the guests in ink. The invitation begins with the name(s) of the writer(s) whose address is placed at the bottom left margin. The date and RSVP are at the lower right margin. Invitations are not signed. The invitation should be placed in an envelope addressed to the recipient.

### Replying to an invitation

1   If the invitation is formal (in third person) reply in the third person.
    1.1   Thank the sender for the invitation.
    1.2   Repeat the original details from the invitation—function, date, time and place.
    1.3   Accept or refuse (if a refusal, give a reason).
    1.4   Where an invitation is from a husband and wife, it is thought more correct to reply to the wife only.
    1.5   No signature is required; put date (if thought necessary) at lower left.
2   If the invitation is informal, reply in a similar form—letter or telephone.

## Italic

The printer uses italic typeface to emphasize certain words (titles of newspapers, books, periodicals, etc) in a printed document. When preparing a typewritten document for the printer, the typist must underscore the words that the printer has to set in italic typeface. Also, when typing from a printed document, the typist must underscore the words that are printed in italic. If you use a single-element typewriter and have an italic printhead, then, of course, you would type the words in italic instead of underlining them.

## Itineraries

### Appointments itinerary

If your employer has appointments outside the office, an appointments itinerary may have to be prepared for him/her, and thus the person will know exactly where he/she should be at any given time. This schedule of a day's appointments should be typed on a convenient size of paper or, preferably, on a card. There are many ways of setting out an appointments itinerary. The headings may be blocked or centred, and three spaces are left between columns.

### Travel itinerary

A travel itinerary usually implies travelling some distance by one or two types of transport and may or may not include certain appointments. Here again, headings may be blocked or centred and three spaces are left between columns.

## Justified right margin

The right margin in typewriting cannot be completely regular as in printing, but for our purposes of display it may be made regular by adopting the printer's method. This is known as 'justifying', ie the space between words is increased (where necessary) so that the last character in each line is typed at the same scale point.

For this purpose a draft must be typed, making certain that no line extends beyond the point at which the right margin is set. On the draft copy, additional spaces are indicated, so that when the passage is retyped and the additional spaces inserted all lines will end at the same scale point.

**NOTE**   It would be wrong to try and justify 'short' lines.

Most word processing machines have a function key that will automatically justify the right margin. See *Aligned right margin*, page 167.

## Labels

See *Envelopes*, page 182.

## Leader dots/leader lines (continuous dots)

See *Forms: 1 Layout, 2 Form completion*, pages 186–187; *Tabulation: 5 Leader dots*, page 211.

## Leaflets

See *Folded leaflets*, pages 184–185.

## Legal documents (Agreements, Wills)

### Margins

Preferably, left 38 mm (1½ inches), right 13 mm (½ inch). Short lines are usually filled in with a typed or handwritten line, or sometimes a series of unspaced hyphens.

I/J/L              Data Bank                        191

# PRODUCTION DEVELOPMENT

See pages **186 187**

## Forms

1 Type the following form on A5 portrait paper in double spacing and take an original and two copies. Use blocked style and margins of 12 pitch 12–62, 10 pitch 6–56. Keep the three copies for use in Integrated Production Typing, Number 1.

> BAYLES AND BAYLES
> Registered Opticians
>
> Please complete the following questionnaire.
>
> Prescription No ...................................
>
> Patient's Surname .................. Initial ....
>
> Address .........................................
>
> ........................... Postcode ...........
>
> Occupation ......................................
>
> Do you drive? ... Do you wear contact lenses? ...
>
> Do you require safety glasses at work? ..........

*TYPIST - Please finish typing the form in the same way w. the following questions. What are yr hobbies? Are you satisfied w. yr present spectacles? Do you use a computer/WP? Have you ever worn progressive or varifocal lenses?*

2 Type the following on A5 landscape paper. Use margins of 25 mm (1 inch) and 13 mm ($\frac{1}{2}$ inch) and take one copy.

READER ENQUIRY SERVICE

*TYPIST - Complete the copy w. the information given in the Data Files (filename FORM) Section A on p. 163*

For further information on advertisements in this issue please enter enquiry number(s) in the box(es) below.

[ ]  [ ]  [ ]  [ ]  [ ]
[ ]  [ ]  [ ]  [ ]  [ ]

Name _____  Position _____

Company/firm _____  No of employees ____

Address _____

_____  Postcode _____

Tel No _____  Fax No _____

(ignore any odd letter) and begin typing at the point to which you have backspaced. To centre THE TOTAL, backspace TH  Espace TO  TA (ignore the L). Say the letters to yourself as you backspace.

No punctuation is inserted at the end of lines unless the last word is abbreviated and full punctuation is being used.

**NOTE**  When the paper is inserted so that the left edge is at 0, note the scale point at which the right edge appears; half that number is the centre of the paper. For example: A4 paper extends from 0 to 100 (elite) or 0 to 82 (pica); the centre would be 50 (elite) or 41 (pica). To find the centre point of the typing line, when the margins have already been set, add the margins together and divide by two. For example, with margins of 20 and 85 the centre point of the typing line is, $20 + 85 = 105 \div 2 = 52$ (ignore the fraction left over).

### 2  Vertical display

2.1  Count the number of lines (including blank ones) that the material will occupy.
2.2  Subtract that figure from the number of line spaces on your paper. On A4 paper there are approximately 70 single spaces; on A5 portrait paper there are 50 single spaces, and on A5 landscape paper there are 35 single spaces.
2.3  After subtracting, divide the remainder by two (ignoring any fraction) to determine on what line to begin typing. For example, to centre eight lines of double-spaced copy on A5 portrait paper:

you need 15 lines, ie 8 typed, 7 blank.

$50 - 15 = 35$ lines left over.
$35 \div 2 = 17$ (ignore $\frac{1}{2}$). Start to type the matter on the next line (18).

## House style

An organization may decide that letters, memos, reports, etc, should be displayed according to certain conventions or style. This would mean that all letters sent to customers and clients would have the same layout. If the organization you work for has a particular house style which differs from your training or preference, you **must** conform to it without deviation.

## Hyphen

This is used to replace the word 'to' in certain instances. Examples:

The firm's address was 19–23 North Street. He lived from 1901–1976. This date could also be typed 1901–76, but you must be careful if the dates spread over two centuries, eg 1707–1806 (NOT 1707–06).

## Income and expenditure account

See *Financial statements*, page 183.

## Input

The first step in the information processing cycle, in which facts or data are entered into the system for processing.

## Inset matter

This refers to matter that has to be typed to the right of the set left margin. It may or may not be inset from the right margin as well. The inset portion starts a minimum of five spaces in from the left margin and there is a clear linespace above and below.

Where the matter is to be inset from both margins, take the following steps:

1  Find the centre point of typing line—add together the scale points at which the margins are set and divide by two.
2  Bring printing point to centre point of typing line and backspace once for every two characters and spaces in the longest line of the matter to be inset. The point reached is the starting point for all items unless indented or hanging paragraphs are being used. Insetting is useful in emphasizing particular aspects of the text.
3  Word processors have a second temporary margin which may be set while retaining the original margin.

## Integrated Production Typing

See pages 32–33 of this textbook.

## Interliner

The interliner lever (sometimes called the ratchet release) releases the platen temporarily from the linespacing mechanism. It may be on the right or left side of the typewriter. Locate it on your machine. When the lever is returned to the original position, the cylinder goes back to the original writing line.

The interliner is used for:

1  Superscripts and subscripts.
2  Double lines underneath totals.
3  Certain combination characters.

**3** Prepare an original and one copy on A4 paper of the following proxy form. Use a 25 mm (1 inch) margin on either side. Turn to the Data Files, pages 163–164, and on the copy type in the information from filename FORM Section B. It is essential to study the wording, etc, to be inserted when preparing the form, so that you leave ample space for the insertions.

E U R O P A C K   C O   L T D
56/60 Lonsdale Road, Caterham, Surrey
FORM OF PROXY

*TYPIST - You will find the postcode on p 15.*

*TYPIST - Replace the shaded, boxed areas w. lines of the appropriate length.*

Share Account No
☐

(Please use BLOCK CAPITALS when completing the form)

I, (Full Name)
☐

of (Full Address)
☐

hereby appoint the chair of the Meeting or, failing him/her,

Full Name
☐

Full Address
☐

as my proxy to attend and vote in my name and on my behalf at the AGM to be held on 30 April 1994, and at any adjournment thereof.

I declare that: (i) I have attained the age of 18 years. *bo.*
(ii) *I am a shareholder of the Co.*
(iii) *I hold shares in the Co. to the value of £100 or more.*

|  | FOR | AGAINST |  |
|---|---|---|---|
| *Resolution No 1* | ☐ | ☐ | *Please place an X in the appropriate box.* |
| *Resolution No 2* | ☐ | ☐ | |
| ~~*Resolution No 3*~~ | ☐ | ☐ | |

*TYPIST - Please make boxes 13 mm (½ in) square.*

SIGNATURE                                    DATE

UNIT 5                    *Forms*                    28

## 2 Main heading

This starts on the seventh single space from the top edge of the paper. The main heading may be blocked at the left margin or centred in the typing line, and is usually typed in **closed** or **spaced** capitals. It is usual to leave one clear linespace after the main heading before starting the text. However, if the paragraphs are blocked with double spacing, then it is better to turn up three single or two double spaces after the main heading before the start of the text, so that it gives a balanced appearance, matching the two or three clear spaces between paragraphs.

Main and subheadings can be effectively displayed if prominence is given to important lines by the judicial use of (a) spaced capitals (one space between each letter and three spaces between each word); (b) closed capitals (one or two spaces between each word; (c) underscore for certain words or lines; (d) emboldening.

Where the main heading 'runs on' into two or more lines, eg:

EXTRACT FROM MINUTES OF THE MEETING
HELD ON 3 JANUARY 1994

it would seem preferable to type the lines in single spacing.

## 3 Paragraph heading

These headings may be typed with initial capitals and lower-case letters and underscored, or in closed capitals with or without the underscore. Paragraph headings may be followed by two clear spaces, a full stop or a colon, when the appropriate spacing must be left after the punctuation mark. These headings may also be typed in 'run on' style where the heading is part of the sentence, but the first few words are underscored or in capitals.

## 4 Shoulder heading

These are always typed at the left margin and may be in capitals or in lower case with initial capitals, when they may be underscored. There is always a clear space above and below a shoulder heading.

## 5 Side heading

They are typed inside the left margin position and usually in closed capitals with or without the underscore. When typing side headings the following steps should be taken:
5.1 First decide on left and right margins.
5.2 Set right margin.
5.3 Set a tab stop at the left margin position.
5.4 From the tab stop in 5.3, tap in once for each character and space in the longest line of the side headings, plus three extra spaces.
5.5 Set the left margin at the point reached in 5.4.
5.6 To type the side headings, use the margin release and bring typing point to tab stop set in 5.3.

**NOTE**  When centring main or subheadings in conjunction with side headings, find the centre point by adding together the scale point where the side headings start and the right margin, then divide by two. If you are using a word processor, you may have the facility for setting a second margin or automatic indent instead of setting a tab stop.

## 6 Subheading

In addition to the main heading mentioned in 2, there may be a subheading(s) following the main heading. This heading(s) may be typed at the left margin or centred and may be in closed capitals or in lower case with initial capitals and underscored. If the main heading is centred, then it seems wise to centre the subheading(s); otherwise, the subheading will look like a shoulder heading.

There is usually one clear space between the main heading and a subheading and one clear space between the subheading and the start of the text. However, when typing blocked paragraphs with double spacing, it is usual to turn up two double spaces after the subheading to match in with the two or three clear single spaces between paragraphs.

## 7 Punctuation

There is never a full stop after a **subheading**, or after a **main**, **shoulder** or **side** heading unless the last word is abbreviated and **full** punctuation is being used.

## 8 Headings with blocked paragraphs

If blocked paragraphs are being used, it is normal practice to use blocked main and subheadings; however, there is no reason why centred headings should not be used with blocked paragraphs, or blocked main and subheadings with indented paragraphs.

# Horizontal and vertical display

## 1 Horizontal display

Headings and displayed items may be centred on the paper or on the typing line. In either case, find the centre point and backspace once for every two letters and spaces that the typed line will occupy

H                                    Data Bank                                    189

**4**

> TYPIST - Prepare a form displaying the following details neatly & accurately.

MEMBERSHIP FORM

Name // Address // Postcode // Home Tel. No

> Typist - a new line is indicated by //

Subscription

£12 individual // £16 joint // £7 under 25 //
£12 local organizations // £350 life // £500 joint life.

> TYPIST - Please type the above subs under one another in 2 columns by the side of a small box
> eg ☐ £12 individ.      ☐ £16 joint
>    ☐ £7 under 25      ☐ £12 local orgs, etc

Donation

☐ I wd like to make an additional gift of £ ___
☐ I encl. a cheque/PO for £ ___ made payable to VERGE

Please return the completed form to Tracy Holliday, VERGE, FREEPOST, 6 St Philips Way, LEICESTER, LE11AA.

---

**5**

> TYPIST - Draft a form containing the following details. Take an original & a copy & complete it w the details in the Data Files (filename FORM, Section C) on p.163.

LEISURE CENTRE - REGISTRY INFORMATION FORM

In order to achieve the highest service, we must keep our records up to date. Please help us by completing the following info & returning the completed form in the envelope provided.

Title (Mr/Mrs/Ms/Miss/Other) // Forename(s) // Surname // Date of birth // Full address.

I participate in the following activities -

Indoor Tennis / Squash / Badminton / Swimming / Judo / Table Tennis *

(* Delete those activities in wh you do not take part.)

Signature // Date // Membership No.

> Typist - type "Judo" before "Swimming".

**UNIT 5**    See Practical Typing Exercises, Book Two, pages 22–23, for further exercises on **Form layout**

space between the whole number and the fraction. In the third example ($3\frac{5}{12}$) turn up 1½ spaces and type the whole number, turn back half a space and type the enumerator; without turning up, type the underscore; turn up one space and type the denominator. When a piece of typing contains underscore fractions, type it in double spacing.

Fractions that are provided on the typewriter may be used with either sloping fractions or underscore fractions. **Never** use sloping fractions and underscore fractions in the same exercise.

### Vulgar fractions

Note the spacing in the following.

```
 5     3     Do not turn up.
12  +  6
   5     1   Turn up 1½ spaces before the whole number.
2 12  -  5   Turn back half a space to insert enumerator.
```

### Fully-blocked and centred styles

When fully-blocked letters were first introduced in *Typing First Course* in 1963, it was more or less taken for granted that everything must be blocked or centred. Over the years, attitudes have changed and it is now somewhat difficult to establish what might be acceptable and what is not acceptable. However, as we have said in previous editions of this textbook, in order to make certain information more easily found (date on a letter at right margin) and to give parts of a fully-blocked document more emphasis, there seems to be no reason why headings should not be centred, matter inset from left margin or from both margins, date at right margin, etc. In business, follow instructions or the house style; in examinations, follow instructions or layout and endeavour to meet the requirements of the examining board.

### Golf ball head

See *Single-element machines*, page 205.

### Half-space corrections

In making a correction (you have typed **the** instead of **that**) how can you squeeze in an extra letter? Erase the word you want to replace. You must now move the word half a space to the left so that only half a space precedes and follows it. To do this, you should keep the carriage/carrier from spacing normally. On manual and electric machines you can, by means of the paper release level, move the paper so that the printing point is half a space to the left of the word you have erased.

Depending on the make of machine, there are several other ways in which you can control the movement of the carriage/carrier.

**1 Electric and some electronic machines**

1.1 Bring the carriage/carrier to the space before the first letter of the word you have just erased.
1.2 Press the half-space key/bar and hold it down while you type the first letter of the word; then release the half-space key/bar.
1.3 Repeat 1.2 for the remaining letters.

**2 Manual machines**

2.1 On some typewriters the space bar can be held down to half-space the carriage. Follow the same procedure as for electric machines above.
2.2 On other machines the backspace key may be used.
   2.2.1 Bring the printing point to the space where the second letter of the erased word was typed.
   2.2.2 Hold down backspacer, type the first letter and then release backspacer.
   2.2.3 Tap space bar once.
   2.2.4 Hold down backspacer, type the second letter, release backspacer and tap space bar once.
   2.2.5 Continue in the same way with the remaining letters to be typed.

### Hard copy

Hard copy or printout is the text printed on paper.

### Headings

**1 Chapter number and heading**

The first page of a chapter may be in the form of a **dropped head**, ie the chapter number, heading, etc, start approximately 51 mm (2 inches) from the top edge of the paper. The chapter heading is usually typed two single spaces below the chapter number.

F/G/H

# Postcards

See page **199**

**6** Type the following information on a postcard.

EUROPACK Co Ltd
56/60 Lonsdale Road  Caterham  Surrey  CR3 8SY

*TYPIST - address the reverse side of the card to yourself*

---

Ref  PG/FY                                          4 May 1994

SUMMER CATALOGUE

We regret that our new summer catalogue has been
delayed at the printer.  We should be receiving
a delivery within the next 2 weeks.

Your name is on our mailing list and you will be
sent a copy at the earliest possible date.

**7** Type the following information on a postcard.

SUNBIRDS  HOLIDAYS
6 High Street  DONCASTER  DN1 3AP

---

*Send PC to:- Mr & Mrs R Smith, 6 Riverside Drive, Doncaster DN4 3FS*

                                        Date as postmark

Would you please call in to this office before (insert a suitable date abt one week fr. today) to collect the tickets for yr holiday to America. The flight departure details are as follows -

Airport          Time           Flight No
Heathrow       1355 hrs         UA 630

You are due to arrive in San Francisco at 1655 hours on the same day.

**8**

*Send a pc to Steve Garner 9 Waterloo St Edinburgh EH6 2BB*

ST/RE                                          Today's date

Yr application for the post of assistant in our postal dept is receiving attention. // In the meantime, wd you please let us hv the following details:

u.c./(a) d.o.b. (in full)
u.c./(b) the date you joined yr present firm.
We hope to receive yr reply asap.

*TYPIST - The name & address of the Co. is the same as in Ex 6 above.*

UNIT 5    See Practical Typing Exercises, Book Two, page 24, for further exercises on **Postcards**

use double spacing. One cannot be specific about the amount of space to leave when inserting dotted lines or the underscore; however, the following suggestions should be helpful.

Surname: 51 mm (2 inches), Forename(s): 76 mm (3 inches), Address: 2 complete lines, Postcode: 25 mm (1 inch), Telephone number: 38 mm (1½ inches), Date: 51 mm (2 inches).

There are one or two cases where there is no space between the typed character and the start of the continuous dots/underscore: after the £ sign and after the letter M for the insertion of the letter(s) in a person's title; eg, £.... and M....

## 2 Form completion

When typing over a dotted line/underscore, the insertion should be typed so that the base of a descending character (p, j, y, g) is just above the dotted line/underscore. For example: go, put
go put
......

Where there is no dotted line or underscore, the insertions should be aligned with the bottom of the printed/typewritten words.

Always leave a minimum of one clear space after the printed/typed headings before the start of the insertions. Always be consistent and leave the same space after each printed/typewritten heading in any one exercise. In completing some forms, it is possible to block the insertions at the same scale point in any one particular section.

If letters/words have to be deleted, use the letter X aligned precisely with the characters previously typed.

## 3 Automation

Word processing technology has eliminated many of the difficulties associated with the preparation and completion of forms and form letters. They can now be prepared and stored in a word processing system, corrections and revisions can be made quickly and easily without having to type the document again, and the form, or form letter, can be retrieved and any variables (including name and address of addressee) automatically inserted.

See also **Standard paragraphs**, page 207.

## Forms of address

1 Courtesy titles must always be used when writing to individuals.
2 Use Mr or Esq (never both) when writing to a male person.
3 Rev, Dr or Sir replaces Mr or Esq.
4 Use Messrs when addressing more than one male person.
5 Use The Misses ... when writing to more than one single lady with the same surname.
6 Address a married lady and a single lady as follows: Mrs L Brown and Miss J Black (if surnames are different), Mrs L and Miss C Brown (if surnames are the same).
7 Married couples—Mr and Mrs J Brown *or* Mr J and Mrs A Brown.
8 Use no courtesy title with impersonal names or those beginning with 'The'.
9 Use no courtesy title for limited or public companies, even if the name incudes a personal name.
10 If the abbreviation 'Snr' (Senior) or 'Jr' (Junior) is used, this comes immediately after the name and before Esq.
11 Letters after a person's name must be arranged in order of importance as follows: (a) Military Decorations; (b) Civil Decorations, eg OBE; (c) University Degrees, eg MA; (d) MP; (e) JP.

**NOTE** Use the courtesy title Ms if it is unclear whether a lady is Mrs or Miss, or if you know that a particular correspondent prefers Ms.

## Fractions

In addition to the $\frac{1}{2}$, most typewriters have keys with the most commonly used fractions. Examine your typewriter to find what fraction keys it has and practise the use of these, noting which ones need the use of the shift key. No space is left between a whole number and a fraction provided on the keyboard, eg $2\frac{1}{2}$, $3\frac{3}{4}$.

When you are required to type fractions that are not provided on the typewriter keyboard, these should be typed in one of two ways.

### Sloping fractions

Type ordinary figures with the oblique, eg 5 twelfths = 5/12; 3 sixteenths = 3/16. Where a whole number comes before a sloping fraction, leave one clear space between the whole number and the fraction; examining bodies will not accept a full stop between the number and the fraction. Example:    5 3/16.

### Underscore fractions

Type the enumerator above and the denominator below the typing line.

eg $\frac{5}{12}$  $\frac{3}{16}$  $3\frac{5}{12}$. Notice that, in this case, there is no

---

F       Data Bank       **187**

## Pre-transcription reading (proofreading)

*See page 202*

9  The following typescript was received by the typist without any corrections on it. The typist read it through before typing and made the amendments. The document now looks as it is below.
(a) Read through the exercise and note the contents and amendments. (b) Type the exercise on A4 paper in single spacing unless otherwise instructed.

PRE-TRANSCRIPTION READING

Proofreading is reading through the matter you have typed to see if there are any mistakes and, if there are, correcting them neatly.

In order to lessen the chance of your making typing errors, and to make quite sure that the finished document is correct in every way, it is essential that you spend a little time reading through the original before you start to copy from it, and to make certain that you follow the instructions precisely.

You may have to decide:

(a) size, kind and quality of stationery (paper to use) — *2 clear, Double spacing*
(b) at what scale points the margins should be set
(c) whether carbon copies are required and how many
(d) whether you will use open or full punctuation
(e) whether you will use blocked or centred style.

When reading through the original, you will watch for:

(a) wrong choice of words where there are 2 words of similar sound, eg, PLAIN/PLANE, CHECK/CHEQUE — *2 clear, Double spacing*
(b) grammatical mistakes
(c) incorrect spelling
(d) incorrect use of words and figures
(e) incorrect punctuation
(f) incorrect use of capitals l.c.
(g) incorrect use of abbreviations
(h) inconsistencies of all kinds.

## Quotation marks

*See page 203*

10  Type the following exercise in double spacing.

MEETING THE CHALLENGE — THE SINGLE MARKET

The Prime Minister said:

"The United Kingdom's Presidency falls at a particularly important time in the evolution of the European Community. We are working through a challenging agenda.

"It is our responsibility to strive with our partners to ensure . . . becomes a reality.

"We have long supported the concept of a unified European market place free of trade barriers. Such a market, based on open and fair competition, will offer us many new opportunities for business. It will also provide a strong and dynamic home base . . ."

*(one clear space)*

UNIT 5    *Pre-transcription reading (proofreading), Quotation marks*    31

next line after the reference in the text, with a horizontal line **above** and **below** it. When the final copy has to be typed, the amount of space required for the footnote(s) at the bottom of the page will then be obvious. The *Oxford Dictionary for Writers and Editors* says that copy for the printer may have the footnotes at the bottom of the page or on a separate sheet with reference figures for identification.

## *Form letters*

Many documents that businesses use will contain similar information and wording and, in order to save time, form or skeleton letters, containing the **constant** (unchanging) information, are prepared and are duplicated or printed and only the **variable** items (name and address, etc) are inserted by the typist in the blank spaces which have been purposely left to accommodate these items.

The electronic keyboard and the VDU have made production of repetitive text very much easier and time-saving. The skeleton letter, containing the constant information, is keyed in and stored on a disk. When required, it can be retrieved by pressing a function key and any insertion can be made quickly and easily (there is no difficulty with alignment when you have a VDU) and the completed letter printed out, so that it looks like an original—as distinct from a duplicated or printed document with the variables added.

When typing in the variables, care must be taken to see that the typeface on the machine used for inserting the particulars is the same size and kind as that used in the duplicated portion, and that the ribbon matches in colour and depth the constant information in the letter.

The following steps should be taken when you fill in a form letter:

1. Insert the form letter into the machine so that the first line of the body of the letter is just above the alignment scale.
2. By means of the paper release, adjust the paper so that the base of the entire line is in alignment with the top of the alignment scale (this position may vary with certain makes of machines) and that an 'i' or 'I' lines up exactly with one of the guide lines, or arrows, on the alignment scale/card holder.
3. Set margin stops and paper guide. The margin stops should be set to correspond to the margins already used in the duplicated letter.
4. Turn the cylinder back two single spaces, and, if not already typed, insert salutation at the left-hand margin.
5. Turn the cylinder back a sufficient number of linespaces to provide the correct space for the reference and name and address of the addressee, and the spaces between, to reach the line for the reference and date.
6. Type the reference at left margin.
7. Type the date.
8. Type the name and address of addressee.
9. Insert any details required and delete any unnecessary letters and/or words.
10. Check carefully.
11. When preparing a form letter, always leave sufficient blank space for the details that have to be inserted. In business, this is not always easy to decide and it is better to be over-generous. However, if you have a form letter in an examination and have to insert given details, then it is obvious that you should study the insertions when deciding on the number of blank spaces to leave.

See als *Forms* (*Automation*), page 187, and *Standard paragraphs*, page 207.

## *Forms*

Forms are printed sheets of paper or cards used to record and transmit information. That part of the information which is always the same is typed or printed in order to save time when completing the form.

### *1 Layout*

When setting out a form, be it on paper or on a card, sufficient space must be left for the information which has to be inserted. Obviously, one would leave more space for a person's surname than one would leave for his/her age; similarly, one would leave more space for a person's address than one would leave for his/her forenames. Columns where figures have to be typed must always be wide enough for the number of figures to be inserted.

Items should always be arranged in a logical sequence and related items, such as personal details in an application form, kept together.

At business, you would have a sample of the completed form and, therefore, would know what space to leave for the items to be inserted. In an examination, you may have to use common sense as to how much space should be left blank for an insertion. The form should look neat and well balanced.

Very often there will be lines of continuous dots/underscore on a form to help a person write in the information clearly. When setting out the form, see that there is one clear space after the last typed character and before the start of the continuous dots/underscore, and one clear space after the last dot and before the next typed character. Where continuous dots/underscore are inserted, always

F     Data Bank     **186**

# INTEGRATED PRODUCTION TYPING

These simulated office tasks are preceded by a Typist's Log Sheet (copy in the *Solutions and Resource Material*). Refer to the Log Sheet for instructions and relevant details before and during the typing of the documents.

## *Timing*

*Applied Typing* was the first advanced British typewriting textbook to recommend a target time, in minutes, for production work. Over the years, with the help of students and teachers, we have been able to suggest timings that came very close to the time taken by the average typist.

Today, because of the number of automatic functions on certain electronic keyboards (as compared with, say, a manual typewriter), it is impossible to set an average timing for any one document. In some typewriting examinations it is essential that you attempt all questions; therefore, we suggest that your objective is to type the Integrated Production Typing in $2\frac{1}{2}$ hours, and, to help you judge just how much **time you can afford to spend on each task**, we have allocated the maximum number of minutes you should devote to any one task in order to finish the paper within the stipulated time. This time includes proofreading the typed page and making corrections where necessary.

Reading the manuscript or typescript through to see that you understand the contents (which is of paramount importance), deciding on linespacing and margins, reading and following instructions, are all essential typing techniques that require immediate decisions and must be carried out speedily and accurately. Therefore, within the timing of $2\frac{1}{2}$ hours, we have left 15 minutes unused so that you can spend the first 10 minutes reading through the complete script, marking the special points to watch for and corrections to be made, deciding on what paper to use, what margins to set, where copies are required, etc, and another five minutes for a final check to see that each task has been attempted and each instruction followed. Of course, it may be that you will take less time than that stated, and this is good as you will then have time in reserve.

Any writer, when preparing a draft or editing a script, may unwittingly make a mistake—it may be a word spelt incorrectly; an apostrophe in the wrong place or no apostrophe at all when there should be one; it may be that the verb does not agree with the subject. You have to correct these mistakes when you are typing. In practice exercises we draw your attention to the words by circling them; in the Integrated Production Typing we do not circle them: you have to watch for the errors and correct them, just as you would do in business.

## *Folders*

Keep the typed documents in a folder marked FOR SIGNATURE, and the folder (with the tasks in document number order, together with the Log Sheet) should be handed to your tutor when you are sure that all the documents (in any one group) are MAILABLE and ready for approval and signature where appropriate. Also, keep a separate folder for the documents that have been approved/signed—file the documents under the Log Sheet number and in document number order.

## *Mailable documents*

The contents must make sense; no omissions (you could have a serious omission and the document may still make sense); no uncorrected errors (misspellings, incorrect punctuation, typing errors, etc); no careless corrections (if part of the wrong letter(s) is showing, the correction is not acceptable); no smudges; no creases. Consistency in spelling, in format, in typing sums of money, etc, is vital. Occasionally, your tutor may return a document marked C & M (correct and mail). This means that there is an error that will not be difficult to correct, and after a neat correction the document may be mailed. Remember to correct any copies.

## *Typist's Log Sheet*

The information in the Typist's Log Sheet will follow a pattern: name of employer will be at the top; the name of the originator and the designation (where appropriate) will be handwritten; the date may or may not be given, but letters and memos must have a date unless there are instructions to the contrary. If you have access to a word processor, a text-editing electronic typewriter, or a correction only electronic typewriter, follow the general instructions given on the Log Sheet against the symbol     Enter your name, date and

**A4 landscape paper folded into three**

| page 1 | page 2 | page 3 |
|---|---|---|

| reverse side of page 3 | reverse side of page 2 | front cover reverse of page 1 |
|---|---|---|

## *Front cover*

This will contain the title or main points of the document and should be given emphasis by the judicial use of centring, blocking, emboldening, capitals, spaced capitals, underlining, etc, so that the result is neat, attractive and eye catching.

## *Inside pages*

It gives a more pleasing appearance if the far left and far right margins are equal, and where there is sufficient space, the margins on either side of the fold should match the left and right margins; however, this is by no means obligatory as long as there is equal space, say 13 mm ($\frac{1}{2}$ inch) on either side of the fold. In exercise 4, on page 52 of this textbook, it will give a more balanced appearance if the display on each page starts at the same distance from the top. The display on the inside left will take up more vertical space than that on the right and should be typed first so that calculations can be made to enhance the presentation by inserting extra spaces, asterisks or a tailpiece on the right-hand page.

## *Back page*

Any wording on this page will contain matter of less importance; nevertheless, it should be displayed attractively.

## *Footnotes*

### 1  Footnotes are used

1.1  To identify a reference or person quoted in the body of a report.
1.2  To give the source of a quotation cited in a report.
1.3  For explanations that may help or interest a reader.

### 2  *Each footnote is*

2.1  Preceded by the reference mark which corresponds to the reference in the text.
2.2  Typed in single spacing.

The reference mark in the text must be a superscript. In the footnote, it is typed either on the same line or as a superscript. In the text, **no** space is left between the reference mark and the previous character. In the footnote, **one space** is left between the reference mark and the first word. The reference mark may be a number, asterisk, dagger or double dagger, and is placed outside the quotation mark and the punctuation mark.

It is now more popular to use one asterisk for the first footnote, two for the second and three for the third, rather than a dagger or double dagger, as the daggers are not always easy to construct on an electronic keyboard. The use of figures (in brackets) as a reference mark is favoured by printers.

In ordinary typewritten work, the footnote is usually placed at the foot of the page on which the corresponding reference appears in the body, and typed in **single** spacing. Care must be taken to leave enough space at the bottom of the page for the footnote, and, if a continuation page is needed, a clear space of 25 mm (1 inch) should be left after the last line of the footnote. It is usually separated from the main text by a horizontal line from margin to margin, and this line is typed by the underscore one single space after the last line of the text, and the footnote on the second single space below the horizontal line. If there is more than one footnote, turn up two single spaces between each. Where the typed text is short and there is plenty of white space on the sheet of paper, you may wish to make a more attractive display by leaving the clear space after the text and before the footnote, with the last line of the footnote ending one inch from the bottom of the page. Some examining bodies do not always insert a horizontal line before the footnote and, in that case, it may be wise for the examination candidate to omit the line, and we suggest that examining bodies should be asked to make the candidate's position clear. There is no horizontal line before footnotes which follow a ruled, tabulated statement.

If the typewriter has an asterisk key, the typed character will be raised half a space, but if a small x and the hyphen key are used, then it will be necessary to use the halfspace mechanism of the typewriter, or the interliner, to raise the mark above the line of typing. All footnote signs should be superscripts if the asterisk key on the typewriter is used. On word processors, there will be a superscript facility for raising characters above the typing line.

When typing a draft of a document which contains a footnote(s), it is helpful to type the footnote on the starting time near the bottom of the sheet. When all the documents have been completed and are ready for approval/signature, calculate and enter the TOTAL TYPING TIME at the bottom of the last column, and also record the date and time of completion.

## *Urgent*

Note that any input marked with an asterisk (*) is urgent and should be dealt with first. Type the word URGENT at the top of the document, and see that it is ready for approval/signature within 40 minutes of your starting time.

## *Stationery requisition*

Before starting the Integrated Production Typing, you should read it through and decide on the quantity and kind of stationery you will require for all the tasks, and then fill in a Stationery Requisition Form which you should hand to your tutor for approval. You will need headed paper for business letters and memoranda; bond white paper for top copies of other documents; bank paper for carbon copies; carbon paper, envelopes, cards, labels, etc. You may allow yourself a few sheets more than you require, but you should in no circumstances give yourself unlimited supplies. Most employers keep a strict control over the use of stationery. In an examination, your supply of typing paper will be limited. Of course, you will have readily available some means for correction of errors, ruler, pen, pencil, dictionary, carbon paper, etc.

## *Distractions*

As an office worker, it is a necessity of life that you should be able to cope with interruptions and distractions which are a normal part of the office scene. Your boss may ask you to make alterations to a script (already in your possession) while you are engrossed in typing an urgent or complicated document; you may be interrupted by the telephone; a client may call to see your boss, etc. You should be sufficiently accomplished to be able to return to your typing unaffected by these distractions. To simulate office conditions, your tutor may interrupt you while you are working on the Integrated Production Typing tasks and give you alterations to an exercise, or hand you an additional task: these alterations/additions are in the *Solutions and Resource Material*. Examining bodies may incorporate this form of distraction during a typing examination.

## *Dates*

A business document is of very little use unless it is dated and has a reference as to its origin. Documents, other than letters and memos, are usually dated at the bottom of the last page with the reference either before or after the date. When you are at business, follow the house style. Typewriting examiners for certain boards may penalize you if you date any document (unless there are instructions to do so) apart from letters and memos.

## *Superfluous wording*

If you add a word(s) not in the script, eg, a reference in a letter when it is not given, then you may be penalized by the examiner. Similarly, if you insert a line before a footnote and there is no line in the script, then you may be penalized.

**Check very carefully to ascertain what the examiner does and does not accept.**

## *Solutions and Resource Material*

The *Solutions and Resource Material* is loose-leaf, and record sheets, printed letterheads, forms, form letters, language arts skills—punctuation, word comparison, subject and verb agreement, word usage, etc, may be copied and these will make your typing much more realistic.

Text-edited copies of the word processing exercises are in *Solutions and Resource Material* and may be used instead of the text-editing instructions on pages 162–163.

### Vertical Balance Sheets

Decide on the margins. Set left and right margin.

From the right margin backspace one for one for the longest item in the money column and set a tab stop. Where an item runs on to two lines, it is usual to indent the second line two spaces. If there are two columns of figures, leave a minimum of three spaces between each column.

## Fit (manuscript)

1. It is sometimes necessary to divide a long manuscript among several typists. If the manuscript is in chapter form, the division should be made at the end of a chapter. If, however, the matter is continuous, the division must be made in such a way that the last line of each typist's section comes to the bottom of a page, so that it may run on without a break to the start of the next typist's section. This is known as 'fit'. To do this, it may be necessary to make some adjustments to the linespacing on the last page.

2. When a manuscript is divided in this way, care must be taken to see that each typist adopts the same margins, style for headings, etc, and that the ribbons and typefaces on all machines match.

3. **Word processors** When preparing long reports, manuscripts for publication, construction proposals, product analyses and legal briefs, several authors may contribute to them. Because information processing means that documents can be revised or reorganized without being completely rekeyed, these, and similar documents, can be prepared more quickly and efficiently (by a team of operators if necessary) than was so when using a manual or electric typewriter.

## Flow charts

A flow chart is a graphical representation of the flow of work, movement of documents, sequence of events, etc. By using lines and (sometimes) standard symbols (circles, diamonds, boxes, etc) a clear picture of a progression of happenings can be followed more easily.

The layout of flow charts varies widely and the design will depend on the characteristics of the particular topic. The aim of the flow chart is to help one complete a specific task step by step, or to identify the way in which a specified job is completed. By studying a flow chart, one can very often eradicate bottlenecks and wasteful operations.

Lines can flow vertically or horizontally provided that they show by letters, numbers or arrowheads the movement of a sequence of activities. Broken lines (continuous hyphens) are used for any function other than progressive flow.

When a flow chart has to be typed, it is usual to employ rectangular boxes for each step.

Flow charts are the foundation of computer programming. A chart has to be prepared so that the machine will execute each step of a particular task in logical succession and does not move forward to the next step until the previous step has been verified.

Before starting to type a flow chart, careful planning is essential. The first problem is to decide on the size of paper—it is better to err on the large side and you may have to use the paper lengthwise. If necessary, type a rough draft quickly to see what the longest horizontal line will look like. Unless otherwise instructed, leave three character spaces between items and at least one clear vertical space. When typing horizontal lines for boxes, turn up once before and twice after, although more, or less, space may be left between items or boxes.

## Folded leaflets

The display and format used when typing a folded leaflet will depend on the way in which the page is folded, the number of lines to be typed and the range of display required for each page. To avoid confusion, mark all pages quite clearly in pencil before inserting the paper into the machine.

**A4 landscape paper folded to give four sheets of A5 portrait paper**

FRONT SIDE OF PAPER UNFOLDED

front page—right-hand side
back page—left-hand side

| back page  | front page  |
| left hand  | right hand  |

page 2—left side of fold
page 3—right side of fold

| page 2     | page 3      |
| left side  | right side  |

# INTEGRATED PRODUCTION TYPING

## BAYLES and BAYLES
### Registered Opticians

OFFICE SERVICES — REQUEST FORM

*Typist's Log Sheet*

This sheet contains instructions that must be complied with when typing the documents. Read the information carefully before starting, and refer back to it frequently.

Originator: *Simon Aspel*    Designation: *Manager*    Date: *21 May '94*    Ext No *2*

Typists operating a word processor, or electronic typewriter with appropriate function keys, should apply the following automatic facilities: top margin; carrier return; line-end hyphenation; underline OR bold print (embolden); error correction; centring; any other relevant applications.

Remember to (a) complete the details required at the bottom of the form; (b) enter typing time per document in the appropriate column; and (c) before submitting this **Log Sheet** and your completed work, enter TOTAL TYPING TIME in the last column so that the typist's time may be charged to the originator.

| Document No | Type of document and instructions | Copies— Original plus | Input form¶ | Typing time per document | Total typing time ¥ |
|---|---|---|---|---|---|
| 1 | Letter to Mr Gregory Shipley, 9 Fellowes Lane, Norwell, Newark Notts NG21 4PR (Type an envelope) | 1 + 2 | AT | | |
| 2 | Postcard to Mr Shipley | 1 original | MS | | |
| 3 | Spectacle Care Guide | 1 original | AT | | |
| *4 | Personal letter (I will give you the place of the mtg shortly. I have to confirm with the Sec. You will need this info for the next task, also.) | 1 + 1 | MS | | |
| 5 | Memorandum — which includes an agenda. | 1 original | MS | | |
| 6 | Form to be completed | 1 original | MS (A print from Data Files) | TOTAL TYPING TIME | |

TYPIST — please complete:
Typist's name:        Date received:        Date completed:
                      Time received:        Time completed:

If the typed documents cannot be returned within 24 hours, the office services supervisor should inform the originator. Any item that is urgent should be marked with an asterisk (*).

¶ T = Typescript   AT = Amended Typescript   MS = Manuscript   SD = Shorthand Dictation   AD = Audio Dictation
¥ to be charged to the originator's department   AP = Amended Print.

*Typist's Log Sheet — No 1*    34

before the addressee's address; eg

Mrs Monica Phillips
PO Box No 4651
47 Market Street
COVENTRY     CV4 9FR

   7.8  BY HAND is typed in the top right corner in capitals.

8  Remember to type the envelopes for any extra copies which may be sent to the other offices or persons for their information.

9  **Optical character recognition**  The Post Office now use OCR machines for reading and sorting mail at a high speed: 35 000 items an hour. However, the machines can be employed only if the POP envelopes are used and methods of addressing, given on page 182, are followed. The OCR machines cannot read script or italic typefaces; addresses typed on envelopes which are not white, buff or cream; proportionately spaced type; or crooked application of address labels. The typeface should be 10, 11 or 12 characters to the inch.

## *Errors*

You will require individual remedial practice based on your needs; therefore, check your work carefully and make a note of the letters on which you made mistakes; then look in the Index under **Drills** and choose the drill(s) that will help you overcome your faulty techniques.

## *Fair copy*

Final copy typed on bond A4 paper in double spacing.

## *Fax*

See page 55 (S/M 10).

## *Figures in columns*

Care must be taken to see that units come under units, tens under tens, etc. Where there are four or more figures, these are grouped in threes starting from the unit figure, a space being left, or a comma inserted, between each group. **Be consistent!**

## *Financial statements*

There are certain accounts which you may be asked to type for your employer, such as Balance Sheet, Income and Expenditure Account, Receipts and Payments Account.

## *Guide to typing*

1  The financial statement may be divided into two sides and may have a line down the middle of the page.

2  Leave the same number of spaces to the left and right of the centre of the page—say 13 mm ($\frac{1}{2}$ inch) clear on either side.

   2.1  With A5 landscape paper or A4 paper, this would mean the centre of the paper is 50(41) and, to leave 13 mm ($\frac{1}{2}$ inch) clear, backspace 6(5) from 50(41) plus the number of figures in the longest item in the figure column—set a tab stop for the start of the longest line in the left-hand figure column.

   2.2  From 50(41) tap in 7(6) and set a tab stop for the start of the items on the right half of the page.

3  Leave left and right margins of 25 mm (1 inch) clear which means the left margin will be set at 13(11) and a tab stop set at 89(73). To find the starting point for the money column at the far right of the page, backspace from 89(73) one for one in the longest line of the column.

4  All headings, on right and left sides, start on the same lines, including the £ signs.

5  Use double spacing between each item. If any item requires more than one line, type the item in single spacing, indenting two spaces for the second and subsequent lines.

6  The totals on both sides must be typed opposite each other on the same line. This may mean leaving a blank space on the shorter side, before inserting the total and the total lines.

7  The horizontal lines above and below the total itself are typed as explained on page 215.

8  Blocked or centred display may be used with open or full punctuation.

## *Balance Sheets*

The method of setting out Balance Sheets is the same as that already explained above, although in some instances two separate sheets are used, the heading of the Balance Sheet running right across the two sheets without a break—half being typed on the Liabilities side and ending close to the right edge of the paper, say 13 mm ($\frac{1}{2}$ inch).

The side containing the larger number of items should be typed first, and, before starting to type the second sheet, you should make a light pencil mark to show the precise point at which the heading is to be continued, to ensure that the two parts of the heading are in line with one another. Also mark lightly in pencil on the second sheet the line on which the £ sign appears, the line on which the first item is to be typed and the exact position for the total, so that the two sides may coincide exactly.

① – 40 mins

TYPIST – Please type the following letter, dated today, on our letterhead paper, & take 2 copies – one for JOHN BAYLES & the other for file. Type an envelope & mark the letter & envelope PERSONAL.

Our ref SA/(Your initials)

Mr Gregory Shipley
(Insert address here)

Dr Mr S——    CATARACTS

You asked me if I could let you have some information about cateracts to alleviate some of the worries you have about your forthcoming operation on ⁁ . I am enclosing a booklet but have also prepared some of the more useful points below. (Insert date here from Task 2)

The operation. In a straightforward hospital operation the lens of the eye can be removed and replaced with a clear lens of transparent material. Cateract operations are generally very successfull and the cateract will not grow again. It is possible to have the operation as an out patient but you will probably go into hospital and have either a ⁁ P complete general or a local anaesthetic. You will stay in hospital for 1-3 days to recover from the anaesthetic, for drops to be given and for progress to be watched.

What is a cataract? The lenses inside our eyes remain clear for most of our life, but sometimes the lens becomes cloudy, light cannot pass thro' well, and we cannot see clearly. This condition is called a cataract.

After the operation.
In the first few days after the operation a purple colour may be noticed but later the vision shd be very much clearer than before the op. New spectacles (or contact lenses if you wish) wl take a little getting used to at first, as the eyes adjust to the new prescription.

Continued/

opening bracket and one space after the final bracket.

## Decimalized enumeration

In addition to the methods of enumeration explained above, it is modern practice to use the decimal point, followed by a figure, for subdivisions. For example, 4(a) and 4(b) would become 4.1 and 4.2; and 4(a) i and 4(a) ii would become 4.1.1 and 4.1.2. When using both full and open punctuation, the decimal point for decimalized enumeration must be inserted. Leave two clear spaces after the final figure.

## Envelopes

| | | |
|---|---|---|
| C5 | 162 × 229 mm ($6\frac{3}{8}'' \times 9''$) | |
| | takes A5 paper unfolded and A4 paper folded once | |
| C6 | 114 × 162 mm ($4\frac{1}{2}'' \times 6\frac{3}{8}''$) | |
| | takes A4 paper folded twice and A5 paper folded once | |
| DL | 110 × 220 mm ($4\frac{1}{4}'' \times 8\frac{5}{8}''$) | |
| | takes A4 paper folded equally into three | |

The above measurements fall within the POP (Post Office Preferred) sizes. The POP envelopes are sorted automatically, whereas larger or smaller sizes are not, and there may be an extra charge for sizes outside the POP range.

## Post Office regulations

1. Post Office regulations require the address to be parallel with the longest side of the envelope.
2. Postal town should be typed in capitals on a fresh line.
3. The postcode should be typed as follows:
    3.1 It is always the last item in the address and should have a line to itself.
    3.2 If it is impossible because of lack of space, to put the code on a separate line, type it two to six spaces to the right of the last line.
    3.3 Always type the code in block capitals.
    3.4 Do not use full stops or any punctuation marks between or after the characters in the code.
    3.5 Leave **one** clear space between the two halves of the code.
    3.6 **Never** underline the code.

EXAMPLE    Open punctuation

Messrs W H Ramsay & Co
Mortimer Street
LONDON
W1N  8BA

Full punctuation

Messrs. W. H. Ramsay & Co.,
Mortimer Street,
LONDON.
W1N  8BA

## Addressing envelopes, labels, postcards, etc.

See also **Forms of address**, page 187.

1. Always be sure to use an envelope sufficiently large to take the letter and any enclosure.
2. Many firms have their name and address printed in the top left corner. This ensures the safe and speedy return of the letter if, for any reason, it cannot be delivered.
3. Always type the envelope for each letter immediately after typing the letter.
4. Single spacing and blocked style are preferable on a small envelope. With larger envelopes the address may be better displayed and more easily read by being typed in double spacing.
5. On most envelopes the address should be started about one-third in from the left edge and the first line should be approximately half-way down.
6. Envelopes for overseas mail should have the town/city and country in upper case.
7. Special instructions.
    7.1 PERSONAL, CONFIDENTIAL, PRIVATE, URGENT should be typed in capitals, two spaces above the name of the addressee.
    7.2 FOR THE ATTENTION OF . . . is typed two spaces above the name and address of the addressee and may be in capitals or lower case with initial capitals when it must be underscored.
    7.3 RECORDED DELIVERY, REGISTERED MAIL and SPECIAL DELIVERY are typed in the top left corner in capitals, or immediately below the return address if there is one.
    7.4 FREEPOST and POSTE RESTANTE are typed after the name of the addressee.
    7.5 The words PAR AVION (BY AIRMAIL) are typed in the top left corner.
    7.6 Care of—typed c/o at the beginning of the line containing (a) the name or number of the house, eg Ms R Sharpe, c/o 21 Market Street, or (b) the name of the occupier, eg Ms R Sharpe, c/o Mrs U Needle, 21 Market Street.
    7.7 An addressee may rent a private box at the normal delivery office so that he or she may call to collect mail as an alternative to delivery by the postman—there is a charge for this service. The box number is typed on the line below the addressee's name and

2

(Date)

Mr. Gregory Shipley

NP/ Generally, it is wise to chose reasonably small frames, as large ones cld mean unduly thick & heavy lenses. Many people find plastic lenses an advantage because they are lighter in weight than glass.

It is often worth considering a **HARD** coating on plastic lenses to reduce the risk of scratching the more steeply curved front surface of post-cataract lenses.

Please dont worry abt having the operation. In next to no time you wl be able to see more clearly than you hv for yrs.

You wl, of course, hv advice from our optician abt the best form of frame for you.

Very best wishes.

Yrs sinc

(My name & designation here)

---

② — 15 mins — Type the following on a postcard, please. Address the reverse side to Mr Gregory Shipley as in Task 1.

BAYLES and BAYLES
Registered Opticians

(Address here)

(Date)

Wd you call in to see Mrs Sara Edwardes, the ophthalmic medical practitioner, at the above address, on Wed 1 June @ 2.30pm.

TYPIST — Change time to 24-hr clock.

I understand you are to hv the operation on 14 June.

**Integrated Production Typing Project — No 1**

5  External memory—any storage medium (disk) which can be removed from the system.
6  Mailing applications.

## *Elision*

This is the omission of a letter (usually a vowel) when pronouncing a word, eg wouldn't, can't, don't. This form of abbreviation must **not** be used in typescript unless you are quoting direct speech, ie using quotation marks, or instruction has been given to use it.

## *Ellipsis (omission of words)*

Words are sometimes deliberately omitted at the beginning, end or in the middle of a sentence. Such omission is indicated by the use of three spaced full stops with a space either side, as follows: . . . . When quotation marks come before the ellipsis, there is a space between the mark and the first full stop. There is also a space before the final quotation mark, eg " . . . ".

## *Embolden*

Electronic typewriters and word processors have a **bold** function key. Usually, this key is depressed before typing the chosen word(s) which will then appear in a much darker print and thus be more emphatic.

## *Emphasis*

See *Effective display*, page 180.

## *Endorsements*

See *Legal documents*, page 191.

## *Enumeration*

An enumeration is a set of numbered/lettered paragraphs or lines that may be displayed in several different ways.

1  The numbers may project to the left of the first line of the paragraph, with the second and subsequent lines blocked underneath the first line of the paragraph—as in this paragraph. Punctuation must not be inserted after a number when typing in open punctuation—leave two clear spaces. Also, leave two spaces after the full stop when full punctuation is used. Indented or hanging paragraphs may be used.

2  In some cases the numbers are put in brackets, eg (2) in which case two spaces and no full stop are left after the final bracket.

3  Letters may be used in place of numbers.

4  Where there are subdivisions of enumerated items, these can be distinguished in order of importance as follows:
   4.1  Capital roman numerals for main division.
   4.2  Upper case letters for first subdivision.
   4.3  Arabic numbers, small letters or small roman numerals for further subdivisions.

5  There must be a clear linespace above, below and between lettered/numbered items.

   **NOTE**  In business, you will find that your employer may prefer you, in order to save space, to leave no space **between** the lettered/numbered items.

6  When roman numerals are used in enumerations, these may be blocked on the left or right. Do not insert full stops when using open punctuation.

   *Left—example with full punctuation.*
   I.    Two spaces should be left after the full stop following the **longest** numeral.
   II.   Therefore, there will be four spaces after I, three spaces after II, two spaces after III and
   III.  three spaces after IV.
   IV.

   *Right—example with open punctuation.*
     I  Two spaces should be left after the numeral.
    II  It will be necessary to indent two spaces before typing I, one space before II, no space
   III  before III, and one space before IV.
    IV

**NOTES**  (a) The punctuation before the start of an enumeration may be a full stop; a colon (most popular); a colon and dash (:-) which is considered old-fashioned; a dash (space before the hyphen).

(b) The punctuation at the end of each enumeration could be no punctuation at all, a comma, a semi-colon, or a full stop, depending on the sense. The final item in a list would normally have a full stop. Always follow instructions, the copy or the house style. **Be consistent!**

## *Continuous prose*

When using enumerations in continuous prose where the items 'run on' (are not listed underneath each other), the numbers or letters should be enclosed in brackets. There is one space before the

③ *TYPIST - Change 'glasses' to 'spectacles' in ea case.*

**25 mins**

Spectacle Care Guide — CAPS

*Please check to see whether or not this word should be hyphenated.*

Please call in within 4 weeks of receiving your new glasses so that we can check there fit. Slight readjustments will be made free of charge. The following guidelines will help preserve the fit and the appearance of your glasses.

*Double spacing between items*

(i) Always take your glasses off with 2 hands to avoid straining the frames.

(ii) Keep your glasses in a case when not in use.

(iii) Never leave them w the lenses lying face down. They may become scratched.

(iv) Clean glasses daily by holding the rim of the frames, not the sides or the bridge.

CAPS (v) Do **not** polish lenses when dry. For the best results spray w a lens cleaner & wipe dry w a high tech cloth.

Yr glasses are an important part of yr life. Loss or damage cd be extremely inconvenient. For a small premium paid at the time of ordering, you can insure them so they can be swiftly replaced if the need arises.

---

④ *TYPIST - Type the following letter on plain paper, please, with one copy. Fold the letter to fit into a window envelope.*

**15 mins**

97 Forest Rd
Norwell Newark Notts NG14 3SP

Mr R Philpot 1 Assington Rd Norwell Newark Notts NG23 6JN

Dr Mr P——  ASSOCIATION FOR THE BLIND

I am writing on behalf of the local branch of the A—— for the B—— to thank you very much for offering to come & talk to our cttee members on (insert date from Task 5 on following page).

It is understood th you wl be able to give us some info abt the care of visually impaired people in the community, the aids or specialized equipment available, holidays for the blind, visiting services, etc.

We look forward to seeing you @ 1930 hrs in

Yrs sinc

(Name)
CHAIR

---

**Integrated Production Typing Project — No 1**

addresses and, on instruction, the machine will retrieve and assemble the paragraphs into a letter. In some cases there may be additions or deletions.

Often-used forms are also stored and are retrieved and completed as and when required.

The electronic keyboard and the VDU have made production of repetitive text very much easier and time-saving. Any variables can be inserted quickly and easily (there is no difficulty with alignment when you have a VDU) and the complete document printed out as an original—as distinct from a duplicated or printed document with the variables added.

## Document presentation

See page x.

## Double underscore

See *Totals*, page 215.

## Draft

If your employer asks you to type a draft copy of a document, it would be wise for you to enquire whether the document is likely to be radically revised or whether the draft is to show how the document will look when completed.

If the document is likely to be extensively revised after typing, then the draft should be in double or treble spacing with wide margins. On the other hand, if the draft is to show how it will look when finished, then it should be typed in the style required for the finished job.

The word DRAFT should always be typed in capitals at the top left-hand margin at least one clear space above the start of the document.

## Dropped head

See *Chapter headings*, page 175.

## Effective display and emphasis

Matter can be effectively and artistically displayed if **emphasis** is given to important lines by the judicial use of:

1. Spaced capitals (one space between each letter and three spaces between each word).
2. Closed capitals (one or two spaces between each word).
3. Underlining of certain words or lines. Instead of underlining spaced capitals, a more pleasing effect may be gained by turning up half a linespace after the heading in spaced capitals before typing the underscore, then turn up two single linespaces before typing the subheading or start of text. (See exercise 3 on page 3.)
4. Initial capitals and small letters with or without underlining.
5. Insetting of lines or items from the left margin or left and right margins.
6. Bold type if this function is available on your electronic machine.
7. Hanging paragraphs.
8. Changing the linespacing.

**NOTE** Care must be taken not to overdo any one of these methods; otherwise, no line will stand out more prominently than another, thus detracting from the general appearance.

## Preparing a layout of a notice

Before typing an unarranged notice or tabulation, or when rearranging a table, etc, prepare a 'layout', ie a rough plan in pencil, showing the best arrangement of the matter and the number of lines required. Keep the layout before you as you type. Where the display or rearrangement is complicated, it is a good plan to type a rough copy of the longest line and/or parts that are not clear.

## Electronic typewriters

While the electric typewriter consists of mechanical parts and electrical wiring, the electronic typewriter has silicon chips to decode the keyboard instructions and operate the editing and storage functions.

On electronic typewriters the printing element is a daisywheel, with the exception of the older IBM machines where the golf ball head is still used.

The following are some of the facilities to be found on electronic typewriters:

1. Automatic—carriage return, underscoring, bold face, vertical ruling, margin sets and additional margin sets, horizontal centring, reverse tabulation, decimal tabulation, justification of right margin, etc.
2. 'Window' display—the typist can read the text line by line before printing it. While the words are in display, the typist can make corrections, add or take away words, etc.
3. 10, 12 and 15 pitch plus proportional spacing.
4. Internal memory—may be stored permanently on a read only memory chip or may be lost when the machine is switched off.

(5) — (20 mins)

MEMORANDUM
To      All cttee members
FROM    S— A—, Chair
DATE

ASSOCIATION FOR THE BLIND

You will all be pleased to hear th an eminent Eye Consultant, Robert Philpot, has agreed to come & talk to us, at our next mtg in June, abt the care of the visually impaired people in the community, the aids & specialized equipment available, holidays for the blind, visiting services, etc.

I give below the agenda for the mtg to be held on 24.6.934 @ 1930 hrs in

(Inset 5 spaces)

←——— A G E N D A
1   Apologies.
2   Minutes of last mtg.
3   Matters arising not dealt with elsewhere on the agenda.
4   Correspondence.
5   Distribution of batteries for the wireless for the blind.
6   Grants & financial assistance.
7   Talk by Robert Philpot.
    (To commence @ approx 1945 hrs).
8   Date of next mtg.

SA/(Yr initials)
_____

(6) — (20 mins)

Please complete a copy of the form on page 27, Ex 1, for Dick Martin of 3 Brent Close, Norwell, Newark, Notts, NG20 9SA.  [MARTIN]

You will find the remaining details in the Data files on page 163 (filename BAYLES).

## Diagrams

See **Allocating space**, page 167.

## Disk

The most common method of storing information in word processing and computing is on a disk. The disk can be **floppy** (usually referred to as a diskette) or **hard**—the **hard disk** has a much larger storing capacity.

## Disk drive

This is the unit in a word processor or micro-computer in which the floppy diskette is inserted so that information may be stored or retrieved.

## Display

### 1 Horizontal

1.1 **Block-centred** Centre the longest line which gives the starting point for all lines.
1.2 **Centred** All lines centred on the paper or on the typing line. To find the centre point of the typing line, add together the points at which the margins are set and divide by two.

With certain electronic keyboards there is usually an automatic centring function which will centre the typed line. The heading, line of text, etc, to be centred is typed at the left margin and the item will be centred between the margins when the appropriate command is given. When using a VDU the appropriate key is depressed and the typed item is automatically centred.

### 2 Vertical

2.1 Find the number of vertical lines on the paper being used.
2.2 Count the number of lines and blank spaces between the lines, in the exercise to be typed.
2.3 Deduct 2.2 from 2.1 and divide by two (ignore fractions).
2.4 Turn up the number of linespaces arrived at in 2.3 **plus one extra**.

See also **Effective display and emphasis**, page 180.

## Distractions

See page 33.

## Distribution lists

See **Business letters, 4.15**, page 172.
Instead of typing cc followed by the names of the persons to whom copies of a document should be sent, your boss may require you to type a distribution/circulation list. An example is given on page 77.

## Ditto marks

When the same word is repeated in consecutive lines of display matter, double quotation marks may be used under the repeated word. If there is more than one word repeated, the quotation marks must be typed under each word. The abbreviation 'do' (with the full stop in full punctuation) may be used under a group of words. When used with blocked style, the ditto marks should be blocked at the beginning of each word; with centred style, the ditto marks should be centred under the word(s). See page 136.

## Division of words

See **Line-end division**, page 192.

## Document assembly

In word processing terms, this is known as boilerplating. Many documents that businesses use will contain similar information and wording and, in order to save time, form or skeleton letters (see page 90) containing the **constant** (unchanging) information are prepared, keyed in and stored. Space will be left for the date, inside address, salutation and any other **variables**.

Each form letter is given a filename so that it can be retrieved easily, and a special code is placed at each point so that the machine will stop and the relevant information can be inserted at the position of the cursor. If the same letter is being sent to a number of customers, the typist keys in the names and addresses, and command keys are used to merge the two banks of information. Each customer will then receive an individually addressed and typed letter. Also, the machine, when instructed, will automatically type the name and address on a label or an envelope.

The author does not have to dictate the letter, she or he simply supplies the typist with the names and addresses of the customers and the filename of the form letter to be typed.

Standard paragraphs (see page 93) are also keyed in and stored. The author will supply the names and

# SKILL BUILDING

Type each line three times and, if time permits, complete your practice by typing each group once as it appears.

Margins:
12 pitch 22–82
10 pitch 12–72

### A  Keyboarding skills

1 Speed    If you can get a good price, you may wish to sell that land.
2 Accuracy Karl was quite vexed to learn that Juliet was not in Zurich.
3 Figures  The dates are: 22.05.90; 03.11.91; 17.12.92; 03.05.93/94/95.
4 Symbols  Peters said, "Do you buy Fry's bacon (ham) from S Fry & Co?"

### B  Improve control of home and third row keys

5 jug fear pear sway sees duke what hives whose horses awakes.
6 rug take fake ford aqua away pale dwarf poked office suggest
7 Patsy and Kay will cross the ford with the horses very soon.
8 We suggest that you visit our office whenever you find time.

### C  Spelling skill—correct the one misspelt word in each line
—see page 161 for answer

9  apiece proceeds receipts companies acknowlege genuineness.
10 pianos potatoes referred annoyance goverments resourceful.
11 They benefited from his achevements over the last 2 years.
12 Both today's advertisments were for the same organization.

### Skill measurement
One-minute timing                Not more than one error

You should now aim at increasing your speed by five words a minute, ie if you have been typing at, say, 35 words a minute, your aim is now 40 words a minute.

```
S/M6  My brothers and I were terrors when we were boys, but I do      12
      not believe we were really bad.  In those days boys were        23
      forced into mischief, for there were not yet any movies or      35
      radio, and television was a mystery of the future.  When the    47
      police chased us for some of our pranks, we always had some-    59
      where to hide.  As we lay breathless in our lair, we often      71
      heard the tread of heavy boots as the policeman went on his     83
      way.                                            (SI 1.27)       84
```

```
S/M7  There has always been a great deal of good advice available     12
      for the person seeking a job.  Much of this excellent advice    24
      lays stress on making a good first impression, and I do feel    36
      that the first few minutes are critical to your chances of      47
      being selected for a job.  This means that you should carry     59
      out some careful planning before the interview.  The clothes    71
      you wear must be neat and clean and suitable for the job for    83
      which you are applying.                         (SI 1.35)       87
```

         1  |  2  |  3  |  4  |  5  |  6  |  7  |  8  |  9  |  10  |  11  |  12  |

Your curriculum vitae/personal data sheet must be perfectly typed and clearly displayed with main, sub, and side/shoulder headings. The following points should be covered: your name and address; date of birth; secondary education/college/university; secretarial/office training; examinations passed; work experience (if any); special interests; name and address of a referee; date on which you are available for interview.

## Cursor

On the screen of a word processor there is a movable dot (hyphen) which indicates the typing point at which the next typed character will appear. This movable dot/hyphen is called the cursor.

## Daisywheel

See *Single-element machines*, page 205.

## Data Files

As well as being an expert typist, it is essential for you to have practice in finding and using information from various sources. Throughout this textbook, there are exercises where it is necessary for you to refer to another part of the book, or to the Data Files, for data to enable you to complete an exercise. The Data Files are on pages 163–64.

## Dead keys

Some typewriters are provided with keys which, when depressed, do not cause the carriage/carrier to move forward the usual single character space. These are known as 'dead keys'. They are usually fitted for foreign accents so that the accent can be struck first and, without the necessity of backspacing, the letter key is then struck.

Electronic machines may have a few dead keys, eg key for inserting vertical lines. Refer to manufacturer's handbook for further details.

## Decimals

1 Always use full stop for decimal point.
2 Leave **no** space before or after decimal point.
3 No punctuation is required at end of figures, except at the end of a sentence.

## Decimals in columns

1 When typing decimal figures in columns, see that the decimal points come under one another.
2 There must be the same number of decimal places in each line of the column, so that where necessary the figure 0 is used to make up the required number of decimal places. For example, if there are two decimal places, type 6.00, 6.60, 6.66. If three decimal places, type 6.000, 6.600, 6.660, etc. If there is no whole number, type 0 before the decimal point, eg 0.66.
3 If pounds and pence are typed in columns, the £ sign is typed over the unit figure of the pounds. No sign appears over the pence or decimals of a pound.
4 If the column contains whole pounds only, the £ sign is centred over the longest item, eg:
 £
 240
5 With blocked display, the £ sign is typed over the first figure of the longest line, or over the £ sign if one is used before the total.

## Decimal tabulation

On electronic machines the decimal tabulation function enables the typist to set a tab stop for the decimal point. No matter how many figures there are before and after the decimal tab stop, the point will always appear at the set scale point and the figures will be in alignment (units under units, tens under tens, etc) before and after the decimal point.

## Degree sign

If the typewriter does not have a special key for the degree sign, it is represented by the small o raised half a space. When typing 20 degrees, type 20° with no space between the figures and the degrees sign; but when typing 20 degrees Fahrenheit or 20 degrees Celsius, type 20 °F or 20 °C—note that there is a space between the figures and the degree sign, but no space between the degree sign and the F or C. Other methods are 20° C and 20°C.

## Deliberate errors

Certain exercises, both in this textbook and in some examinations, contain deliberate errors of spelling, punctuation and relationship between subject and verb. These errors may or may not be indicated by encircling the incorrect word(s). Your knowledge of the use of words, spelling, etc, should be such that you notice and correct the errors when typing. As a typist in business you will be expected to correct any spelling errors accidentally made by the author.

C/D  Data Bank  178

# PRODUCTION DEVELOPMENT

> See pages **207**
> **187**
> **188**

## Superscripts, Subscripts and Fractions

1  Type the following exercise on a sheet of A5 landscape paper.

$$\frac{x+1}{2} + \frac{x+2}{3} + \frac{x+3}{4} + \tfrac{1}{4} = 0. \qquad \frac{ty+1}{2} - \frac{y-7}{5} = \frac{y+4}{3}$$

$$48 \text{ miles} = \frac{48 \times 8}{5} \text{ km} = 76.8 \text{ km}. \qquad SP = \pounds\frac{450}{1} \times \frac{84}{100} = \pounds 378$$

$$\text{Simplify: } \frac{1\tfrac{1}{4}}{2\ 2/3} - \tfrac{1}{8} - \tfrac{3}{4} + 1\tfrac{1}{2} - 1$$

2  Type the following exercise on a sheet of A5 landscape paper.

In any right-angled triangle, the square on the hypotenuse is equal to the sum of the squares on the other 2 sides.

$$\text{Hypotenuse} = \sqrt{\text{perpendicular}^2 + \text{base}^2}$$

$$H = \sqrt{p^2 + b^2}$$

## Footnotes and Italic

> See pages **185**
> **191**

3  Type the following exercise on a sheet of A4 paper in 1½ or double spacing.

    5.6  VOLTAGE DOUBLERS*

Several requirements occur in electronics for voltages which are greater than normally available. The principle of *voltage doubler* circuit is shown in Fig 5.14(a). During the first half cycle of the ac supply diode $D_1$ charges capacitor $C_1$ to approximately $V_{max}$. During the second half cycle, diode $D_2$ charges capacitor $C_2$ to $V_{max}$. Since $C_1$ and $C_2$ are connected in series, $V_{out}$ is approximately *twice* $V_{max}$.

Alternatively, in Fig 5.14(c), $C_1$ is charged through $D_1$ during the negative half cycle of the supply. This dc potential is now in series with the ac supply so that during the positive half cycle $C_2$ is charged to a voltage equal to the sum of $V_{max}$ and the voltage across $C_1$. Thus $V_{out}$ is approximately equal to *twice* $V_{max}$.

However, when loaded, each of these circuits produces a large ripple voltage. This means that their use is restricted to low-current applications.

---

  * Extract from page 55 of *Practical Electronics* by Barry Woollard published by McGraw-Hill Book Company (UK) Limited.

UNIT 6      *Superscripts, Subscripts, Fractions, Footnotes, Italic*

## Correction of errors

Correct the error as soon as you know you have made a mistake and read through the whole exercise when you have finished typing it in case there is an error you had not noticed before.

There are various methods which may be used to correct errors:

### 1 Rubber

1.1 Turn up the paper so that the error is on top of the platen or paper table.
1.2 Press the paper tightly against the cylinder or paper table to prevent slipping.
1.3 Erase the error by rubbing gently up and down, blowing away rubber dust as you do so. (Too much pressure may cause a hole.)
1.4 If you are using a new or heavily inked ribbon, erase with a soft rubber and then with a typewriter eraser.
1.5 Turn paper back to writing line and insert correct letter or letters.
1.6 Always use a clean rubber.

**NOTE** If the typewriter has a carriage, move it to the extreme right or left to prevent rubber dust from falling into the mechanism of the machine.

### 2 Correction paper

These specially coated strips of paper are placed in front of the printing point over the error on the original and between the carbon paper(s) and the copy sheet(s). The incorrect character(s) is (are) typed again through the correction paper(s) which will cover up or lift off the incorrect character(s). Remove the coated strips and type the correct character(s).

### 3 Correction fluid

Correction fluid is produced in various shades to match the typing paper and is applied with a small brush. The incorrect letter is obliterated and when the fluid is dry, the correct letter may be typed over the top. The liquid may be spirit- or water-based. If the spirit-based liquid is used, it is necessary to add thinner to the bottle as, after a time, the original liquid tends to thicken. Spirit-based liquid dries more quickly than water-based. Avoid unsightly blobs. Use tissue paper to wipe the brush.

### 4 Correction ribbon

Some electric typewriters and most electronic typewriters are fitted with a correction ribbon. When making a correction with a correction ribbon, it is necessary to:

(a) Backspace to the error.
(b) Press the correction key—the error is then removed.
(c) Type the correct letter(s).

### 5 Correction on electronic typewriters

Electronic typewriters are equipped with a memory and may have a thin window display so that automatic corrections can be made—from a few characters to ten or more lines. The correction is made by backspacing the delete key and then typing in the correct character(s). Electronic typewriters may be fitted with a relocate key which, when depressed, returns the carrier to the last character typed before the correction was made.

### 6 Corrections on word processors/computers

To make a correction on a word processor/computer, one would use the automatic overstrike, delete or erase functions.

## Curriculum vitae: a brief account of one's career

When you apply for a job, your prospective employer will require a summary of your education and training. He or she will want to know what academic qualifications you have, what specialist qualifications you have, what your main interests are, what recreational activities and hobbies you have, etc. Sometimes this information is referred to as a personal data sheet or a curriculum vitae.

No two people are alike and no two personal data sheets should be exactly the same. It is possible that you will arrange your personal record of your career in a somewhat different way when applying for different jobs. You will always wish to emphasize the qualities and qualifications that would make you valuable in the particular job for which you are applying.

If you have worked—for a salary or as a volunteer—you should mention this. Your work need not have been closely related to the work for which you are applying, but it may indicate to your prospective employer a measure of your intelligent thinking, dependability, resourcefulness, etc. Always list temporary or part-time work (holidays and Saturdays only).

It is usual to include the name and address of one referee. See that you give the person's name—correctly spelt—his/her title (Mr/Mrs/Miss/Ms) and correct address and telephone number. **Never**, in any circumstances, give as a reference a person whose permission you have not asked in advance.

# Modification and rearrangement of material

See page **195**

**4** Type the following exercise and take one copy.
Remember to leave a space between the numbered items.

> AREA CODES
>
> *Their local nos. wl also be extended by the addition of an extra digit @ the start of the existing no.*
>
> On "Phoneday" - 16 April 1995 - one digit is to be added to all UK area codes.*
>
> 1  All UK geographic area codes will have a 1 inserted after the initial 0.
> 2  For example, the London codes will change from 071 to 0171 and 081 to 0181, etc. *(Renumber accordingly)*
> 3  Bristol, Leeds, Leicester, Nottingham and Sheffield will each have entirely new codes.
> 4  At the same time, all international dialling codes will change from the 01 prefix to 00. This will bring the UK into line with the rest of Europe.
>
> * *Because of the continuing growth in the range of telecom services, the availability of new tel nos in the UK is to be increased.*

**5** Key in document 4 (filename DIGIT) for 10-pitch print-out. When you have completed this task, save under filename DIGIT, and print an original and one copy. Recall the document and follow the instructions for text editing on page 162.

## Brace

See page **206**

**5** Type the following exercise.

> EC VAT SYSTEM (1)
>
> Physical controls have been abolished on the movement of goods between member states. However, it is essential to:
>
> (a) Quote the customer's VAT number )   For those trading
>     on each invoice.                  )   elsewhere in the EC.
>                                       )
> (b) Provide a quarterly return        )
>     showing total sales to each       )
>     registered customer.
>
> The following personnel must be aware of their responsibilities: (2)
>
> Financial Directors
> Sales Directors
> Tax Managers           } and others involved
> Commercial Managers
> Freight Managers
> Systems Managers
>
> *(Alpha order please)*
>
> (1) *From 1 Jan '93*
> (2) *By not applying the new systems properly, a business wl be open to tax assessments, penalties + investigations, possibly in several countries.*

UNIT 6 — Modification and rearrangement of material, Brace

## 5 Signature

The person writing the letter may or may not sign it. If the writer is signing, type the complimentary close, etc, in the usual way. If the writer is not signing, type Yours faithfully and company's name* in the usual position, turn up two single spaces and type the writer's name, then turn up two spaces and type the designation.

\* If the company's name is not being inserted, turn up two single spaces after Yours faithfully and type the name of the writer, then turn up two spaces and type the writer's designation.

## 6 Tear-off portion

Sometimes a letter or circular will have a tear-off portion at the foot so that a customer may fill in certain details and return the tear-off portion to the sender.

The minimum space to be left after the complimentary close or signatory is one clear space. In other words, turn up a minimum of two spaces and then type from **edge to edge*** of the paper **continuous dots** or **continuous hyphens**, then turn up two spaces and type the information on the tear-off portion.

Where blank spaces are left for details to be filled in, use **continuous dots** (or the **underscore**) and **double spacing**. Remember to leave one clear space after the last character typed before starting the dots or underscore and one clear space at the end of the dots or underscore before the next typed character if there is one, eg:

```
            (space)              (space)
Surname  ↙ . . . . ↘ Forename(s) ↙ . . . . . . .
```

The exception to this is when the dotted line (or underscore) follows the sterling sign, eg £_____, and if the first letter of the courtesy title has been typed, eg M_____ . Of course, the first figure must be typed close to the £ sign, and the first letter close to the M.

\* This is not always possible on a word processor.

## 7 Deletions

It is often necessary to delete letters or words in a form or circular letter. For instance, a circular letter may start **Dear Sir/Madam** and if the letter is being sent to a lady, the word **Sir/** would be deleted. To delete previously typed characters such as the foregoing, use an X aligned precisely with the characters already typed.

## 8 Ruled or dotted lines

In some form letters and forms you may have to type on ruled or dotted lines. You must type slightly above the line so that none of the descending characters touches the line. For example:

<u>going</u>     going
              . . . . .

## 9 Word processor

The word processor has made production of repetitive text very much easier and time-saving. The skeleton letter, containing the constant information, is keyed in and stored on a disk. When required, it can be retrieved by pressing a function key, and any insertion made quickly and easily (there is no difficulty with alignment when you have a VDU) and the complete letter printed out, so that it looks like an original—as distinct from a duplicated or printed document with the variables added.

## Clean and uncreased work

Typed work that is accurate and quickly produced can be spoilt by dirty finger-marks, smudges and, particularly on the carbon copy, creases. It is important to be organized and methodical. Keep your workstation neat and tidy with everything within easy reach; this will aid you in producing neat and clean documents.

## Combination characters

See **Special signs, symbols and marks**, page 206.

## Continuation sheets

See **Business letters, 4.17**, page 173 and **Pagination**, page 196.

## Continuous stationery

Invoice sets are usually in continuous form with perforations between the sets which may be NCR (no carbons required) paper or one-time only carbon paper. Paper for word processing print-outs may also be in continuous form edged by sprocket holes for use on the tractor-feed device. The paper may be letterheads, invoice forms, payslips, etc.

## Copy

To distinguish the copy of a document from an original, type the word COPY at the top, and the word (SIGNED) (in brackets) before the signatory's name (if typed).

## Draft copies

See page 180

6 Type an original and take one copy of the following on A4 bond paper.

D R A F T

The Citizen's Charter* — **Emphasize**

The Citizen's Charter covers all public services:

[Alpha order] schools, hospitals, council housing, police services, courts, prisons, postal services, tax offices, benefit offices, jobcentres, railways, roads, Whitehall and town halls.

It also covers services - like gas, electricity, water and telecoms - that are now in the private sector. The Charter aims to improve public services right across the board, by extending consumer choice & widening competition. The Charter also promises to improve services by setting standards and publishing them, giving the citizen more information about services, and a remedy if standards *are* not met. ‡

Some of the *improvements* include - [2 spaces]

[TYPIST - if you do not hv a bullet mark on yr m/c type 2 small o's, eg oo]

• A Courts Charter setting out the standards of service that such people as witnesses and jurors can expect when they attend court. (1)

• A new Act of Parliament which gives the regulators of gas, water, telecoms and electricity stronger powers to make sure services are improved, with compensation where guaranteed standards are not met. (5)

• Courtesy & helpfulness from public servants. We are beginning to see, as normal *practice*, names being given in letters & on the telephone, & name badges being worn. (3)

• Wider powers for the Social Services Inspectorate. (4)

• A new Schools' Inspectorate. (2)

\* Launched in 1991

‡ If things go wrong, an apology, a full explanation, & a swift & effective remedy (should be given).

[TYPIST - Display the bulleted items in the order indicated, but do not type the figures. Omit bullet. (4)]

6 Key in document 6 (filename CHART) for 12-pitch print-out. When you have completed this task, save under filename CHART, and print one original and one copy. Retrieve the document and follow the instructions for text editing on page 162.

UNIT 6 — See Practical Typing Exercises, Book Two, pages 25–26, for further exercises on **Modification and rearrangement of material, Draft copies**

Some organizations use different coloured paper for different departments so that copies are instantly recognizable. For example, white copies for Sales Department, yellow copies for Works Manager, green copies for Company Secretary, etc.

## Cards

The typist will have to type cards for a variety of purposes such as a mailing list, telephone index, credit sales index, etc.

When cards are to be filed in alphabetical order, then the filing 'word' must start near the top edge of the card, say, 13 mm (½ inch) down. Other information on the card should be suitably displayed with at least 13 mm (½ inch) margins all round, unless the contents are such that it is not possible to leave margins.

A fair amount of practice in typing cards is essential and a great deal of care is necessary in order to see that the card does not slip, or become out of alignment, when turned up/down. A backing sheet will help; otherwise, fold over about 13 mm/25 mm (½ inch/1 inch) at the top of a sheet of A4 paper, place the card underneath the fold and feed into the machine.

## Catchword

In memos and other documents a catchword is sometimes used. When a continuation sheet is necessary, the first word or two of the text appearing on the continuation sheet is sometimes typed at the foot of the preceding page below the last line and aligned at the right margin. CONTINUED or PTO may be used instead of the catchword, but not the number of the next page.

## Chairperson's Agenda

The Chairperson's Agenda may contain more information than the Agenda for the other committee members. The right side of a Chairperson's Agenda may be left blank, so that he or she can write in the decisions reached on the various points. The word **notes** may be typed (either centred or blocked) on the right-hand side and the items re-numbered at the centre of the typing line. Open or full punctuation may be used.

## Chapter headings and chapter numbers — dropped headings

Leave 25 mm (1 inch) clear at the top of the page before typing the chapter number. Alternatively, you may use a 'dropped head', ie the chapter number is typed 51 mm (2 inches) to 76 mm (3 inches) from the top edge of the paper in roman numerals or arabic numbers. The heading is typed in capital letters two single spaces below the chapter number. The chapter number and heading may be centred on the typing line or blocked at the left margin.

## Charts

See **Flow charts**, page 184 and **Organization charts**, page 196.

## Circular letters

Circulars, or circular letters, are letters of same contents which are sent to a number of customers or clients.

Where individually typed circular letters are required, they can be prepared on a word processor. A function or command key will tell the printer how many originals you need.

1   **Reference**

In usual position.

2   **Date**

Typed in various ways, eg:

21 October 1994
October 1994 (month and year only)
Date as postmark. (These words are typed where you normally type the date.)

3   **Name and address of addressee**

3.1  Space may be left for this, and in that case the details are typed on individual sheets after they have been copied. When preparing the master (or draft), turn up eight single spaces after the date (leaving seven clear) before typing the salutation.

3.2  Very often the name and address of addressee are not inserted and, if this is so, no space need be left when the master is prepared. Turn up two single spaces after the date.

4   **Salutation**

4.1  Dear        , the remainder of the salutation is typed in when the name and address are inserted.

4.2  Dear Sir, Dear Madam, Dear Sir(s), Dear Sir/Madam. See 'Deletions' on page 176.

C                       Data Bank                       175

# SKILL BUILDING

Type each line three times and, if time permits, complete your practice by typing each group once as it appears.

Margins:
12 pitch 22–82
10 pitch 12–72

### A  Keyboarding skills

1  Speed      On Tuesday I will return the books you gave to me yesterday.
2  Accuracy   She quoted for six dozen oranges and a few bottles of juice.
3  Figures    I sold 3 lb (1.36 kg) of salt and 21 lb (9.52 kg) of pepper.
4  Symbols    Peter said, "Please send May's books to Jane's new address."

### B  Improve control of home and bottom row keys

5  bad cad mad had name cake lake sake fake hake bake make rake
6  man van bomb comb numb buzz axed lynx annex zinc coma civics
7  The man's van can be left by the lake.  Has Jacky gone away?
8  Vince can make a vase exactly like the ones sold by Jacques.

### C  Spelling skill—correct the one misspelt word in each line
—see page 161 for answer

9   fare assent muscle picnic height truly fulfil fierce ernest
10  believe exercise necessary definitly sufficient information
11  The incident occurred when they quarrelled with my gardner.
12  Sue had already ordered the stationry from the Chief Clerk.

13  To develop your proofreading skills, turn to page 157, exercise 3.

### Skill measurement           Two-minute timing           Not more than two errors

S/M8  Electronic mail sends, receives, and stores messages and the    12
      main reason for using it is to speed the delivery of large      24
      amounts of information: it offers immediate delivery if this    36
      is required.                                                    38

      There are 3 or 4 points you should remember about other         50
      means of communication.  To start with, different pieces        61
      of electronic equipment can communicate with each other —       73
      telephone lines, telegraph lines, satellites are examples.      84
      Further, the information between communicating machines is      96
      in the form of electronic signals, not a copy on paper.        106

      If desired, information may be sent to a location and stored   119
      until it is needed by the receiver.  Also, the receiver may    131
      view the message on a screen or print it out as and when       143
      a copy is required.  This means a great saving, in paper,      154
      additional copies, and mailing costs.           (SI 1.56)      161

      1 | 2 | 3 | 4 | 5 | 6 | 7 | 8 | 9 | 10 | 11 | 12 |

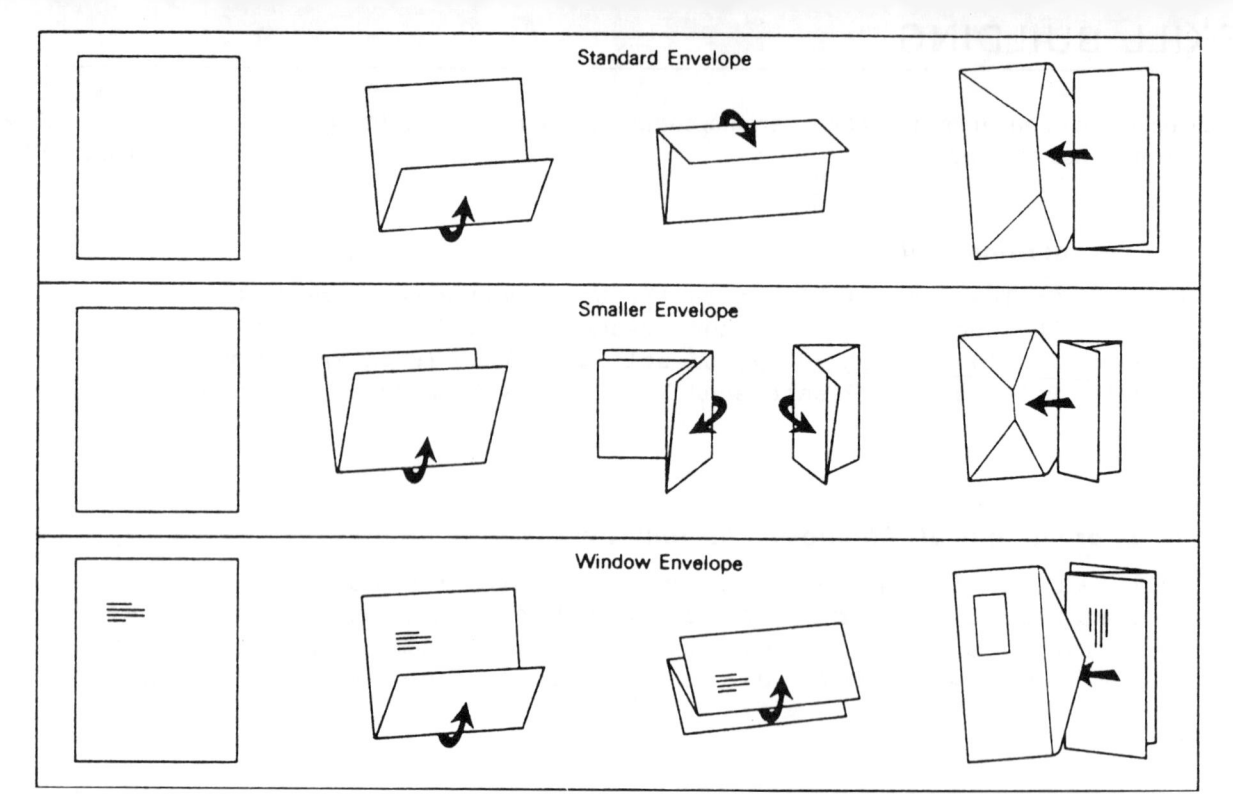

### 6 Overseas mail

6.1 For quicker delivery, **all** letter mail to destinations outside the United Kingdom (apart from the Channel Islands and the Isle of Man) should be marked AIRMAIL (PAR AVION). Airmail postage to all EC countries is at a cheaper rate than to non-EC European countries, and dearer still to destinations outside of Europe.

6.2 In a business letter the words BY AIRMAIL are typed two single spaces after the last line of the reference, or the date if it is typed at the left margin. On the envelope the words are typed in the top left-hand corner. For example:

BY AIRMAIL
(PAR AVION)

                PERSONAL

                Mr Paul O'Connor
                P R O'Connor & Sons
                24 Kenmore Road
                KILLARNEY
                Co Kerry
                REPUBLIC OF IRELAND

6.3 **Letters to the United Kingdom**

Ms A Halcrow
12 Scotland Avenue
PENRITH
Cumbria
UNITED KINGDOM
CA11 7AA

**NOTE** For overseas mail, the name of the **town** and the name of the **country** should be in capitals.

## Carbon copies

See **Business letters—4.14–4.16**, pages 172–173.

## Carbon film

Light-weight carbon film produces the sharpest impressions and can be used for between five and seven copies. Medium-weight carbon film is most commonly used for making three or four copies. Carbon film has a plastic backing instead of a paper backing and is therefore more durable. The following factors need to be considered when choosing carbon film:

1 The size of the typeface: 10 pitch will give a much clearer impression than, say, 15 pitch.
2 The condition of the typewriter and whether it is manual, electric or electronic.
3 The weight of the letterhead sheets and second sheet.
4 The number of carbon copies usually made.

Usually top right- or left-hand corner of carbon paper is cut away and you should, when taking a number of carbon copies (manifolding), always place the carbon paper so that the cut-off corners are together. When the typing has been completed, hold the pages above the cut-off corners and the carbons will drop on to the desk.

# PRODUCTION DEVELOPMENT

## *Allocating space*

See page **167**

**1** Type the following on A4 portrait paper.

VIRTUAL REALITY PHONE

Desktop models of the telephone of the future should be on sale very soon.

The virtual reality phone has a screen about the size of A5 paper. It has no dial or keypad, but can connect you to whoever you want to speak to by a touch of the pictures (or icons) on the screen.

It will also display information and send or receive pictures, eg, estate agents could project pictures of property for sale to potential customers.

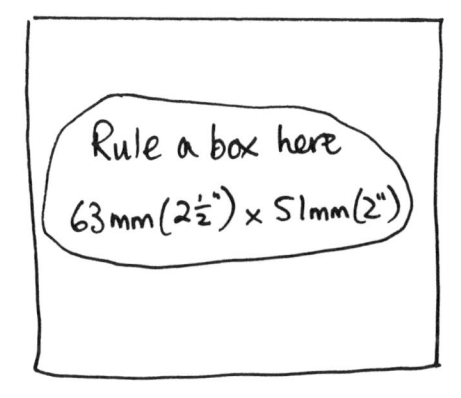

*[Rule a box here 63mm (2½") × 63mm (2½")]*

*[Rule a box here 63mm (2½") × 51mm (2")]*

THE PERSONAL COMMUNICATOR

The latest buzzword in industry is the personal communicator which is a hand-held device linked via wire or a wireless network that allows users to communicate by voice, fax or electronic mail. // As yet they have not been mass-produced but eventually they will allow communications between users of all personal communicators regardless of manufacture.

ELECTRONIC LUGGAGE TAGS

The frustration of arriving at yr holiday destination to find th yr luggage is lost may soon be over, thanks to an ingenious electronic luggage tagging system. When fully in use it wl consist of an identification tag carrying a unique no attached to the luggage & the passenger. This electronic no can be monitored very closely with ease & speed. The system wl notice if a passenger who has checked in luggage does not board the aircraft.

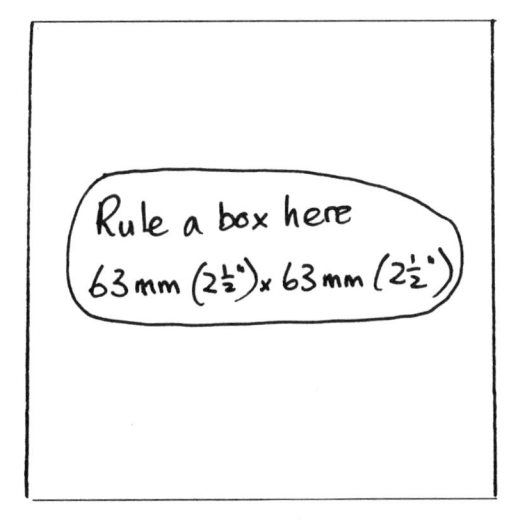

*[Rule another box here please — 63mm (2½") × 76mm (3")]*

**UNIT 7** — *Allocating space* — **44**

Many organizations do not now use a title such as Miss/Mrs/Mr; this is especially so within an organization when copies of documents are being sent to employees—in such cases the names would appear as follows:

| | | |
|---|---|---|
| bcc Harry L Jones | or | bpc HLJ |
| Greta Petersen | | GP |
| Rose Stone | | RS |

**Always** follow the housestyle.

See also **Carbon film**, page 174 and **Repetitive printing**, page 203.

4.17 **Continuation sheets**   A long letter may require a second sheet. This is called a continuation sheet, and sometimes the name or initials of the sender are printed in the top left corner. Otherwise, always use a plain sheet of the same size, colour and quality as the previous page. The only details which you should type are the following: name of addressee, page number and date, starting on the fourth single line from the top. In fully-blocked letters, all these details are typed at the left margin in double spacing, in the following order: page number, date, name of addressee. In indented letters, the name of the addressee is typed at the left margin, the page number is centred in the typing line, and the date ends at the right margin. The letter is continued on the third single space below the continuation sheet details.

When a continuation sheet is needed, the letter must be so arranged that at least three or four lines are carried to the second page. On no account must the continuation sheet contain only the complimentary close and name of writer. Also, at least two lines of a paragraph should be left at the bottom of the first page. Do not divide a word from one page to the next.

If the reverse of the paper is used for the continuation sheet, then the margins must also be reversed, eg first sheet: left margin 38 mm ($1\frac{1}{2}$ inches), right margin 25 mm (1 inch); continuation sheet: left margin 25 mm (1 inch), right margin 38 mm ($1\frac{1}{2}$ inches).

**NOTE**   The word 'CONTINUED' or 'PTO' is seldom used in letters. A catchword is sometimes used, ie the first word of the text appearing on a continuation sheet is typed at the foot of the preceding page. The number of the next page must not be used as a catchword.

4.18 **Signing letters on behalf of the writer**
   4.18.1   Your employer may ask you to type and sign a letter on his or her behalf. The complimentary close in this case would be:

      Yours faithfully
      J R BLACK & CO LTD

      *Helen M Grant*

      for John Black
      Director

      or

      Yours sincerely,
      J. R. BLACK & CO. LTD.

      *Helen M Grant*

      Dictated by Mr. Black
      and signed in his absence

   4.18.2   Your employer may ask you to write a letter on his behalf and sign it, or circumstances may necessitate your writing on behalf of your employer, eg 'Mr Black has asked me to thank you for your letter dated 21 June, etc'. The complimentary close would be:

      Yours faithfully
      J R BLACK & CO LTD

      *Helen M. Grant*

      Helen M. Grant (Mrs)
      Secretary to J Black, Director

      or

      Yours sincerely,

      *Helen M. Grant*

      Mrs. Helen M. Grant
      Secretary to J. Black, Director

4.19 **Titled persons**   The less formal wording is now generally used, eg the salutation: Dear Lord Newton; complimentary close: I am, Sir, Yours sincerely/respectfully/faithfully, etc.

## 5   *Folding letters and documents*

Always use an envelope of suitable size so that letters and documents are not folded more than is necessary. A document folded many times is difficult to read and looks untidy.

**B**        *Data Bank*        **173**

**Continuation sheets**

See pages 173, 196

2  Type the following on A4 paper following the linespacing shown. Take one copy.

*Correct any circled errors.*

THE HEDGEHOG ← Sp caps
(*Erinaceus europaeus*)

Recognition: ← CAPS

*Inset 6 spaces:*

Unmistakeable; the only spiny British mammal.

Head/body length: 150 - 300 mm, depending on age; tail about 10 - 20 mm.

*TYPIST: Leave a space here approx 63mm (2½") by 51mm (2") please.*

Weight: Up to 2 kg; heaviest in autumn.

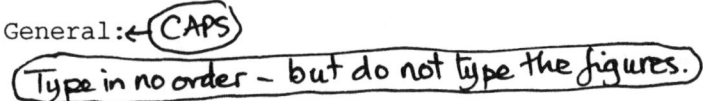

General: ← CAPS

*Type in no order – but do not type the figures.*

(4) Hedgehogs travel about 1-2 km each night, males more than females. They return to the same day time nest for a few days then use another, perhaps returning to an old nest at a later date.

(1) The hedgehog is common in parks, gardens and farmland throughout /trs mainland Britain + Ireland. They prefer woodland edges, hedgerows and suburban habitats where there is plenty of food for them.*

(2) Females have litters of 4 - 5 young (sometimes more) between April and September. They need to weigh at least 450 g (1 lb) or they is not fat enough to last the winter.

(3) Hibernation usually begins about November and ends around ~~Easter~~ March, but is much affected by the weather. The winter nest is made of leaves, tucked under a bush, log pile or a garden shed.

(5) Hedgehogs carry several diseases, but none are dangerous to humans. They carry flees though not the same sort as found on cats or dogs.

UNIT 7          Continuation sheets          45

to type three unspaced dots in the left margin opposite the line(s) in which the enclosure(s) is mentioned. This may not be possible with a word processor.

4.13 **Postscripts** Sometimes a postscript has to be typed at the foot of a letter, either because the writer has omitted something he wished to say in the body of the letter, or because he wishes to draw special attention to a certain point. The postscript should be started two single spaces below the last line of the complete letter and should be in single spacing. Leave two character spaces after the abbreviation. PS has no punctuation with open punctuation, but a full stop after the S with full punctuation.

4.14 **Carbon copies** (See also *Photocopying*, page 198.) It is necessary to keep in the office for filing purposes at least one carbon copy of each letter or document typed. To produce a carbon copy, take the following steps:

    4.14.1 Place face downwards on a flat surface the sheet on which the typing is to be done.

    4.14.2 On top of this place a sheet of carbon paper with the coated surface upwards.

    4.14.3 On top of these place the sheet of paper on which the carbon copy is to be made. Pick up all sheets together and insert in machine with coated surface of carbon paper facing the cylinder.

    4.14.4 All carbon copies must be a **true copy** of the original, ie any handwritten alterations made on an original must also be made on the carbon copies.

    4.14.5 Many organizations do not take carbon copies; instead the originals are photocopied. When **photocopies** have to be made, it is usual to type on the original: pc or p/c followed by the number of copies required, eg pc 6.

    4.14.6 NCR (no carbon required) paper has been chemically treated and the characters printed on the original carry through to the copies. The required number of sheets are usually bound at the top. (See also *Continuous stationery* on page 176).

    **Word processors** The printer component of a word processing system may be either a non-impact or an impact printer. Like typewriters, impact printers apply a hammer mechanism to strike an image (character) on to paper and will produce an error-free original and five or six carbon copies quickly and economically. Non-impact printers create an image on paper by laser or ink-jet mechanisms, and, therefore, cannot produce carbon copies. (See also *Repetitive printing*, page 203.)

4.15 **Additional copies** A copy may be required for filing and, in addition, copies of a document may have to be sent to individuals who have an interest in the subject matter. If a copy of a letter is sent to someone other than the addressee, the letters **cc** (carbon copy) or **pc** (photocopy) are typed at the bottom left margin followed by the name of the recipient. Where a copy is being sent to more than one person, the names are typed one underneath the other (usually in alphabetical order, but not necessarily so) and the name of the person to whom the copy is intended is either ticked at the side or underlined on individual copies, eg:

| (First copy) | (Second copy) |
|---|---|
| cc <u>Mr Jones</u> | cc Mr Jones |
|     Mrs Stone |     <u>Mrs Stone</u> |
|     Mr French |     Mr French |
|     File |     File |

| (Third copy) | (Fourth copy) |
|---|---|
| cc Mr Jones | cc Mr Jones |
|     Mrs Stone |     Mrs Stone |
|     <u>Mr French</u> |     Mr French |
|     File |     <u>File</u> |

The term **filing** meant that a copy of a document was placed in a drawer or filing cabinet in a particular order (alphabetical, numerical, etc). If you use a **word processor**, you record and store the text on a disk or put it into the computer memory. If the document is properly referenced, it can be retrieved easily.

4.16 **Blind copies** It sometimes happens that the writer does not want the addressee to know what copies have been distributed, in which case the machine operator types **bcc** (blind carbon copy) or **bpc** (blind photocopy). When the letter is finished, the carbon copies or photocopies are re-inserted into the machine. At the foot of these copies the operator then inserts the bcc/bpc note at the left margin, as follows:

bcc Mr H L Jones    or    bpc Mr H L Jones
    Miss G Petersen                 Miss G Petersen
    Mrs R Stone                      Mrs R Stone

marking the name of the recipient(s) as before. The bottom copy on which the cc/pc/bcc/bpc notes appear is the one kept for filing.

2

Conservation:** ← CAPS

The biggest threat to hedgehogs is probably habitat loss, with the change from pastoral farming to arable crops, over the past 30 years. The use of chemicals for intensive farming kills the creatures hedgehogs need for food and may also poison them directly. Hedgehogs may become locally scarce or even disappear, but nationwide extinction is unlikely.

*Please leave at least 25 mm (1") clear, here.*

Hedgehogs survive well in gardens, particularly assisted by food put out for them. This shd be encouraged because modern gardens may not otherwise provide sufficient food. Hedgehogs hibernate under bonfire heaps. These shd always be turned over before being burnt. Hedgehogs swim well but can easily drown in garden pools with smooth sides. Ponds (+ swimming pools) shd hv something — perhaps a piece of chicken wire — dangling into the water to help the animals climb out.

---

\*   They eat beetles, worms, caterpillars, slugs and almost anything they can catch, but little plant material. *(Retain abbreviation)*

\*\*  Hedgehogs are protected under the Wildlife & Countryside Act and may not be trapped without a licence from the Nature Conservancy Council.

*TYPIST — Please address a label to Mr & Mrs S W Britton. You will find their address on page 17.*

---

**7** Key in document 2 (filename HOG) for 15-pitch print-out. When you have completed this task, save under filename HOG, and print out original and one copy. Recall the document and follow the instructions for text editing on page 162.

**UNIT 7** See Practical Typing Exercises, Book Two, pages 27–28, for further exercises on ***Allocating space, Continuation sheets***

4.5 **Name and address of addressee**  See also *Forms of address*, page 187 and *Window envelopes*, page 216. Typed in single spacing usually on the second/third single space below the reference, date, any special instructions, or 'For the attention of'.

    4.5.1 May be typed in single spacing at the foot of the page at the left margin.

    4.5.2 If the letter finishes with the complimentary close, turn up nine single spaces before typing the name and address of the addressee.

    4.5.3 If the letter finishes with the name and designation of signatory, turn up two single spaces before typing the name and address of the addressee.

    4.5.4 If you are using a continuation sheet and the name and address of addressee has not been typed before the salutation, then it may be typed at the bottom of the **first** page, two single spaces after the last typed line and ending 25 mm (1 inch) from the bottom of the page.

    4.5.5 If you type the name and address of the addressee at the bottom of the page and the letter is marked for the attention of a particular person, the attention line is typed before the salutation. Similarly, any special instructions must be typed in the usual place and not at the bottom of the page.

    4.5.6 In a one-page letter with the name and address of the addressee at the bottom, the enclosure notation should be placed two spaces after the last line of the address.

4.6 **Salutation**  Typed on the second single space below the last line of the address and blocked at the left margin. If the correspondent wishes to write the salutation in ink, leave plenty of space. It is suggested that you turn up nine single spaces after the last line of the address before starting the body of the letter.

4.7 **Subject heading**  In fully-blocked letters, the subject heading is typed at the left margin, preferably in capitals without underscore. If lower case letters are used, the heading should be underscored. The heading must be centred if the indented style of display is being used.

4.8 **Body of letter**  Start on the second single space after the salutation or the subject heading.

4.9 **Displayed matter**  When matter is to be displayed in a fully-blocked letter, all the lines usually start at the left margin, one clear space left above and below the matter. If the display is in columns, it is usual to leave three spaces between each column. If definite instructions are given for the matter to be inset, then it must be inset, even in a fully-blocked letter. The matter is usually centred in an indented letter.

4.10 **Complimentary close**  Typed on the second single line below the last line of the body of the letter. When a letter starts Dear Mr . . . , Dear Miss . . . , Dear Mrs . . . , Dear Mary . . . , etc, the complimentary close should be 'Yours sincerely'. A letter with the salutation Dear Sir(s), Dear Madam, should end 'Yours faithfully' which may be followed by the organization's name typed in upper or lower case, but capitals are preferable for clarity—it is **never** underlined. Sometimes the name of the organization is typed after the signatory/designation.

**NOTE**  The practice of typing the organization's name after the complimentary close is less popular with the authors of today's business letters as these are much less formal and more personal. In any case, the name of the organization was really only inserted after 'Yours faithfully' never after 'Yours sincerely'.

If the name of an organization has to be inserted, turn up one single line only after the complimentary close.

**Always** follow the layout/instructions given to you by your employer/examiner.

4.11 **Name of signatory**  Whether you type the name and designation of the writer will depend on how well the writer knows the addressee. Follow the style in previous correspondence or ask the writer. In business letters a male person does not append the word 'Mr', before his name. However, it is common practice for ladies to put 'Miss', 'Mrs' or 'Ms' before their name or in brackets after.

4.12 **Enclosures**  After the last line of typing, turn up a minimum of two spaces, and type Enc at left margin. If there is more than one enclosure, then type Encs. Some organizations list the enclosures. A few employers, and some examining bodies, prefer the abbreviation Att when the word 'attached' is used in the body of the letter, eg 'We attach a copy of our price-list.' If there is more than one attachment, a note must be made of the number, eg Att 3. Another method of indicating an enclosure, or enclosures, is

# *Dropped headings, Ellipsis and Pagination*

See pages 175
181
196

**3** Type the following extract from a book. As it is a new chapter, leave a top margin of at least 51 mm (2 inches).

CHAPTER 19 ← (Roman numerals)

**EVANS THE BRIDGE**[1]

TYPIST: Correct the circled errors.

by *John Dossett-Davies*

trs/ The only building of any age at all in Pontypridd is the Old Bridge built in 1575. It is the only item left from the 18th century and was prized, at least civically, by being included in the Town's Coat of Arms.

For me, whenever I saw it in the distance, the Bridge signified one of the most enigmatic and puzzling characters I ever met. He was known as Evans the Bridge. A small, dark, NP/ precise man of great respectability. // Actually Mr Evans was the local bank manager but he wasn't called Evans the Bank because we already had a Manager with that nickname in the (in full) town before the 2nd Evans arrived. So the name Evans the Bridge was invented for him because he lived near the old bridge. I was the secretary of the Towns local historical society and Evans the Bridge was the treasurer.

Bank Managers, in the more relaxed and laid-back days of the early 1950s were people of some consequence and considerlc/ able standing in the community; Men whose advise we usually heeded and whose cautious words stopped many a local chairman and secretary of societies from getting too ambitious and too big for there boots. Besides I had an overdraft with another Bank in the town, so I always took care to be polite and on my guard whenever Evans the Bridge was at one of the historical society committee meetings.

"His affairs were in a shocking state. He's made no will; I cann't find his insurance policies, the deeds of his house are missing. I cann't trace who he owes money to . . ."

He paused for breath.

"Really," I said, at a loss for words. "Just fancy that."

*I recall one day after a mtg when we were relaxing over a cup of coffee, he gave me some advice based on a customer's affairs he had bn dealing with th day.*

---

[1] Extract from *Memories of a Social Worker*

UNIT 7     *Dropped headings, Ellipsis and Pagination*     47

Semi-blocked (sometimes called 'indented').

Date and complimentary close as shown, with first line of each paragraph indented.

## 2 Punctuation

2.1 **Full punctuation** When typing a letter with full punctuation, punctuation marks are inserted in the appropriate places in the reference, date, name and address of addressee, salutation, complimentary close and after all abbreviations.

2.2 **Open punctuation** When typing a letter with open punctuation, no punctuation marks are inserted in the reference, date, name and address of addressee, salutation, complimentary close or abbreviations. The grammatical punctuation in the body of the letter must be inserted. If a name and address appear in continuous matter, the items are separated by a comma, or two character spaces.

## 3 Printed heading

If you are using paper with a printed heading, turn up at least two single spaces after the last line of the printed heading before starting to type. If you are using plain A5 portrait paper, or A4 paper, turn up seven single spaces.

**Word processors** Some organizations provide plain paper for business documents. The letterhead is stored on a disk and copied on to a sheet of paper as and when the heading is required.

## 4 Parts of a business letter

4.1 **Reference** If the words 'Our Ref' are already printed on the letterhead, type the reference in alignment with the print and leave at least **one** clear character space before typing the reference. If 'Our Ref' is not printed, turn up two single spaces after the printed letter heading and type at left margin. Turn up two single spaces and type 'Your Ref' if it is needed.

**Word processors** Many documents are stored (filed) on disks and, therefore, a disk number plus type and number of the document serve as a reference. For example: D12/L31/JB/TH as a reference would mean that the document is on Disk 12; L31 tells us that it is a letter numbered 31; JB are the author's initials and TH are the initials of the operator.

4.2 **Special marks applying to letters** The words PRIVATE, CONFIDENTIAL, PERSONAL, URGENT, RECORDED DELIVERY, REGISTERED, SPECIAL DELIVERY, BY HAND or AIRMAIL are typed at the left margin at least two single spaces after the last line of the reference, or the date, if the date is typed at the left margin. FREEPOST, POSTE RESTANTE (to be called for) and a private PO Box No are all typed on the line after the name of the addressee.

4.3 **Date** Typed at least two single spaces after the reference, blocked at left margin, or typed on the same line as the reference and blocked at right margin.

4.4 **For the attention of** It is the custom with some firms to have all correspondence addressed to the firm and not to individuals. If, therefore, the writer of a letter wishes it to reach a particular person or department, the words, 'FOR THE ATTENTION OF . . .', are typed at the left margin. In a letter, for the attention of a particular person may be typed above, or below the name and address, but it is placed **above** on the envelope; therefore, as the special marks **must always** be typed on the envelope, and the operator usually copies the details from the letter, we suggest that 'for the attention of' is typed above the name and address of the addressee.

When a letter is addressed to a business organization and marked for the attention of a particular person, eg, Mrs E Holiday, the salutation **must** be **Dear Sirs**. If the writer wishes the salutation to be **Dear Mrs Holiday**, the attention line should not be used, and **Mrs E Holiday** should be typed on the line preceding the name of the organization. The result of the present informality is that the salutation **Dear Sirs** is seldom used, thus avoiding the implication that members of the organization consist of only male persons. In business, the operator should follow the housestyle, and in an examination, the suggestions given in the typewriting syllabus for the particular examining body.

B     Data Bank     170

2

"He was also a treasurer of a local club, & I can't tell wh is the club's cash & wh is his own. Its a real nightmare." He thin/ pursed his/lips in disapproval.

"Really," I said, politely.

"John, make sure you make a will & put all yr affairs in order." He paused & sipped his coffee. "The secretary's petty cash & our society's shd be kept quite apart from yr own money. Do you do this?"

He stared at me with his dark brown eyes.

"Oh, yes ... yes," I hastened to add. "Of course."
I was going hot.

6 mths later on a hot Sat evening in Aug, Evans the Bridge dropped dead whilst mowing his lawn.

Now the interesting thing is this. He left no will; there was the greatest difficulty in finding the deeds, duplicate copies of his insurance policy had to be sent for, & it was not known if he owed money or if anyone owed money to him. of his house

And the local historical society? To my knowledge we had £150 to our credit, but so intertwined were the society's financial affairs with those of Evans the Bridge th we had to write off all the cash & start again.

So, whenever I see the old bridge in Pontypridd, I recall my dead friend & his good advice.

---

**UNIT 7** See Practical Typing Exercises, Book Two, pages 29–31, for further exercises on *Dropped headings, Ellipsis*

## Borders (ornamental)

Display work, such as programmes, menus, etc, can be made more artistic by the use of a suitable ornamental border or corners, such as the following. You should be able to make up other artistic borders, but in doing so take care not to make the border too heavy, as this will detract from the general appearance.

```
* * * * * *     0:0:0:0:0:0     ***   ***
*         *     :          :     *     *
* * * * * *     :          :     *     *
                0:0:0:0:0:0     *     *
                                 *     *
                                ***   ***
```

## Brace

See *Special signs, symbols and marks*, page 206.

## Brief notes

You may be asked, in the office or in an examination, to type a letter or memo from brief notes. The following procedure should be adopted:

1. Type a rough draft, making sure you get the points in the correct order, usually in the order they are given in the brief notes.
2. Avoid short, disconnected sentences and decide where to paragraph.
3. There is no need to correct typing errors in the rough draft as it will waste time, but verify dates, people's names, etc, and type them accurately.
4. Remove paper from machine and read very carefully what you have typed, making any further amendments that may be necessary.
5. Insert a fresh sheet of paper and type a final copy ready for despatch.
6. When using a word processor, compose the rough draft on the screen and edit the soft copy before printing out.

## Bring forward reminders

Very often it is important for a person to ascertain by a particular date that a certain action has been taken. The action may be the result of outgoing correspondence, incoming correspondence, a telephone call, etc. A special file, which has a variety of names such as bring-forward, bring-up file, tickler file, follow-up file, etc, is kept for this purpose.

As a typist it may be one of your duties to keep a bring-forward file, and for that purpose you may have a concertina file with a space for each month of the year and, at the front, pockets for each day of the current month. In the various sections you will keep papers, documents and notes, that require attention on a particular date. At the end of each month, you should transfer the contents of the next month's pocket into the daily pockets. You must train yourself to look in the bring-up file each morning and take out that day's reminders so that action may be taken.

Your employer may ask you to make a note, on a file copy or on a special copy kept for the purpose, of the date on which a certain document should be brought forward—see page 136. In this case, the author of the document wishes to check to see if further action is required.

## Bullet mark

This is a heavy dot, used mainly in printing and desktop publishing, to draw the reader's attention to a particular line, section, or paragraph. When this facility is not available on your machine, type two small oo's or use the asterisk.

## Business letters

### 1 Layout

Letters can be displayed in various ways, the styles most commonly used are illustrated below.

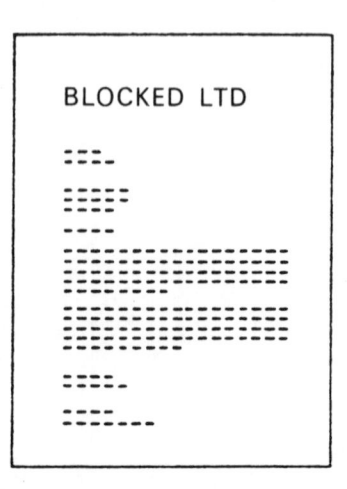

Fully-blocked (sometimes called 'blocked').

Begin every line at the left margin.

# SKILL BUILDING

Type each line three times and, if time permits, complete your practice by typing each group once as it appears.

Margins:
12 pitch 22–82
10 pitch 12–72

### A  Keyboarding skills

1  Speed      When we reach town, we will visit the open market and shops.
2  Accuracy   When temperatures fall below freezing, avid sports fans ski.
3  Figures    Remember: 1603 1707 1815 1837–1901 1918 1936 1939 1945 1952.
4  Symbols    12% discount; 30 @ £5 each; R Holmes & Co Ltd; 9' = 2.743 m.

### B  Improve control of right- and left-hand keys

5  hip limp imply nylon nippy pupils puny puppy minimum million
6  vet zest debts vexed waxed aware barge zebra sweater average
7  Ada ate that egg yolk.  It is better to add onions to taste.
8  It seems a million years since I saw Eva and Jim — it is 20!

### C  Spelling skill—correct the one misspelt word in each line
—see page 161 for answer

9   planned editing admitting signature unequalled unnecessarily
10  receive furious refference companies signatures approximately
11  The assessors valued the company's propperty at £125,850,000.
12  Unless you substantiate your arguements, you will lose votes.

### Skill measurement          Three-minute timing          Not more than three errors

S/M9 Perhaps you have seen typists' jobs advertised in the papers    12
     and wished you could apply.  Or you may have spent some time    24
     in an office and have an idea of the different types of work    36
     the typist has to tackle.                                       41

   For the better-paid typist's job you should have appropriate      53
   qualifications: a Stage III in typing, Stage II/III in Audio      65
   Transcription; and a good knowledge of English.  This job         77
   usually demands common sense, initiative, and tact.  However      89
   rushed you may be, you will have to be pleasant to the bore       101
   who will often deviate from the topic and perhaps waste your      113
   time.  If you have a query, always ask for advice — never         124
   undertake a job unless you are sure you know what is meant.       136

   You may be required to deal with internal and external tele-      148
   phone calls and to make certain decisions.  The typist often      160
   has to operate a photo-copying machine and to maintain a          171
   filing system.  Typing is also a means of providing input         183
   for word processors and computers and it may be that you          194
   will have extra pay for operating these machines.                 204

   Employment prospects for typists are excellent.  Thousands        216
   of typists are added to the work-force each year, and the         227
   typist who is familiar with processing equipment has an even      239
   better chance.                                    (SI 1.40)       242

   1 | 2 | 3 | 4 | 5 | 6 | 7 | 8 | 9 | 10 | 11 | 12 |

insert a new paragraph, to type words or lines in capital letters or spaced capitals, etc. Most work in offices, and in examinations, will be edited in some way, and it is part of the typist's job to be able to interpret these amendments and make the necessary corrections. Time spent in reading and understanding the copy will mean speedier and more accurate presentation of the final document. See also **Proofreaders' marks**, page 201.

## Backing sheet

To prevent damage to the cylinder of the typewriter/ printer, use a backing sheet. Other uses of the backing sheet are:

### 1 Typing on cards and memoranda

When typing on cards and memoranda, you may have, of necessity, to type near the bottom. To ensure that the cylinder grips the card (paper) and thus prevents the bottom line(s) from 'running off' the paper, use a backing sheet. In fact, whenever you have to type within one inch of the bottom, use a backing sheet which extends below the bottom of the page.

### 2 Aid to centring

On the backing sheet rule a vertical line down the centre and also a heavy horizontal line across the centre. This will help you when centring material on a page.

### 3 Top and bottom margins

With the underscore type a line on the seventh single space from the top edge of the paper. This will remind you that you always turn up seven single spaces before you start to type. Likewise, one inch from the bottom of the backing sheet draw a dark horizontal line to remind you that you are nearing the bottom of the page.

With some word processors, you may use the automatic paper insertion key.

## Balance sheets

See **Financial statements**, page 183.

## Bank/bond paper

See **Paper**, page 196.

## Bibliography

A bibliography is a list of books, magazines, or newspaper articles, included in footnotes at the end of a chapter or book to show the source from which the information has been taken or as a reading list for people who want to go further into the subject. The items are listed alphabetically according to the author's last name which is typed in upper and lower case. The author's name is typed first followed by the forename(s) or initials: see example on page 123. With full punctuation, use the comma and full stops as follows:

Drummond, A. M. and Coles-Mogford, A., *Keyboarding and Document Processing, First Course*: McGraw-Hill, Maidenhead, 1992.

With blocked style, it is usual to block all lines although the second and subsequent lines for any one item may be inset five to ten spaces. The titles of the books are typed in upper and lower case and underlined, or in sloping type, because the printer will set them in italic.

## Bills of Quantities

A Bill of Quantities is a document showing the details and prices of materials to be used in building, etc. Its purpose is to obtain tenders for the work to be done and materials required. It also enables the architect to make an accurate estimate of the work to be carried out.

A4 paper is used and the vertical lines ruled over the full length of the paper. Follow the layout given. When typing between the vertical lines, every endeavour should be made to see that the characters do not touch the lines.

Short Bills of Quantities are folded from left to right and endorsed on the uppermost side, ie with folded edge to the left. Long Bills of Quantities are bound and endorsed on the front page.

(Please see notes under **Specialized typing**, page 207.)

## Boilerplate

See **Document assembly**, pages 179–180.

## Bold print

Word processors have a facility that enables the operator to print characters with a much darker type than the normal printing. This emboldening is a very useful device for emphasizing text.

# PRODUCTION DEVELOPMENT

*See pages 169, 179, 180*

## Effective display, Emphasis and Borders

1  Type the following attractively and effectively on A4 paper. Type an ornamental border.

```
* / * / * / * / * / *
```

Desktop publishing
Write, design and print
Your own advertising features

*[Use any form of emphasis available to you to make these 3 lines stand ~~out~~]*

Desktop publishing software turns your computer screen into a 'paste-up' board. Text & artwork are transferred from files on disk & manipulated until the correct design effect is achieved.

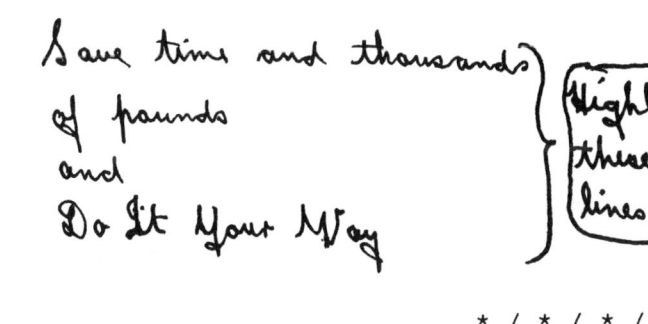

Save time and thousands
of pounds
and
Do It Your Way

*[Highlight these lines]*

```
* / * / * / * / * / *
```

## Brief notes

*See page 169*

2  Compose a memo from Sam Pascoe, Sales Manager, from the following notes. Insert today's date and a reference which will consist of Mr Pascoe's initials followed by your initials.

Send a memo to Merel [MEREL] Frampton, our Marketing Manager, enclosing the above leaflet, & ask if there are any amendments she wishes to make. I need it back tomorrow (insert date) as it has to be sent to the printers.

(Insert a subject hdg DESKTOP PUBLISHING)

---

**UNIT 8**   *Effective display, Emphasis, Borders, Brief notes*

## Agenda

When the Notice of a Meeting is sent out, it is normal practice to include the Agenda, which is a list of items to be discussed at a Meeting, these being listed in a certain order and numbered for easy reference as follows:

1 Apologies
2 Minutes of the last Meeting
3 Matters arising out of the Minutes
4 Correspondence
5 Reports
6 Any special points for discussion
7 Any other business
8 Date of next Meeting

As is the Notice of a Meeting, the Agenda is sent to all who are entitled to attend. It is usually duplicated and care should be taken to have available additional copies for members who may forget to bring a copy to a meeting.

The word AGENDA is blocked at the left margin or centred on the writing line, usually in spaced capitals. The numbers may be blocked or, if indented from the left margin, the longest line may end the same number of spaces from the right margin.

## Align

To arrange typed letters in a straight line. If the base of a character appears above or below the normal line of type, it is said to be out of alignment. This is most unsightly and should be avoided at all costs. Also, to align vertically means that all lines start at the same scale point.

On word processors the align facility is used when figures are required to line up under a decimal point or when rearranging the line endings or left margin after text editing.

## Aligned right margin

Programmes, display, financial statements, etc, sometimes have a right column and the last character of each line of this column may have to end at the same scale point. To do this:

Decide on the exact scale point at which you wish the last character to be typed, and set a tab stop one space to the right of that point. From the tab stop, backspace once for each character and space in the line to be aligned; from the point reached, type the word(s)/figure(s). This is sometimes referred to as justifying, but justifying really means inserting extra spaces between words so that the lines of the text all end at the same scale point. Word processors may have a 'flush right' facility to allow the information to be typed so that it will end automatically at the right margin.

## Alignment scale (sometimes known as line indicators)

Close to the cylinder, behind the ribbon on each side of the printing point, there is sometimes a number of vertical marks, the tops of which indicate the base of the typing line. Also, a red vertical line, or arrow, indicates where the next character will print vertically on the paper. There are a variety of indicators on word processors.

## Allocating space

You may be asked to leave blank spaces for the insertion of photographs, etc, or you may have to draw geometrical figures. The diagram or blank space left must be the exact size indicated. For instance, if you were asked to leave a **blank** space of 51 mm (2 inches) you should turn up 13 (**thirteen**) single linespaces. However, if you have to **insert lines** and use the **underscore** for the horizontals, you would turn up the exact number of lines. For example, if you had to draw a square 51 mm (2 inches) deep, and you were using the underscore for the horizontal lines, you would type the first horizontal line, turn up 12 (**twelve**) and type the second horizontal line.

Horizontal and vertical lines may be drawn in ink or by means of the underscore. Alternatively, the horizontal lines may be typed by the underscore and the vertical lines drawn in ink, provided the ink is the same colour as the lines typed by the underscore.

When typing from complicated copy, it is a good plan to type a draft quickly to see how much space the typing, drawing, etc, is likely to take up. When a diagram has typing before and after it, there should be a blank space before the first line and after the last line.

## Amendments to text

Draft work, whether typewritten or handwritten, invariably contains amendments in some form. This can include matter to be transferred from one portion of the text to another, items deleted and replaced with other information, an instruction to

3  Type the following on A5 portrait paper, emphasizing any words you feel necessary to make the notice attractive. Type an ornamental border.

```
                    Somertown's

                    Largest Car Boot Sale


                    Every Sunday at 9.0 am

                    Turn your unwanted
                    items into cash

                    Station Lane, Somertown


                    Just turn up
                    (no booking required)

                    Ring Darren Peachey on
                    (0404) 1089
```

*(Turn your unwanted items into cash / Station Lane, Somertown — to be moved, arrow indicates new position)*

**8**  Key in document 3 (filename BOOT) for 10-pitch print-out. When you have completed this task, save under filename BOOT, and print out original. Recall the document and follow the instructions for text editing on page 162.

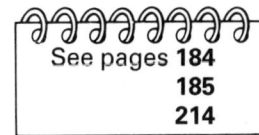

## *Folded leaflets, Tailpiece*

*See pages* **184**, **185**, **214**

4  Type the following leaflet on A4 paper, folded to form two sheets of A5 portrait.

*(FRONT COVER)*

```
                  M A I L    O R D E R


                  STRIKING FASHION

                  for

                  AUTUMN 1994


                  Make sure you are up to date
                  and eye catching
                  wearing the latest fashions


                  You can order -

                  24 hours a day, 7 days a week


                  Telephone free:
                  (0800) 49614
```

UNIT 8 — *Folded leaflets, Tailpiece* — 51

SCF (S.C.F.) = Save the Children Fund
WCT (W.C.T.) = World Championship Tennis
(UKROFS) = United Kingdom Register of Organic Food Standards

### 4.2. Always used

| | | |
|---|---|---|
| ad lib (ad lib.) | = *ad libitum* | = at pleasure |
| eg (e.g.) | = *exempli gratia* | = for example |
| Esq (Esq.) | = Esquire | = courtesy title |
| etc (etc.) | = *et cetera* | = and others |
| et seq (et seq.) | = *et sequentes* | = and the following |
| ie (i.e.) | = *id est* | = that is |
| Messrs (Messrs.) | = Messieurs | = courtesy title |
| Mr (Mr.) | = Mister | = courtesy title |
| Mrs (Mrs.) | | = courtesy title |
| NB (N.B.) | = *Nota bene* | = note well |

**NOTE** Miss is not an abbreviation and does not require a full stop; likewise Ms does not require a full stop.

### 4.3 Used with figures only

| | | |
|---|---|---|
| am (a.m.) | = *ante meridiem* | = before noon |
| HP (H.P.) | = hire purchase | |
| No, Nos (No., Nos.) | = number, numbers | |
| pm (p.m.) | = *post meridiem* | = after noon |
| % (%) | = per centum | |
| v, vol (v., vol.) | = volume | |
| *in (in.) | = inch or inches | |
| ft (ft.) | = foot or feet | |
| *oz (oz.) | = ounce or ounces | |
| *lb (lb.) | = pound or pounds (weight) | |
| *cwt (cwt.) | = hundredweight or hundredweights | |
| *m | = metre, metres | |
| *mm | = millimetre, millimetres | |
| *cm | = centimetre, centimetres | |
| *g | = gram, grams | |
| *kg | = kilogram, kilograms | |

* These do not require an s in the plural.

**NOTE** It would seem preferable to add an s for the plural of yd and qr (yds/yds. qrs/qrs.). This style is recommended by the *Oxford Dictionary for Writers and Editors*; however, the British Standards Institution gives both examples without the s. Follow the author's copy and/or house style.

### 4.4 Used in cases indicated

& (&) = ampersand = and. Used in names of firms and numbers [Nos 25 & 26 (Nos. 25 & 26)] never in ordinary matter.

BA (B.A.) = Bachelor of Arts. Degree after a person's name.
Bros (Bros.) = Brothers. In names of firms or companies only.
bf (b.f.) = brought forward (accounting) or boldface (word processing)
c/o (c/o) = care of. Used only in addresses. (Sometimes the word 'at' is used instead of c/o.)
Co (Co.) = Company. Used in names of companies.
cod (c.o.d.) COD (C.O.D.) = Cash on delivery. Used on invoices.
DSc (D.Sc.) = Doctor of Science. Degree after person's name.
E & OE (E. & O. E.) = Errors and omissions excepted. Used in invoices.
Jr or Junr (Junr.) = Junior. Used in addresses after a man's name to distinguish from senior [Snr (Snr.)].
Ltd (Ltd.) = Limited. Used in the name of a private limited company.
PS (PS.) = Postscript. Abbreviated form used at end of letter and memo only.
PLC (P.L.C.) plc (p.l.c.) = Public Limited Company. Used after the name of public limited company.
pro tem = *pro tempore* (for the time being). Used after a designation, eg Secretary pro tem.
Ref (Ref.) = Reference. Used in letters and memos.
SERPS = State Earnings Related Pension Scheme. (May be in full or abbreviated.)

### *Accents*

Machine operators may have to type documents in a foreign language and the use of various accents may be necessary. If these are not part of the keyboard, the following should be inserted by hand in black ink.

 ́   ̀   ̂   ̃
acute  grave  circumflex  tilde

Usually typed as combination characters are:

diaresis and umlaut = quotation marks (") typed over letter;
cedilla = type letter c, backspace and type comma.

A | Data Bank | 166

(INSIDE LEFT) ← (CAPS)

Essential Style ← (CAPS)

Traditional tweeds are updated in rich, nobbly cloth with strong colours - bright lime, lemon, red and purple checks.

Subtle tailoring is used with assured elegance to work with delicious shades of sorbet.

Texture makes its presence felt in rich bouclés, soft mohairs and luxurious angora.

In the comfort of your own home, sit back and relax and enjoy your mail order shopping, any day or evening of the week.

Essential accessories made for us in Italy are available, including handbags in fine leather in the new, autumn colours of olive, fuchsia and burgundy.

(INSIDE RIGHT)

How to order

Order by telephone for immediate service

or

Order by post -

1  Peel off the label from the back cover of the catalogue and attach to the order form.

2  Use the attached pre-addressed envelope when you post your order, and don't forget to include your cheque, postal order or credit card details.

3  Sign the order form.

o - o - o - o - o - o
    o - o - o - o - o
      o - o - o
        o

*Use any form of emphasis available to you to make this last page attractive and eye-catching.*

---

**UNIT 8**     *Folded leaflets, Tailpiece*     52

# DATA BANK

**NOTE** Throughout this textbook we have referred to word processors where we felt it appropriate, and we hope you will find the suggestions and exercises useful. The text-editing instructions are given on pages 162–163 in the textbook; however, to make your text editing more realistic, you may wish to use the edited exercises from the *Solutions and Resource Material*.

Also in the *Solutions and Resource Material* you will find a guide to **language arts skills**.

This **Data bank** is in alphabetical order and gives up-to-date, precise and clear information about typewriting conventions, display and layout—in other words, a guide to present-day practices and document presentation. In word processing terms, the Data bank will suggest a suitable **format** or style (page layout, margins, indentations, linespacing, etc).

## Abbreviations

In typewritten work, abbreviations should not, as a rule, be used. There are, however, a few which are **never** typed in full, and others which may be used in certain circumstances.

### 1 Open and full punctuation

When using **open** punctuation, no full stops are inserted after initials or in abbreviations, eg Mrs Y W T St George-Stevens is Managing Director of Y W T Stevens and Co Ltd. With **full** punctuation, full stops are inserted after initials and in abbreviations, eg Mrs. Y. W. T. St. George-Stevens is Managing Director of Y. W. T. Stevens and Co. Ltd.

Notice the spacing in the following:

**Open** punctuation   Mrs S J Hudson MA BSc—where an abbreviation consists of two or more letters, there is no space between the letters but one space between each group of letters.

**Full** punctuation   Mrs. S. J. Hudson, M.A., B.Sc.—space between the groups is replaced by a comma, followed by a clear space.

1.1 However, with **full** punctuation, full stops need not be inserted in the following cases:

 1.1.1 **Acronyms** (words formed from initials): VAT, PAYE, UNESCO, NATO, BUPA, OPEC, NUPE, ACAS, etc.

 1.1.2 **Names** of **well-known** companies, states, countries, radio and television broadcasting stations, unions and many government departments: ICI, GKN, USA, UK, RSA, EEC, BBC, IBS, DES, etc.

 1.1.3 In metric measurements: 12 mm, 4 m, 6 kg, 30 km, etc.

### 2 Imperial measurements

No punctuation is inserted with open punctuation, but with full punctuation the full stops are inserted, eg 2 lb., 2 ft. 4 in.

### 3 Longhand abbreviations

These are used in handwriting, but the words must be typed in full. Examples: dept = department; st = street; shd = should; sh = shall; w = will; wh = which; th = that; etc. Great care must be taken to verify the correct spelling when typing abbreviations in full, eg accom = accommodation; gntee(s) = guarantee(s); recd = received; def = definitely; sep = separate; rec(s) = receipt(s); temp = temporary; etc. Days of the week and months of the year, eg Wed, Fri, Jan, Sept, etc, **must** be typed in full. Where the names of persons, towns, countries, associations, etc, are repeated in any group of tasks, the author may write only the initial(s) or use the initial(s) followed by a long dash to represent the word(s). For example: in a letter addressed to Mrs R Green, the handwritten salutation may read, Dear Mrs G———, and the typist would be expected to type Dear Mrs Green.

### 4 Standard abbreviations

Lists of standard abbreviations, with their uses, are given below. Study the lists so that you will know when and when not to use the abbreviations. Full punctuation is given in brackets, although the tendency today is to use open punctuation.

4.1. **Common abbreviations**   Usually abbreviated, but may be typed in full. It is wise to follow the style used by the author and/or house style. **Be consistent**.

| | |
|---|---|
| EC | = European Community |
| Ecu | = European currency unit |
| EU | = European Union |
| EMS | = European Monetary System |
| Hon Sec (Hon. Sec.) | = Honorary Secretary. Typed in full. |
| IQPS | = Institute of Qualified Private Secretaries |
| MEP (M.E.P.) | = Member of the European Parliament |
| MoD (M.o.D.) | = Ministry of Defence |
| mph (m.p.h.) | = miles per hour |
| RMO (R.M.O.) | = Resident Medical Officer |
| RNLI (R.N.L.I.) | = Royal National Lifeboat Institution |

A                            Data Bank                          165

**5** Type the following on A4 landscape paper, folded in two. The front cover will be typed on the back of page one.

*Names of speakers & their designations to be blocked at right margin, please.*

**Page 1 - Inside left**

*Insert date*

TUESDAY     JUNE 1994

*leave 5 clear spaces*

| | |
|---|---|
| 1030 | Registration |
| 1200 | Lunch |
| 1330 | 'AIM FOR THE TOP' |
| | Kirsty Reynolds |
| | Recruitment Consultant |
| 1430 | |
| 1500 | 'OFFICE PLANNING AND DESIGN' |
| | Oliver B Cobb |
| | Managing Director |
| 1600 | |
| 1630 | 'PERSONAL EFFECTIVENESS' |
| | Rebecca Halls |
| | Career Analyst |
| 1730 | |
| 1900 | Dinner |
| 2030 | FASHION SHOW FOR THE |
| | SUCCESSFUL BUSINESS WOMAN |
| | Jonquil Fashions |

*Insert the date of the Date title on 164, filename SEMIN.*

---

**FRONT COVER**

-----ooo0ooo-----

S E M I N A R

for

SECRETARIES OF THE 90s

-----ooo0ooo-----

To be held

at

THE MOAT
CONFERENCE CENTRE
London   E1 8DX

from

   June 1994

to

   June 1994

-----ooo0ooo-----

### HEALTH

Two people working in the cardio-vascular clinic are:

Nurse Sam Rixstead
Nurse René Turner

### HIST

Local visit—to be confirmed at AGM

### HOTEL

The date for the birthday luncheon is Saturday 13 August 1994
*Beverages* (To be inserted on leaflet)
Pot of hot chocolate for one person   £1.80
Each additional person - £1.00
Glass of chilled milk - £0.80

### INS

Vet's fees   £20 premium
Recovery costs   £5 premium

### MTG

2.2.3 Ensure that the attendance register is signed, if appropriate

### PROP

Mr and Mrs Clements' address is:
35 Long Meadow   Folkestone   Kent   CT20 1ZA

### Rushbridge

Mrs Mo Rushbridge   13 High Street
Taunton   Somerset   TA3 8FV

### SEMIN

from Tuesday 14 June 1994 to
Thursday 16 June 1994

### SMITH

Pete Smith   49 Holly Lane
Taunton   Somerset   TA7 5TP

### STAND

SP1  We thank you for your Order No     dated     and regret that we are temporarily out of stock of the     you require. We will forward them by express delivery on     and trust that this arrangement will meet your requirements.

SP2  Further to your telephone call on

SP3  Thank you for your letter dated     with which you enclosed a cheque for     in part payment of your account for the period up to

As you still owe us the sum of     we must ask you to pay this amount by the

SP4  Please accept our apologies for the delay.

SP5  We are pleased to tell you that your Order No     was/will be despatched on

SP6  We look forward to receiving your cheque.

SP7  As there is a balance of     still outstanding on your account for     , we feel you may not have received our Statement of Account, and we enclose a copy.

### TAKA

Dr and Mrs Raymond Morley
26 Longmeadow Road
Rye   East Sussex   TN29 8FE

Ms Charity Colton
Sea View Cottage
High Hill
Rye   East Sussex   TN30 9WP

The balance due by 2 weeks today (insert date) is £867

### VITAE

Ms F Paling   Headmistress
Crayfield Comprehensive School   Bellend Road
Wellingborough   Northants   NN6 4TY
(Telephone: 0933 220889)

Mr Toby Glazebrook
Chief Administrative Officer
Northamptonshire Education Department
Dale End
Northampton   NN2 7OP
(Telephone: 0933 664876)

(TYPIST: Please type these two addresses side by side.)

*Data Files*

[Page 2 - Inside right] [Insert date]

**WEDNESDAY    JUNE 1994**

| | |
|---|---|
| 0800 | Breakfast |
| 0930 | 'PERSONALITY PROFILE' — Amanda Smythe, Consultant Psychologist |
| 1100 | 'TODAY'S SECRETARY — TOMORROW'S MANAGER' — Stanley P Anders, Personnel Director |
| 1230 | Lunch |
| 1415 – 1615 | 'THE AUTOMATED OFFICE' — Demonstrations to include — Word Processing Today, Desktop Publishing, Fax and Telex _updated_ |
| 1615 | Tea and free time |
| 1900 | Dinner |
| 2030 | 'BEAUTY CARE DEMONSTRATIONS' by Style |

[trs] [uc/]

[Back cover] [Insert date — June 1994]

**Thursday**

| | |
|---|---|
| 0800 | Breakfast |
| 0930 – 1030 | 'THE SUCCESSFUL SECRETARY OF THE 90's' — Judith Maddox, PA to Sir James McWithers MP [// stet] |
| 1100–1200 | 'INTERVIEW TECHNIQUES' — Pauline Whittacker, Senior Lecturer |
| 1230 – 1.30 | 'THE TECHNOLOGY OF THE 90's' — Andrew Walden, RCK Components Limited |
| 1.45–2.45 | Lunch |
| 3.00–4.00 | 'AIM HIGH – YOUR FUTURE' — Neil Adams, Careers Adviser |
| 4.00–4.30 | Final forum and discussion — all speakers |
| 4.30 | Tea |
| | Close of Conference |

Display back cover in the same form as pages 1 & 2. Change times to 24-hr clock.

---

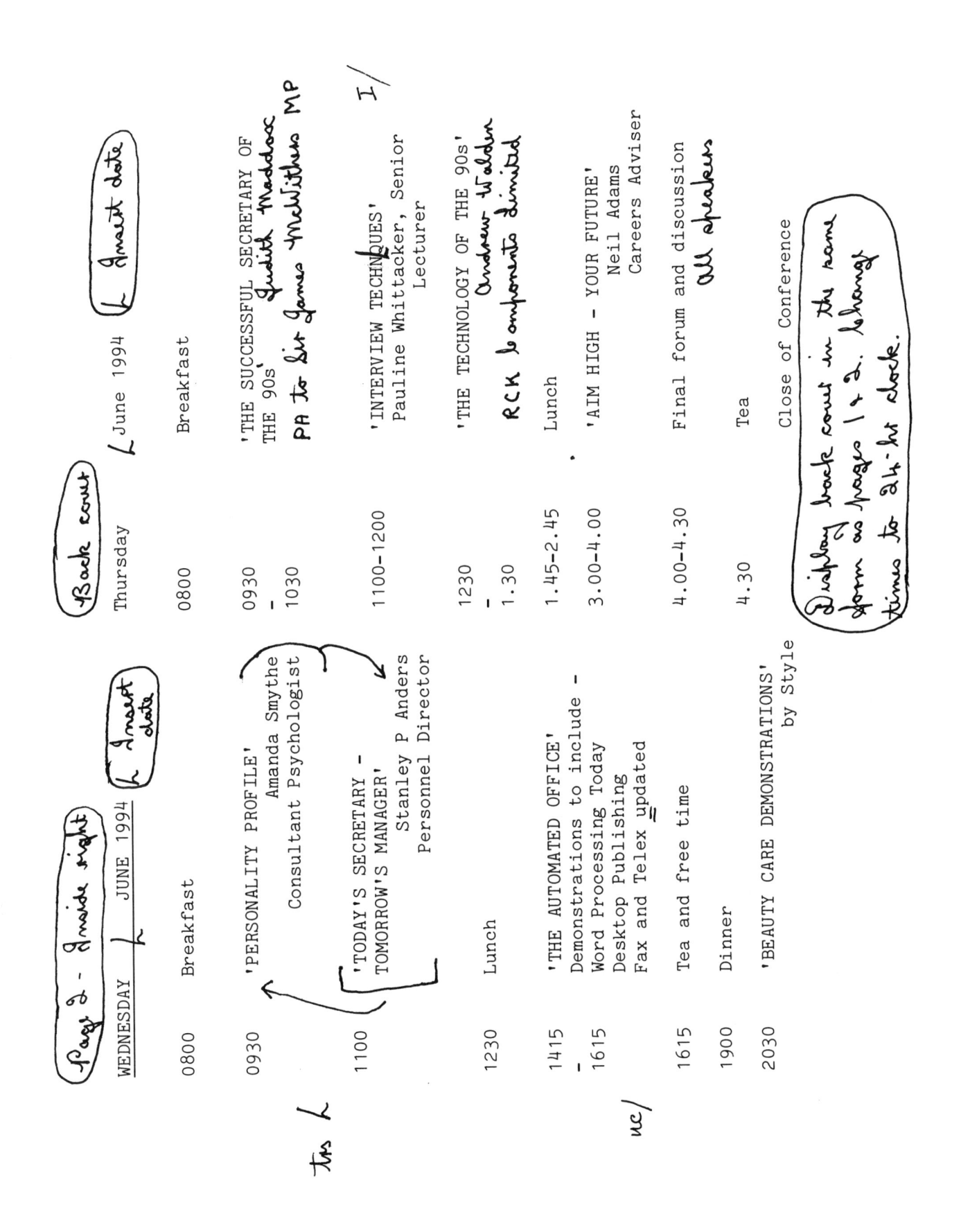

**9** Key in document 5 (filename SEMIN) for 10-pitch print-out. When you have completed this task, save under filename SEMIN, and print out original. Retrieve the document and follow the instructions for text editing on page 162.

**UNIT 8**   See Practical Typing Exercises, Book Two, pages 32–35, for further exercises on ***Folded leaflets***

*Page 72*
Recall the document stored under filename INTER. Transpose the 1993 and 1992 columns. Proofread soft copy and, if necessary, correct. Print out an original in 12 pitch, but omit the 1993 column.

*Page 79*
Recall the document stored under filename EURO. Change the discount to $33\frac{1}{3}$ per cent and alter the figures accordingly. Change to fully-blocked style (including the table) with justified right margin. Proofread soft copy and, if necessary, correct. Print out one original in 12 pitch; then print one original of the subject heading and the table (ignore the other parts of the letter).

*Page 86*
Recall the document stored under filename RATES. Transpose **Banks** and the information that follows with **National Savings** and text that follows. Proofread soft copy and, if necessary, correct. Print out one original of columns 1, 2, and 3 (omit the last column) plus the footnote with the single dagger (omit the asterisk footnote).

*Page 117*
Recall the document stored under filename POET. Centre the main and subheadings and the title of the poem. Indent the paragraphs and type in single spacing. Justify the right margin except for the poem. Proofread soft copy and, if necessary, correct. (a) Print an original of the complete document; (b) print an original of poem and its title centred on the page.

# DATA FILES

The following office files contain information that you will need when typing certain documents.

---

**AGENDA**

**Section A**
Visit to Millfield Home for the Elderly

**Section B**
1  Apologies for absence
2  Compulsory redundancies
3  Duties and reorganization of remaining staff
4  Customer complaints

**Section C**
6  Financial statement.

---

**BAYLES**

Prescription No. S489475
Mr Martin is a welder who does drive a car and wears safety glasses for his job. He doesn't wear contact lenses but does have glasses for reading, but he isn't completely satisfied with them. They do not have progressive or varifocal lenses. He does occasionally use his son's computer, rides a bike and plays bowls in the summer.

---

**CAR**

Agreement No. 401 374342-21

---

**EURO**

Mr & Mrs F Rollison's address is:
102 Longstretton Road   Gildersome
Leeds   LS24 2FP
(c) The home has no more than 5 bedrooms;
(d) The home is self-contained;

---

**FORM**

**Section A**
Enquiry Nos: 2187, 4096, 3209
Name: Simon Aspel   Position: Manager
Company: Bayles and Bayles   No of employees: 6
Address: 26 Ossington Road   Norwell
Newark   Notts   NG23 6JW
Tel No: 0636 41114   Fax No: 0636 14441

**Section B**
Share Account No: 461058
Insert your own name and address
Your proxy's name is Jonathan Smythe who lives at 15 High Street   Caterham   Surrey   CR2 4FU
You wish to vote 'for' Resolution 1, but against Resolution 2

**Section C**
Type your own title, name, address and date of birth. You participate in squash, swimming and table tennis, and your membership number is BR 43078. Sign the form and type today's date.

---

**GOV**

(e)  Foundation Governors appointed by the body which established the school (usually the church).
(f)  Minor authority Governors appointed by town, district or parish councils.
(g)  Headteachers are automatically Governors of the school unless they choose not to be.

# SKILL BUILDING

Type each line three times and, if time permits, complete your practice by typing each group once as it appears.

Margins:
12 pitch 22–82
10 pitch 12–72

### A  Keyboarding skills

1  Speed     Few can now say why she and her son did not get off the bus.
2  Accuracy  We advocated and specialized in acquiring the maximum speed.
3  Figures   Dividend: 1987 £1,950,000; 1986 £1,450,400; 1985 £1,275,300.
4  Symbols   I spent $19.69 and had ¢31 left.  20 - 11 = 9.  8 + 31 = 39.

### B  Language arts—use of apostrophe
—see explanation on page 161

5  My clerk's new word processor has many useful function keys.
6  All our clerks' income tax records were in the Staff Office.
7  The company's new laser printers were very swift and silent.
8  The directors' cars were parked just in front of the office.

9  To develop your proofreading skills, turn to page 158, exercise 4.

### Skill measurement         Four-minute timing          Not more than four errors

S/M10  A FAX or facsimile machine is a copier which will transmit          12
       a document by electronic means usually over telephone lines         24
       from one location to another.  At the distant end it appears        36
       as a printed copy, or facsimile, of the original.                   46

       Almost anything that can be put on paper can be transmitted         58
       by facsimile — text, graphs, charts, etc, can be sent and           69
       also received.  Quotations, orders, price-lists, delivery           80
       schedules, specifications, etc, are just a few examples.            91
       As originally used it was slow and the quality was certainly       103
       poor.  The equipment used today takes advantage of today's         115
       technology which means that it is much faster and of good          126
       reproduction.  Today, many new special-purpose systems will        137
       transmit a page in as little as 15 seconds; however, all           148
       high-speed transmission equipment is expensive.                    157

       One of the great advantages of facsimile is the reduction of       169
       keyboarding errors because if the original copy is correctly       181
       prepared, no further typing or checking is necessary, and no       193
       carbon copies, envelopes, postage, etc, are required.  Also,       205
       you will know that the document cannot get lost in the post.       217

       These machines have answering devices and other automatic          229
       mechanism which means they can receive documents without an        241
       individual being present, and documents may be sent when           252
       phone prices are at a lower rate, such as in the evening.          263
       Up until 1987 most electronic mail was transferred on inter-       275
       nal networks by individual companies.  However, towards the        287
       end of 1987, an American company started to develop, in            298
       Great Britain, a public worldwide electronic mail service.         310
       It would seem that in the years ahead facsimile will be a          321
       major means of transmitting information.       (SI 1.59)           329

   1  |  2  |  3  |  4  |  5  |  6  |  7  |  8  |  9  |  10  |  11  |  12  |

## Text-editing instructions

**NOTE** Text-edited copies of the exercises listed below are given in *Solutions and Resource Material* and may be duplicated for class use.

*Page 12*
Recall the document stored under filename AGENDA. Inset left margin 13 mm ($\frac{1}{2}$ inch). Substitute (a), (b), etc, for the roman numerals. Before number 9, insert another item, **Vote of thanks to The Chair**. Proofread soft copy and, if necessary, correct. Print out original only in 12 pitch.

*Page 16*
Recall the document stored under filename FAB. Inset left and right margins 13 mm ($\frac{1}{2}$ inch). Move date to the left margin. Transpose the words **patterns** and **colours**. Inset the column items (cowslip, etc) 25 mm (1 inch) from left margin. After the sentence ending . . . **designs in a variety of settings**. insert **Please telephone or fax our Sales Department if you would like a copy**. Proofread soft copy and, if necessary, correct. Print original and two copies in 10 pitch.

*Page 19*
Recall the document stored under RENT. Put today's date on the same line as reference, aligned with right margin. Embolden the shoulder headings and delete underscore. Move Myra Bradley's name and details and insert after Nigel Blount and before Martin Grant. Delete **We would advise you that** and start new paragraph with **As your** . . . . Proofread soft copy and, if necessary, correct. Print out original in 10 pitch.

*Page 20*
Recall the document stored under filename HIST. Change the venue of the lectures to the Athenaeum Room in the Guildhall. Change the date of the AGM to 8 July (at 7 pm) and put the three items in chronological order. Add a final sentence to the final paragraph, **If so, I should be very grateful if you would let me know in time for the announcement to be made at the AGM**. Proofread soft copy and, if necessary, correct. Print out an original and one copy in 12 pitch.

*Page 41*
Recall the document stored under filename DIGIT. Add an additional item 4, **All phones and faxes that have pre-set numbers will need to be re-programmed. In most cases, BT will not charge for modifications to equipment which is covered by a BT maintenance contract**. Change the enumeration to small roman numerals, and use double spacing (except for the footnote). Proofread soft copy and, if necessary, correct. Print out original and one copy in 10 pitch.

*Page 42*
Recall the document filed under filename CHART. Remove the bullet marks and inset the bulleted items 13 mm ($\frac{1}{2}$ inch) from left and right margins and underscore the first three words of each paragraph of the inset items. Remove the horizontal line before the footnotes. Proofread soft copy and, if necessary, correct. Print out original only in 12 pitch.

*Page 46*
Recall the document stored under filename HOG. Embolden the words: **Recognition**, **General**, and **Conservation**. Insert the following on page 2 as a final paragraph after the handwritten portion, *Strimmers* **(cutters with a rotating strip of cord) cut back rank vegetation in the very places hedgehogs lie up during the day, causing serious wounds to the sleeping animals**. Change to single spacing and leave double where appropriate. Proofread soft copy and, if necessary, correct. Print out original and one copy in 15 pitch.

*Page 51*
Recall document stored under filename BOOT. Use the automatic centring function to centre each line. Type 25 mm (1 inch) from left edge of paper **£4.00 in advance in aid of Comic Relief** (emphasize in some way), and on right-hand side of paper type today's date ending 13 mm ($\frac{1}{2}$ inch) from right-hand edge of paper. Change filename to SALE. Proofread soft copy and, if necessary, correct. Print out original only in 10 pitch.

*Page 54*
Recall document stored under filename SEMIN. Replace the first lecture on Wednesday with the first lecture on Thursday and move the 0930 lecture on Wednesday to Thursday. Adjust the text so that the right-hand margins are aligned and the first and last lines of each page are in alignment with each other. Proofread soft copy and, if necessary, correct. Print out original in 10 pitch.

*Page 58*
Recall the document stored under filename HOUSE. Add an extra item in correct alphabetical order: **Cedarhurst A[1] nil B[2] 7 C[3] 14 D[4] and E[5] nil**. Remember to enter and cross-check the new totals. Proofread soft copy and, if necessary, correct. Print out original only in 12 pitch.

*Page 60*
Recall the document stored under filename VITAE. Embolden all underscored headings and delete underscore. Add the following at the end of the paragraph headed **1981–1992**; **I was responsible for arranging meetings, taking minutes, keeping accounts, liaising with school staff, and arranging activities and outings**. In the paragraph dealing with the years **1977–1981**, delete the words **by telephone**, and the words **at reception**. Under heading **EMPLOYMENT**, arrange the dates in ascending order, ie, start with **1977–1981**. Proofread soft copy and, if necessary, correct. Print one original and two copies in 12 pitch.

*Page 62*
Recall the document stored under filename ITIN. Head this notice **DRAFT** and leave a right-hand margin of 64 mm ($2\frac{1}{2}$ inches). In the text after 1000 hours, delete the word **floor**, put a dash after **Manager** and add **demonstration of new machinery**. Leave five clear spaces between the **s** in **hours** and the start of the text, and two clear spaces between each timing. At 1100 hours delete the word **brief** and replace the words **workings of particular components** with **operation of certain machinery**. Proofread soft copy and, if necessary, correct. Print out original in 15 pitch.

*Page 71*
Recall the document stored under filename FINAN. Embolden the main heading. Alter the figure for subscriptions to £1 292.20, and the cash at bank will be £1 252.62. The totals will need to be changed. Proofread soft copy and, if necessary, correct. Print out original in 10 pitch.

# PRODUCTION DEVELOPMENT

*Tabulation with ruling and leader dots*

See pages **208**, 209, 211

**1** Type the following ruled tabulation.

    L U G G A G E[1]

For airline travel

| REF NO | LUGGAGE | SIZE cm | WEIGHT kg |
|---|---|---|---|
| A420 | Travel case[2]<br>Tourer case | 75 x 53 x 23<br>65 x 43 x 20 | 3.6<br>3.2 |
| B632 | Overnight case<br>Flight bag | 51 x 37 x 17<br>38 x 29 x 18 | 2.0 |
| F310 | Garment carrier<br>Wheeled case<br>Tote | 58 x 53 x 18<br>62 x 40 x 23<br>50 x 39 x 24 | 2.5<br>3.0<br>2.0 |
| G190 | Organizer case | 28 x 20 x 7.5 | |

[1] 2-year guarantee.

[2] All cases made of tough fabric in black, navy and tan.

**2** When typing the following ruled table, use any form of emphasis available to you for the main heading and subheading. Insert leader dots as shown.

Price Buster Sale      Order Direct *(Subheading)*

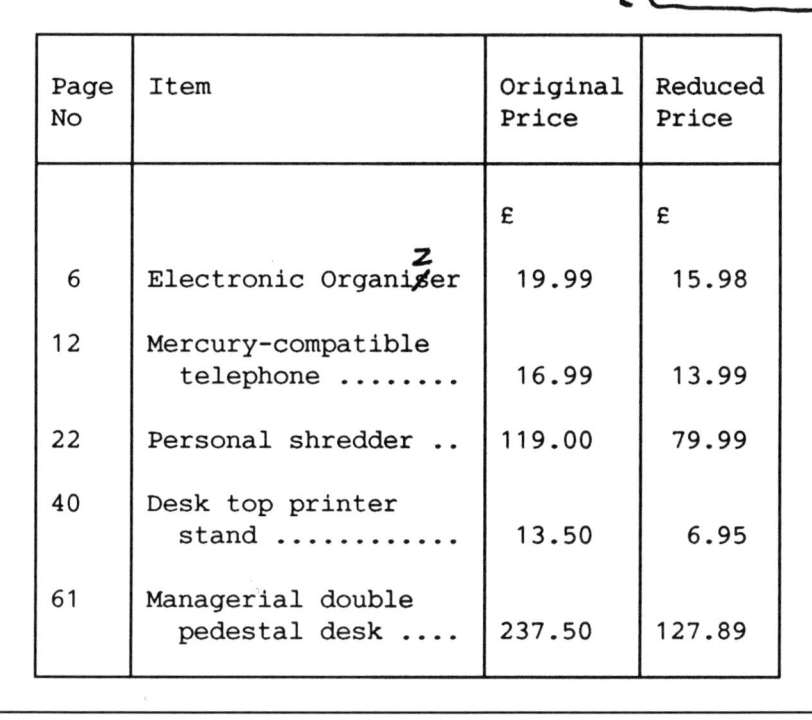

| Page No | Item | Original Price | Reduced Price |
|---|---|---|---|
| | | £ | £ |
| 6 | Electronic Organizer | 19.99 | 15.98 |
| 12 | Mercury-compatible telephone ........ | 16.99 | 13.99 |
| 22 | Personal shredder .. | 119.00 | 79.99 |
| 40 | Desk top printer stand ........... | 13.50 | 6.95 |
| 61 | Managerial double pedestal desk .... | 237.50 | 127.89 |

**UNIT 9**    See Practical Typing Exercises, Book Two, page 36, for further exercises on *Tabulation with ruling and leader dots*

## Answers to proofreading

### Page 156—exercise 1
FIELD WALK; 10 April; Shân; Mow'; A4057; Route; reference; SU637856).; hear; binoculars; $3\frac{3}{4}$ miles. (two spaces before) Suitable.

### Page 156—exercise 2
GCSE; General Certificate of Secondary Education; Visual Display Unit (without the semicolon); RSA; Cultural; Organization; Beginners'; Telegraphy; Errors and Omissions Excepted.

### Page 157—exercise 3
Brook-Little; PB-L/TSEv; SEPTEMBER 1989 TO DECEMBER 1989; enrolment; run,; follows–; underline column headings; type the whole line 'Audio Typing' before 'Beginners' Typing'; 25.9.89; 20.9.89.; B207; I shall be glad; dates and times.

### Page 158—exercise 4
Address; Installed; Due; Treatments; Tel: (0603) 623091; postcode on the same line as Norwich; Computer; November; (0272); BS16 1RP; 10A; Felton; Peterborough (without the full stop); April (without the comma).

### Page 159—exercise 5
countryside; town. (2 spaces after full stop, omit s); obedient; dog-training; know; told,; which is hard to break; line space between each numbered item; dog's lead; when there are farm; and (not the ampersand).

### Page 159—exercise 6
manufacturers; Their furniture; companies; e.g.,; executive's; approximately; £981.50; The colours; yellows, (2 errors—delete apostrophe, add comma); inset 5 spaces for second paragraph; year's; breaking; 27.7%.

### Page 160—exercise 7
Prestel; and (in full, not the ampersand); British; world's; service. (2 spaces); computers; you are given; modem; device; do not indent the third paragraph; stories; advertisements; information,; etc.; goods,.

### Page 160—exercise 8
all day; headaches,; miscarriages; worries; stress comes highest; that not 'than'; breaks; possible; detachable; swivel; screen; (one space after semi-colon); adjust; processor; typewriter.

## Answers to spelling skill and language arts exercises

### Spelling skill—words misspelt
Page  1—desirable, accommodation, ingenious
Page  9—livelihood, separated, benefited, companies
Page 14—monopolies, unnecessary, miscellaneous, benefited
Page 21—debatable, temporarily, catalogue, committee
Page 39—acknowledge, governments, achievements, advertisements
Page 43—earnest, definitely, gardener, stationery
Page 49—editing, reference, property, arguments

### Language arts—apostrophe

| | | |
|---|---|---|
| Page 55— | Lines 5 and 7 | Singular (one only) noun not ending in **s**, add an apostrophe **s**. |
| | Lines 6 and 8 | Plural noun ending in **s**, add an apostrophe. |
| Page 70— | Lines 9 and 10 | If the singular noun ends in **s**, or an **s** sound, and the addition of an apostrophe **s** makes the word **difficult to pronounce**, add the apostrophe only. What one considers difficult to pronounce is debatable. |
| | Lines 11 and 12 | Plural nouns (children, men) **not** ending in **s**, add an apostrophe **s**. |
| Page 74— | Line 9 | The contractions **don't** and **it's** require the apostrophe to show the omission of **o** and **i**. The pronoun **its** (The dog chased its tail.) does not require an apostrophe. |
| | Line 10 | The apostrophe is sometimes used in place of quotation marks to indicate the exact words of a speaker or writer. |
| | Line 11 | Used as the sign for feet. Is also the sign for minutes: 1' equals 60". |
| | Line 12 | To avoid confusing the reader, the apostrophe is used around the word 'embarrass' and between the single letter and the **s** that follows. Electronic typewriters usually have an emboldening facility and one would then embolden the word(s)/letter(s) instead of using the apostrophe. |
| Page 83— | Line 9 | The apostrophe is not now used (to show omission) before words such as **bus** (omnibus), **phone** (telephone), and other everyday words. |
| | Line 10 | The apostrophe is not used in the pronouns: hers, yours, ours, theirs and its. |
| | Line 11 | **Do not** use the apostrophe for the plural of abbreviations and plural of figures. |
| | Line 12 | The apostrophe is not used in expressions such as **Works Manager**, **Engineers Association**. |

### Language arts—agreement of subject and verb

| | | |
|---|---|---|
| Page 89— | Line 5 | **daisywheel** (singular noun) requires singular verb **is**. |
| | Line 6 | **disks** (plural noun) requires plural verb **are**. |
| | Line 7 | A plural verb is always necessary after **you**. |
| | Line 8 | Although **s** or **es** added to a noun indicates the plural, **s** or **es** added to a verb indicates the third person **singular**. |
| | Line 9 | When singular subjects are joined by **nor**, the verb must be singular. |
| | Line 10 | Singular subjects joined by **and** require a plural verb. |

# Tabulation—Subdivided column headings

See page 211

**3** Type the following ruled table on A4 paper in double spacing.

FAX   PAPER

<u>from £3.90 per roll</u>*

| Code | Machine group | Roll size | | Price | |
|---|---|---|---|---|---|
| | | Length (mm) | Width (mm) | Per roll | Per carton |
| | | | | £ | £ |
| 20/2 | 3 | 100 | 210 | 7.80 | 48.64 |
| 20/4 | 3 | 100 | 210 | 8.20 | 50.10 |
| 20/8 | 2 | 35 | 210 | 3.90 | 44.80 |
| 20/18 | 2/3 | 80 | 210 | 8.57 | 49.26 |

* Special rates for larger quantities.

**4** Type the following ruled table on A5 landscape paper.

Insurance Premiums

Domestic Animals

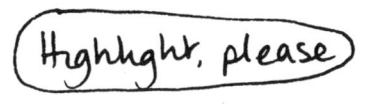

(Highlight, please)

| | Type of animal | |
|---|---|---|
| | Cats and dogs | Horses and ponies |
| Death by accident | £4 per £100 sum insured | £2 per £100 sum insured |
| Vet's fees | £6 premium | Insert information here from the Data Files, page 164, filename INS |
| Recovery costs | £1 premium | |

UNIT 9    Tabulation—Subdivided column headings    57

## Exercise 7

**Proofreading target: 7 minutes**
**Typing target:    4 minutes**

The following exercise contains 15 errors. A correct version is not provided, so you will have to identify the errors by using your knowledge of typing layout, spelling, punctuation and correct grammatical expression. When you have noted all the errors, type a corrected version, proofreading your typed copy very carefully.

```
P R E S T E L

Prestal is a collection of specialist, educational and general databases which
provide a wide range of information & services for a variety of users.  It
is part of british Telecom and was the worlds first viewdata service. At
the end of 1987 there were about 300,000 pages of information and interactive
services held on Prestel's own computors, from more than 1,000 organizations.

When you subscribe to Prestel you is given an identity number and password
and a telephone number to dial to connect you to the Prestel network.  The
information is held on mainframe computers situated in different parts of the
country and linked together to form a network.  The services are made available
to your microcomputer via the telephone and modem at local call telephone rates.
The moden is a devise which allows a computer to be connected to a telephone
line.

     The information includes news articles, storys, advertisments, reference
information statistics, ect.  A Prestel user can book holidays, send messages
to other subscribers, order goods; etc.
```

## Exercise 8

**Proofreading target: 5 minutes**
**Typing target:    3 minutes**

The following exercise contains 14 errors. A correct version is not provided, so you will have to identify the errors by using your knowledge of typing layout, spelling, punctuation and correct grammatical expression. When you have noted all the errors, type a corrected version, proofreading your typed copy very carefully.

```
HEALTHY VDU SCREENS?

Is it safe to sit in front of a visual display unit allday?  Or does it cause
eye strain, backache, headaches frozen shoulders, or even misscarriages?

If there are any health worrys, it may be that stress come highest on the
list caused by sitting with a fixed posture in front of a screen for more
than four hours a day on work than is repetitive and requires a high degree of
accuracy.  It is wise to take plenty of brakes, get up and walk around a little,
or do a different type of work for a short time, if poss.  Make sure the
lighting and ventilation in your office are adequate, and that your chair is
adjustable so that you are sitting in a comfortable position; a detatchable
keyboard is useful, as is a tilt and swivle screen;  ajust the brightness of the
print on the screen to suit your eyes.  Remind yourself how lucky you are to
have all the advantages of typing on a word processer!  Or would you prefer to
use an old manual type writer?
```

*Proofreading*                                                                                                                          **160**

5  Type the following table on A4 paper, with the name of the properties in alphabetical order.

*(Please insert the final total figure)*

HOUSING STOCK AND RENT LEVELS

1988–89

| Name of property | House types ||||| Total number of properties |
|---|---|---|---|---|---|---|
|  | A[1] | B[2] | C[3] | D[4] | E[5] |  |
| High Beeches ......... |  |  | 24 |  |  | 24 |
| Woodleigh Court ....... | 12 | 12 | 12 |  |  | 36 |
| Kingsmead ............ |  |  |  | 20 | 20 | 40 |
| The Laurels .......... | 10 | 22 | 12 |  |  | 44 |
| Cherry Bright Buildings | 15 |  |  | 30 | 10 | 55 |
| Maxstoke Gardens ...... |  | 30 | 40 |  |  | 70 |
| Orchard Court ........ |  | 15 | 15 |  |  | 30 |
| Greville Drive ....... | 8 | 12 | 20 |  |  | 40 |
| Total ................ | 45 | 91 | 123 | 62 | 42 |  |

*(Gordonstone Ave — D[4] 12, E[5] 12, TOTAL 24)*

1  Bedsits

2  One-bedroomed flats

3  Two-bedroomed flats

4  Disabled units

5  Elderly schemes

Key in document 5 (filename HOUSE) for 12-pitch print-out. When you have completed this task, save under filename HOUSE, and print out original. Recall the document and follow the instructions for text editing on page 162.

**UNIT 9**   See Practical Typing Exercises, Book Two, pages 37–38, for further exercises on
*Tabulation — Subdivided column headings*

## Exercise 5

Proofreading target: 5 minutes
Typing target: 3 minutes

The following exercise contains 12 errors. A correct version is not provided, so you will have to identify the errors by using your knowledge of typing layout, spelling, punctuation and correct grammatical expression. Read the exercise and mark the errors with standard proofreaders' marks and then type a corrected version, proofreading your typed copy very carefully.

```
WALKING DOGS IN THE COUNTRYSIDE

It is just as important to keep your dog under control in the country-side as it
is when walking him in a towns.  Your dog should be trained to be obediant.  There
are dog - training classes in most areas.  Take your dog - both you and he will
enjoy it, and it will give you confidence to now that you can control your dog.
He should stay when he is told come when called, sit and walk to heel on command.

Remember the following points when in the country -

1  Never allow your dog to chase anything - it is a bad habit which are hard
   to break.
2  The dogs lead should always be on when their are farm animals about, and do
   not allow him to run on to cultivated fields.
3  Make sure you know the country code yourself, & then you can train your dog
   in countryside awareness.
```

## Exercise 6

Proofreading target: 5 minutes
Typing target: 4 minutes

The following exercise contains 14 errors. A correct version is not provided, so you will have to identify the errors by using your knowledge of typing layout, spelling, punctuation and correct grammatical expression. When you have noted all the errors, type a corrected version, proofreading your typed copy very carefully.

```
     Staverton International Ltd., office furniture and equipment manufactures,
have reported losses for a number of years, but have now staged a strong recovery.
They were in good form last year, breaking the £1 million pre-tax profit barrier
for the first time.  There furniture is modern and functional and within the
price bracket of the smaller companys, eg, an executives desk in mahogany will
sell for approximatly £981.50p. the colours are bright and imaginative with
yellow's blues and greens being used for the upholstery.

Last years record braking results reflect a 27.7 % return on shareholders' funds.
This year has started strongly and there is a good order book.
```

**Proofreading**

# SKILL BUILDING

Type each line three times and, if time permits, complete your practice by typing each group once as it appears.

Margins:
12 pitch 22–82
10 pitch 12–72

### A  Keyboarding skills

1  Speed     Thank you very much for your letter which arrived on Monday.
2  Accuracy  Moreover, the hazy sunshine was quite unexpected in Morocco.
3  Figures   Account Nos: 12890, 23567, 34568, 19283, 28456/57, 02035/36.
4  Symbols   F (Fahrenheit) = 1.8 °C (Celsius) + 32°.  8' 6" = 2590.9 mm.

### Skill measurement    Five-minute timing    Not more than five errors

(**NOTE**   The following is an extract from chapter 10 of the book *The Practical Secretary* by Bea Holmes and Jan Whitehead, published by McGraw-Hill Book Company (UK) Limited.)

**S/M11**  We receive constant reminders of the importance of good com-  12
munication.  Vast sums are expended by both individuals and  24
organizations to convey a desired message or image to the  35
public.  Politicians and their parties engage the services  47
of high-powered promotion experts to sell their message;  58
companies employ advertising agents to put forward the qual-  70
ities of their products; PR people devote their expertise to  82
enhancing the reputation of organizations; individuals in  93
the public eye use the media to create a particular image so  105
that some manage to make a lucrative career merely out of  117
being a personality or well-known figure, recognized for who  129
or what they are rather than for what they do.  All these  140
interests are devoted to using professional communicators  152
to promote a particular message in order to provoke the  163
intended response.  167

Individual members of staff will also play a part in enhanc-  179
ing or detracting from the impression given by the organiza-  191
tion.  You will be able to think of examples such as using  203
a snack bar regularly because of the pleasant staff or  214
deciding not to return to a shop because of the surly off-  226
hand manner of an assistant.  You may think of occasions  237
when you were trying to obtain information but were discour-  249
aged by being kept waiting on the telephone or having to  260
prise answers from an unhelpful clerk.  Perhaps you have  272
experienced difficulty in understanding the manual accom-  283
panying an unfamiliar piece of equipment or despaired of  294
filling in an application form neatly because of its poor  306
design.  Alternatively, you may have noticed examples of an  317
attractively written invitation or good presentation in a  329
notice or advertisement.  Such experiences almost certainly  340
influence your response to the company concerned and may  352
determine whether you wish to have further dealings with  363
them.  364

In a secretarial role you should be especially conscious of  376
the vital importance of conveying the desired message in an  388
appropriate form.                                (SI 1.61)  392

1  |  2  |  3  |  4  |  5  |  6  |  7  |  8  |  9  |  10  |  11  |  12  |

**UNIT 10**                    *Skill building*

## Exercise 4

Proofreading target: 5 minutes
Typing target: 7 minutes

The details given in the handwritten exercise 4(b) are correct. There are a number of errors in the typewritten version in exercise 4(a). Read 4(a) and mark the errors with standard proofreaders' marks and then type the corrected version, making sure that you proofread your own typed copy very thoroughly.

### Exercise 4(a)

ADDRESSES OF PREMISES WHERE OUR EQUIPMENT IS INSTALLED

| Name | Addresses | Date Instaled | Inspection due on |
|---|---|---|---|
| P M Coker & Sons<br>Tel: (0373) 62445 | Watermore House<br>21 Castle Street<br>Frome<br>Somerset BA11 3AS | September 1986 | January 1989 |
| Acoustic Treatment PLC<br>Tel: (0603) 624091 | Castle House<br>Norwich<br>NR2 1PJ | January 1987 | September 1989 |
| Batley Computor Services Ltd<br>Tel: 0272 548967 | 2 Old Gloucester Road<br>Hambrook<br>Bristol BS16 1RP | March 1987 | Nov 1989 |
| Dandy Agency plc<br>Tel: (0733) 653312 | 10a High Street<br>Old Fleton<br>Peterborough. PE2 9DY | April, 1987 | December 1989 |

### Exercise 4(b)

ADDRESSES OF PREMISES WHERE OUR EQUIPMENT IS INSTALLED

| Name | Address | Date installed | Inspection Due on |
|---|---|---|---|
| P M Coker & Sons<br>Tel: (0373) 62445 | Watermore House<br>21 Castle Street<br>Frome, Somerset BA11 3AS | Sept 1986 | Jan 1989 |
| Acoustic Treatments PLC<br>Tel: (0603) 623091 | Castle House<br>Norwich NR2 1PJ | Jan '87 | Sept 1989 |
| Batley Computer Services Ltd<br>Tel: (0272) 548967 | 2 Old Gloucester Road<br>Hambrook<br>Bristol BS16 1RP | Mar '87 | Nov 1989 |
| Dandy Agency plc<br>Tel: (0733) 653312 | 10A High Street<br>Old Fletton<br>Peterborough PE2 9DY | April 1987 | Dec 1989 |

Months in full please

Do NOT type postcodes on a separate line

# PRODUCTION DEVELOPMENT

## Curriculum vitae

1  Type the following cv and take one original and two copies.

See page 177

        C U R R I C U L U M   V I T A E

    PERSONAL DETAILS

    Mrs Kathy Grosvenor            Date of Birth: 2 November 1960
    35 Connaught Grove
    Wellingborough
    Northants      NN3 8FR         Telephone: 0933 540983

    _____

    EDUCATION AND TRAINING

    1971 - 1976        Mount Comprehensive School  Wellingborough
    1976 - 1977        College of Commerce  Wellingborough
    1993               'Working Towards Employment' - Full-time
                         course at Wellingborough College

    _____

    QUALIFICATIONS

    'O' Level passes in English Language, History, French, Art
    RSA Stage II Typewriting (1993)
    Word Processing Stage I (Wordstar) (1993)
    College Leaving Certificate (1993) - Business Calculations and
       Financial Record Keeping, Audio Transcription, Micro-Computer applications

    _____

    EMPLOYMENT    *TYPIST - Please leave one clear linespace after ea. of these hdgs & emphasize them in some way.*

    1994 to date
    Crayfield Comprehensive School.  Four mornings a week, cash
    handling, record keeping and word processing.

    1981 - 1992
    At home bringing up my daughter.  During this time I was
    secretary of the Parent Teacher Association at my daughter's
    school, a post which I still hold.

    1977-1981
    Northamptonshire County Council Education Department.  My duties
    included: collation and distribution of post, filing, liaison
    with other departments by telephone, dealing with the general
    public at reception.

    _____

    PERSONAL INTERESTS    Gardening, horse riding, home brewing

    REFEREES
    *TYPIST: You w/ find the names & addresses of the referees in the Data Files (filename VITAE) p.164. Please type them here.*

**11**  Key in document 1 (filename VITAE) for 12-pitch print-out. When you have completed this task, save under filename VITAE, and print out original and two copies. Recall the document and follow the instructions for text editing on page 162.

UNIT 10    See Practical Typing Exercises, Book Two, page 39, for further exercises on
*Curriculum vitae*

**Exercise 3**

Proofreading target: 4 minutes
Typing target: 5 minutes

The details given in the handwritten exercise 3(b) are correct. There are a number of errors in the typewritten version in exercise 3(a). Read 3(a) and mark the errors with standard proofreaders' marks and then type a corrected version, making sure that you proofread your own typed copy very thoroughly.

*Exercise 3(a)*

MEMORANDUM

FROM  Paula Brooke-Little, Head of Department           DATE  11 September 1989

TO  Giles Ladell                                                              REF   PB-L/TS/Eve

TIMETABLE FOR THE WINTER SESSION – SEPTEMBER 1989–DECEMBER 1989

Following enrolement, I am pleased to tell you that we have sufficient students
for your two evening classes to run as follows:

| Subject | Day | Time | Starting Date | Room No |
|---|---|---|---|---|
| Beginners' Typing | Monday | 6.30–8.30 pm | 18.9.89. | B204 |
| Audio Typing | Wednesday | 6.15–8.15 pm | 25.9.89. | H207 |

I should be glad if you will confirm with your senior lecturer that you are
still willing to take these extra classes, and that the times and dates are
suitable for you.

*Exercise 3(b)*

MEMORANDUM

FROM Paula Brook-Little, Head of Department DATE 11 September 1989

TO Giles Ladell                                          REF BB-L/TSEV

TIMETABLE FOR THE WINTER SESSION – SEPTEMBER 1989 TO DECEMBER 1989

Following enrolment, I am pleased to tell you tht we hv sufficient students for yr two evening classes to run, as follows –

| Subject | Day | Time | Starting Date | Room No |
|---|---|---|---|---|
| Beginners' Typing | Monday | 6.30–8.30pm | 25.9.89 | B204 |
| Audio Typing | Wednesday | 6.15–8.15pm | 20.9.89 | B207 |

I shall be glad if you wl confirm with yr senior lecturer tht you are still willing to take these extra classes, & tht the dates & times are suitable for you.

*Proofreading*  157

## Letter of application

2  Type the following letter of application on plain bond paper with one copy. Correct any circled errors.

*[Type Kathy Grosvenor's address here. (You will find it on p.60)]*

16 June '94

M J Singh Esq
Personnel Officer
Educational Services Incorporated
43 High Street
Wellingborough
Northants        NN3 4GH

Dear Sir

I am looking for a position in an office where I can use my qualifications and experience, and I understand, from an article in the Evening Post on 13 June 1994, that your firm is planning to expand in the near future. I should like to be considered for any suitable vacancies which may arise.

Enclosed is a copy of my CV *[In Full]* which gives details of my education & experience. I wd be happy to attend for interview at any time.

Yrs ffly

Kathy Grosvenor (Mrs)


3  Type the following letter from Kathy Grosvenor to Ms F Paling whose address is in the Data Files (filename VITAE) on page 164.

30 June '94

Dr Ms P——

Thank you very much for giving me a ref for the post of word processor operator with Educational Services Inc *[In Full]*.

NP  I am delighted to tell you tt I hv an interview next wk. ~~I wl write to let you know whether or not I am successful.~~ If I am successful I wl write & let you know.

Yrs sinc.

K—— G——

---

**UNIT 10**  Letter of application  **61**

# Proofreading

**Answers on page 161**

The proofreading exercises on pages 156–160 are also printed in *Solutions and Resource Material* and may be duplicated for class use.

## Exercise 1

Proofreading target: 3 minutes
Typing target: 2 minutes

The information given in exercise 1(a) has been typed from exercise 1(b), given below. Exercise 1(b) is accurate, but there are 12 errors in exercise 1(a). Read 1(a) and mark the errors with standard proofreaders' marks and then type the corrected version. Proofread your own typed version very thoroughly and compare with exercise 1(b).

### Exercise 1(a) — to be corrected

FIELD WALK

Sunday, 9 April                                                    Leader: Shan Porter

Meet at car park opposite the 'Barley Mow; turn off A4047 Wallingford–Reading road at Black Root Farm. (Map ref SU637856) 8.30–10.30 am. A walk to see marsh marigolds and here snipe drumming. Wellies advised, binoculers useful. No dogs. Length of walk approximately 3½ miles. Suitable for all ages.

### Exercise 1(b) — correct copy

F I E L D   W A L K

Sunday, 10 April                                                   Leader: Shân Porter

Meet at car park opposite the 'Barley Mow'; turn off A4057 Wallingford–Reading road at Black Route Farm. (Map reference SU637856). 8.30–10.30 am. A walk to see marsh marigolds and hear snipe drumming. Wellies advised, binoculars useful. No dogs. Length of walk approximately 3¾ miles. Suitable for all ages.

## Exercise 2

Proofreading target: 5 minutes
Typing target: 4 minutes

The details given in exercise 2(b) are correct. There are 11 errors in exercise 2(a). Read 2(a) and mark the errors with standard proofreaders' marks and then type a corrected version, in alphabetical order, making sure you proofread your own typed copy very thoroughly.

### Exercise 2(a)

| | |
|---|---|
| PAYE | – Pay As You Earn |
| GSCE | – General Certificate in Secondary Education |
| VDU | – Visual Display Unit; |
| R.S.A. | – Royal Society of Arts |
| UNESCO | – United Nations Educational, Scientific and Culture Organisation |
| BASIC | – Beginners All-Purpose Symbolic Instruction Code |
| FAX | – Facsimile telegraphy |
| EFTA | – European Free Trade Association |
| PTO | – Please Turn Over |
| E & OE | – Errors & ommissions accepted |

### Exercise 2(b)

| | |
|---|---|
| BASIC | – Beginners' All-Purpose Symbolic Instruction Code |
| E & OE | – Errors and Omissions Excepted |
| EFTA | – European Free Trade Association |
| FAX | – Facsimile Telegraphy |
| GCSE | – General Certificate of Secondary Education |
| PAYE | – Pay As You Earn |
| PTO | – Please Turn Over |
| RSA | – Royal Society of Arts |
| UNESCO | – United Nations Educational, Scientific and Cultural Organization |
| VDU | – Visual Display Unit |

# Itineraries

*See page 191*

**4** Type the following on A4 paper.

```
NOTICE FOR ALL STAFF                            11 October 1994


TOUR OF PLANT AND OFFICES BY SIR JAMES BROWNE-ALLEN MP

I T I N E R A R Y

Thursday 27 October 1994

    0915 hours    Arrival at main entrance.  To be met by Managing Director

    0930   "      Coffee and informal discussion with Board of Directors

    1000   "      Tour of factory floor with Jasver Patel, Works Manager

    1100   "      Observation of various aspects of production.  The follow-
                  ing to be ready to give brief explanations of the workings of
                  particular components -

                  Geoff Parkes, Maurice Downing, Winston Lascelles

    1230   "      Lunch in the staff canteen

    1400   "      Tour of offices with Muriel Amerson, Office Manager

    1530   "      Tea in the Board Room, & final discussion with Board of
                  Directors

Sir James Browne-Allen wishes to observe a typical day; work will
therefore proceed as usual.
```

**12** Key in document 4 (filename ITIN) for 15-pitch print-out. Use the 'flush right' key for aligning the date at the right margin. When you have completed this task, save under filename ITIN, and print out original. Recall the document and follow the instructions for text editing on page 162.

**5** Type the following itinerary on a postcard.

```
         I T I N E R A R Y

    MRS ELAINE FRANKLIN'S VISIT TO SOUTHAMPTON

    13 October 1994

       8.30 am    Train departs for Southampton, Platform 6
       9.30 am    Meeting at Frampton & Sons, Rickards Buildings,
                  30-36 Eden Place.  To be met by Mr Alan Miles
      12.30 pm    Lunch with Ms Lisa Lewis to discuss possibility
                  of opening a branch office in Southampton
       2.30 pm    Meeting with Gray, Burchill and Townsend, Solicitors
       4.00 pm    Train departs from Southampton, Platform 3
```

**⑦ — 25 mins**

*Justify right margin.*

Would you type a card please with the advert you hv just typed for the new car — but slightly altered.

No picture, of course. Just type the information in the right column from "Unparalleled in... etc." Make that stand out & type the price of the car underneath it. Then continue — "Right now ...", down to "... 3 new models."

Set it out neatly & attractively so it will fit in the space available. I think the card is abt 152 mm × 101 mm — that's 6" × 4" isn't it?

Address the reverse side to Mrs Mo Rushbridge. Her address is in our ~~Data~~ Files — under her surname — on p 164.

Thank you

# INTEGRATED PRODUCTION TYPING

## INTERNATIONAL CLIFFTOP HOTEL

OFFICE SERVICES—REQUEST FORM

This sheet contains instructions that must be complied with when typing the documents. Read the information carefully before starting, and refer back to it frequently.

**Typist's Log Sheet**

Originator *J. R. Bosanquet* Designation *Banqueting Manager* Date *6 July '94* Ext No *8*

Typists operating a word processor, or electronic typewriter with appropriate function keys, should apply the following automatic facilities: top margin; carrier return; line-end hyphenation; underline OR bold print (embolden); error correction; centring; any other relevant applications.

Remember to (a) complete the details required at the bottom of the form; (b) enter typing time per document in the appropriate column; and (c) before submitting this **Log Sheet** and your completed work, enter TOTAL TYPING TIME in the last column so that the typist's time may be charged to the originator.

| Document No | Type of document and instructions | Copies— Original plus | Input form¶ | Typing time per document | Total typing time ¥ |
|---|---|---|---|---|---|
| 1 | Letter on A4 letterhead paper to Mrs E Archer | 1+2 | MS | | |
| 2 | Folded leaflet | 1 original | MS | | |
| *3 | Conditions of Trading (2-page document) | 1 original | AT | | |
| 4 | Menu — I will let you have this as soon as I hv confirmed the details | 1+1 | MS | | |
| 5 | Menu with ornamental border | 1 original | MS | | |
| 6 | Table of International hotels | 1 original | MS | TOTAL TYPING TIME | |

TYPIST—please complete:

Typist's name:       Date received:       Date completed:
                     Time received:       Time completed:

If the typed documents cannot be returned within 24 hours, the office services supervisor should inform the originator. Any item that is urgent should be marked with an asterisk (*).

¶T = Typescript      AT = Amended Typescript      MS = Manuscript      SD = Shorthand Dictation      AD = Audio Dictation
¥ to be charged to the originator's department      AP = Amended Print.

*Typist's Log Sheet—No 2*

This may be the case in some instances. However, the majority of crimes are committed by the less determined, or 'opportunist' criminal. The 'opportunist' thief is constantly on the look-out for the tell-tale signs of an empty house, which could be anything from milk bottles left out to uncollected newspapers and unkempt lawns. If we can take measures which ensure that the thief must -

(a) make more noise;
(b) take more time;
(c) look more conspicuous,

then there is more chance of his being deterred.

Some simple preventative measures would include -

1. **DOOR LOCKS** — Good quality locks should be properly fitted.

2. **WINDOW LOCKS** — These should be fitted to all downstairs windows which are easily accessible from adjacent climbing points or roofs.

3. **LIGHTING** — Lighting should be used as a deterrant, both inside and outside the house. Timer activated lamps inside are ideal for year-round use, whilst the new range of 'low-power, high light output' units, activated by dawn-to-dusk sensors should be used to illuminate the outside dark corners.

The foregoing information is a basic introduction to domestic security.

Further advice and information can be obtained from the Crime Prevention Officer at your local Police Office.

## II In the Garden and around the House

Do not leave tools and valuable equipment lying about. Lock them away in the house, garage or garden shed. It only takes a few seconds.

If this cannot be done, then arrange for some kind of security device, such as a chain and padlock, to secure equipment to a permanent fixing.

1. Fit heavy-duty close-shackle padlocks.
2. Do not expose fixing screws on padlock fixing brackets. A thief with a screwdriver will make short work of that.
3. Fit good 'Dawn-to-Dusk' lighting to cover your back garden. It will deter prowlers and prospective thieves.

These items can be obtained locally. If in doubt, a reputable ironmonger will advise.

For further security advice contact your LOCAL CRIME PREVENTION OFFICER.

1  (25 minutes)

TYPIST - Two copies please. Mark one for file & one for Amy Smith, Catering Manager

Our ref JRB/LM/D22/L35

(Date)

Mrs E Archer  100 Camborne Rd  NEWQUAY  Cornwall  TR5 1NZ

Dear Mrs A

BIRTHDAY LUNCHEON

Further to our mtg yesterday, I hv pleasure in confirming the details we discussed abt yr sisters birthday luncheon to be held at this hotel on (TYPIST - insert date here please. You wl find it in the Data Files (filename HOTEL) page 164) // The format is agreed as follows:   (Leave 5 spaces here)

12 noon  Arrival of guests.

On arrival we wl serve one glass per person of medium, sweet or dry sherry @ £1.25 per glass. ← For those who wld prefer a soft drink we wl hv fruit juice available

Any other drinks to be purchased on a cash basis from the Warwick Suite Bar.

12 30 hours  Lunch for 90 to be served in the Warwick Suite. Please see menu enclosed.

Price per person: £20.00.

Liquers & cigars to be purchased on a cash basis.

Dinner wine: 1½ glasses per person @ £1.25 per glass - choice of red or white housewine.

Menus to be headed -

BIRTHDAY LUNCHEON ← (Sp. Caps)

Margaret - Congratulations & good wishes! ← (Caps)

Pink serviettes.

Flowers to be supplied.

Round tables x 10 (formal sit down) -

Suggested table arrangement as agreed.

Microphone available for any speeches.

After-lunch drinks to be purchased on a cash basis.

Cont'd.....

> I went to a very interesting talk on Crime Prevention the other evening & I thought it wd be useful for everyone to hv a copy of the notes we were given. Will you type a draft of the following please. Omit those parts marked # & emphasize any word(s) in larger print from the main part.

# CRIME PREVENTION CAMPAIGN

## I Postcoding of Property

Postcoding of property by marking it with an ultra-violet pen with the postcode and house number can assist the Police in returning the property should it be lost or stolen.

A property marking kit, containing an ultra-violet sensitive marking pen, a diamond tipped stylus, and other aids to property marking, can be purchased at many good stationery supplies. Should this prove difficult, then many local Crime Prevention or Neighbourhood Watch panels offer 'kits' for loan or sale.

It is not recommended that antiques, silverware or valuable jewellery be postcoded, as this may affect the value.

To safeguard these items it is more satisfactory to photograph them - in colour - with a ruler in front to give an indication of size.

Items such as pedal cycles can be postcoded by stamping the postcode on the underside of the frame. Larger items of garden furniture & power tools can also be marked in this way.

All items of unidentified property coming into the care of the Police are checked by ultra violet light for postcode markings. This very much simplifies the task of tracing the lawful owners.

**Make YOUR mark against crime - POSTCODE NOW**

(Leave approx 25mm (1") before part II)

## III Practical Home Security

The subject of home security is very often of no concern to us until it is too late and our homes have been broken into. The most common excuse for this lack of action is - "If they want in, nothing I do will make any difference".

2
(Date)
Mrs E Archer

1500 hours  Finish
      Guests depart
      Room Hire £50.00  } (single spacing)

✓ All ~~prices~~ amts are inclusive of VAT at current rate & the invoice shd be settled within 7 days. ↵

If the a/c is not pd by the due date, we reserve the right to charge interest on all overdue amts @ a rate of 3% over the current bank base rate. // I hope tht these arrangements wl meet with yr approval & we look forward to welcoming you to the International Clifftop Hotel on yr sister's brthday on (insert date)

Yrs sinc.
(My name & designation here, please)
PS Please let me know if you require any further info.

(2)  (35 minutes)   (FRONT PAGE)

INTERNATIONAL  CLIFFTOP  HOTEL
(TYPIST - Please insert address & tel no. here from Task 3)

Afternoon tea menu ← (sp caps)
Served daily
from
3.0 - 5.30 pm.

            (INSIDE LEFT)

Beverages ← (caps)
Pot of tea for one person     £1.30
(ea. additional person - 50p)
Pot of coffee for one person  £1.50
(ea. additional person - 75p)

(TYPIST - please type the remaining items in the same way. You wl find them in the Data Files (filename HOTEL) on p.164)

**5** — 20 mins

> Send a memo to Dave Fogden abt the advert for the new car. I'm not too sure abt the price so don't type the memo until I've checked with the MD — shd be abt 30 mins. Can you check for spelling errors — not my strong point!

Advertisement for local gazette ← *Make this line stand out*

I suggest something like the following wording for the advert to go in the local press / — *half a page.*        *In full*

---

UNBELIEVABLE PART-EXCHANGE
PRICES AGAINST THIS SUPERB
NEW CAR

(I suggest a picture of the car here, Dave. What do you think?)

PRICE: *Insert*

Unparalled in it's class — unbeleivable in it's price

Right now you can have one of these stylish new cars from just *Insert the price here* on the road. AND, for a limited period only, it's available with 0% finance over 12 months or low rate flexible finance (maximum APR 9.7%). The car is available in catalysed *petrol, diesal + turbo diesal options, so you can choose the model th suits yr style of driving. Now the range is even more appealing, with the addition of 3 new models.*

| Example: | 306 3-door 1.1i Catalyst — 0% APR over 12 mths |
|---|---|
| On the road price | £ *insert price* |
| APR/Flat rate | 0.0% / 0.0% |
| 50% deposit | £ *insert figure* |
| 12 monthly payments | £ *— ditto —* |
| Finance charges | Nil |
| TOTAL AMOUNT PAYABLE | £ *insert figure* |

If you hv any suggestions or alterations, wd you come to see me sometime today, please — otherwise we wl miss the deadline.
TW/*Yr initials*

(2 cont'd) (INSIDE RIGHT)

## Sandwiches (uc)

[Double spacing]
- Egg
- Cheese
- Ham or beef
- Prawn*
- Smoked salmon*

[Insert leader dots]

£1.60
£1.60
£1.80
£3.50
£4.00

* Please be kind enough to allow at least 15 mins for these orders.

CAKES & PASTRIES

Please choose from the selection of cakes & pastries displayed on the trolley.

Freshly baked scones served with butter & preserve £1.30

Dairy ice cream
(chocolate, strawberry and/or vanilla)

------oOo------

Strawberries & fresh cream
(when in season)

(BACK COVER) (Emphasize)

Please enquire @ Reception for details of arrangements for —

[Inset 5 spaces & leave 2 blank lines between ea. item]
- Dinner Dances
- Wedding Receptions
- Private Dinner Parties
- Accommodation Rates
- Christmas Festivities
- Conference & Business

(4) — 10 mins

Send a letter to a customer of ours & tell him that I can now get him the car he was wanting to test drive if he would like to call in & see me — preferably within the next day or two, because it has been advertised in the local press & is very much in demand. Enclose a copy of the advertisement in case he didn't see it. His name is Pete Smith

You will find his address in our Data Files — under his surname — p 164.

Type our ref (my initials followed by your own) & type my name (but not my designation) after 'With kind regards'. No other complimentary close.

Type an envelope & mark the letter & envelope urgent.

Thank you

INTERNATIONAL CLIFFTOP HOTEL
Narrowcliff  Newquay  Cornwall  United Kingdom  TR7 1BU
Telephone: (0637) 105568            Fax: (0637) 124778

---

**Conditions of trading**

All bookings are accepted by the hotel on the basis that the client has accepted all the conditions of trading set out below.

**Minimum numbers guaranteed for banquets and private facility catering**

i   The numbers confirmed in writing at the time of booking for banqueting functions will be allowed to fall by up to 10% without financial penalty.

ii  We reserve the right not to cater for more than a 10% increase on the original, agreed, confirmed numbers.

iii Final numbers for banqueting and private catering are to be confirmed to us a minimum of 10 days in advance of the function.

*These are the nos. for wh we expect to cater & charge.*

**Inclement weather**

We would recommend that you always consider insuring against cancellation due to inclement weather, or you may wish to hire our marquee which can be erected in the grounds of the hotel, as pictured here.

[Double spacing]

[TYPIST Rule a box here 51mm (2") x 51mm (2")]

**Damage**

Any damage caused by the clients to the fabric of the building or grounds, roadways and car parks, will be fully charged in respect of both labour and materials in making the necessary repairs (inclusive of sub-contractors working on your behalf).

**Credit cards**

The quotation you have received is made on the basis that payment will be made by cheque or cash. Payment by credit card may incur a surcharge.

If you wish to use this method of payment, please contact the hotel manager.

③ — 15 mins

Type one top & two copies of the following form, please, & type a label with our address

GILMORE & THOMAS CO LTD ← Abbreviations in full
Station Yard   Taunton   Somerset TA2 6HB

PERSONAL DETAILS

Change Form ← (centre)
Current details:

⌐                    ⌐



└                    ┘

Purchase date of present vehicle ———
Model ———
Vehicle registration no ———
lc/ Chassis No ———
Fleet Code (Company cars only) ———

Changes:
Name
Address (in full)
Purchase date of new vehicle
Model; Vehicle reg no
Chassis no; Fleet code (Co cars only)

TYPIST
Display this information by the side of the above.

**Integrated Production Typing Project—No 6**  150

2

Fire precautions  *(TYPIST Allow a top margin of 51 mm (2") on the second page, please)*

♂ For conferences involved in building conference 'sets' at the hotel, please ensure that in all respects your construction meets with legal requirements relating to fire and safety.

THANK YOU.

---

4. *(Memo — 10 minutes)*

---

5. *(15 mins)* *(Type the following menu with a simple ornamental border)*

INTERNATIONAL — Hotel

BIRTHDAY LUNCHEON

*(This line to be as given in Task 1, page 64)*

MENU

*(Display the following items as attractively as poss.)*

Hungarian Mushroom Soup; Roast Prime Rib of Beef; Yorkshire Pudding + Horseradish Sauce; Broccoli with Lemon + Red Peppers; Brussels Sprouts; Glazed Carrots; Potato Strudel; Parsley Potatoes; Walnut Salad with Red + Green Endives; Frozen Cranberry Soufflé with Spun Sugar Cranberry Wreath; Cheese + Bscs.

Coffee + Florentine Mints.

② — 35 mins

SMALL & COMPACT CAR TELEPHONES

| Code No | Product | Description | VAT 17.5% £ | Item Price £ | Item Price (inc VAT) £ | Total (CAPS) |
|---|---|---|---|---|---|---|
| SC3 | De luxe | Desk-top charger | 45.50 | 260.00 | Insert Item Prices | |
| SC4 | Super de luxe | Battery adaptor | 49.00 | 280.00 | | |

DELIVERY

| | | |
|---|---|---|
| Packaging, insurance & delivery | 9.80 | 56.00 | Insert figure |

INSTALLATION

| | | | |
|---|---|---|---|
| At customer location | 14.00 | 80.00 | 94.00 |
| At service centre | 9.25 | 50.00 | 59.00 25 |

TOTAL AMOUNT

NETWORK SERVICES

Please tick appropriate box    Newphone ☐    Phonex ☐

Surname (Mr/Mrs/Miss/Ms)                Initials

Address

6 (30 mins)

# THE INTERNATIONAL GROUP OF HOTELS

International hotels can be found in key business locations throughout the UK + /mainland/ Europe. Each has it's own style + character yet all share the same commitment to high standards of service + facilities. [1]

TYPIST — List hotels in British Isles in ascending order according to the price of the single room.

| HOTEL [2] | Valid until | Rates [3] Single | Twin |
|---|---|---|---|
| **British Isles** | | | |
| The Royal, London | 12/94 | £145.00 | £145.00 |
| The Swallow, Cambridge | 12/94 | £95.00 | £75.00 |
| The White Horse, Cheltenham | 11/94 | £85.00 | £70.00 |
| The George, Hastings | 2/95 | £57.00 | £75.00 |
| **Europe** | | | |
| The Ritz, Madrid | 11/94 | 46,880 pta | 58,240 pta |
| Novotel, Berlin | 12/94 | 200 DM | 170 DM |
| Holiday Inn, Rome | 12/94 | L 162,400 | L 150,800 |

1 Guests hv a choice of spacious Classic or Connoisseur accomodation.
2 Just phone or fax yr booking details
3 Per person / per night; includes breakfast

(TYPIST: please insert leader dots)

① 15 mins

Please type the following on our letterhead paper, using semi-blocked style. Take one copy & fold the letter for our window envelope.

In all correspondence please quote: TMW/K744PRT

Ms Lucy Rochester
6 Camomile Green
TAUNTON
Somerset
TA10 2RF

Can you check this no in the Data Files (filename CAR) on page 163, please.

Dr Ms R

**Yr Agreement Number: 401-397442-21**

I am pleased to confirm th the above agreement has now bn completed, & wd like to thank you for the way you conducted your a/c with us. Whether you are looking for assistance as a private individual, someone who is self-employed, a partnership or a small business, please remember th we offer a wide range of vehicle funding facilities — ea precisely tailored to suit your exact needs. Credit is available to anyone aged 18 or over. A guarantee may be req'd.

Once more we thank you for yr custom & look forward to being of service to you in the future. Wishing you safe & happy motoring

Yrs sinc

(My name & designation here, please)

PS You may be interested to know th we are now able to offer extremely competitive terms on new & used cars. For an immediate quotation telephone us on 0832 460317 — quoting ref FBI. In every case we are ready to provide no-obligation written quotations on request, as well as discussing yr particular needs.

Integrated Production Typing Project — No 6

# SKILL BUILDING

Type each line three times and, if time permits, complete your practice by typing each group once as it appears.

Margins:
12 pitch 22–82
10 pitch 12–72

### A  Keyboarding skills

1  Speed     Next week they will have some more pens from that nice shop.
2  Accuracy  Relaxation exercises specialized in freeing you from qualms.
3  Figures   Sales: £25,846,000; Profit: £1,985,794; Assets: £13,451,469.
4  Symbols   240 - 120 - 2 × 3 - 100 + 20 = 300 + 90 - 200 × 2 - 108 + 2.

### B  Improve control of second and third fingers

5  oil kin ink link look joke polo lose kick polly lime knocks.
6  dew cow sew seed exit side care sews disk wider sweet domes.
7  The door was blown down by the west exit.  Lead the way out.
8  Knock on Dickens' window.  Ask Edward Wellers for the holly.

### C  Language arts—use of apostrophe
—see explanation on page 161

9   Mr & Mrs Bob Cross's house was put up for sale on Wednesday.
10  Kenneth Andrews' farm was put up for auction on 21 November.
11  My children's playground was unusable because of the floods.
12  The men's cricket bat will be found near the pavilion gates.

13  To develop your proofreading skills, turn to page 159, exercise 5.

### Skill measurement        One-minute timing        Not more than one error

You should now aim at increasing your speed by five words a minute, ie if you have been typing, say, 45 words a minute, your aim is now 50 words a minute.

S/M12  Are we correct in believing that you have changed your mind     12
       about the coat which you wished to be dyed dark red?  Please    24
       let us know immediately as we have asked our works by tele-     36
       phone to place your coat on one side, but as the coat has       47
       already left our shop, we are not certain that your request     59
       can be carried out.  In the meantime, we would like to point    71
       out that the charge for dyeing to a special shade is double.    83
                                                        **(SI 1.24)**

S/M13  Half a dozen climbers roped together had struggled for hours    12
       up one of the Swiss heights, and the summit lay only half a     24
       mile ahead.  Behind them a snow slope fell steeply away for     36
       more than a third of a mile.  The group was nearly across       47
       the slope when they heard a deep tearing noise, and a crack     59
       appeared in the snow five yards above them.  The snow on        71
       which they stood began to move, but suddenly all was well.      82
                                                        **(SI 1.24)**

        1 | 2 | 3 | 4 | 5 | 6 | 7 | 8 | 9 | 10 | 11 | 12 |

**UNIT 11**                    *Skill building*

# INTEGRATED PRODUCTION TYPING

## GILMORE AND THOMAS COMPANY LIMITED

### OFFICE SERVICES—REQUEST FORM

*Typist's Log Sheet*

This sheet contains instructions that must be complied with when typing the documents. Read the information carefully before starting, and refer back to it frequently.

Originator: **Tim M Waller**   Designation: **Sales & Marketing Director**   Date: **Today's**   Ext No: **24**

> Typists operating a word processor, or electronic typewriter with appropriate function keys, should apply the following automatic facilities: top margin; carrier return; line-end hyphenation; underline OR bold print (embolden); error correction; centring; any other relevant applications.

Remember to (a) complete the details required at the bottom of the form; (b) enter typing time per document in the appropriate column; and (c) before submitting this **Log Sheet** and your completed work, enter TOTAL TYPING TIME in the last column so that the typist's time may be charged to the originator.

| Document No | Type of document and instructions | Copies— Original plus | Input form¶ | Typing time per document | Total typing time ¥ |
|---|---|---|---|---|---|
| 1 | Letter to Ms Rochester | 1 + 1 | MS | | |
| 2 | Table of car telephones | 1 original | MS | | |
| 3 | Form — change of personal details | 1 + 2 | MS | | |
| *4 | Letter from brief notes | 1 + 1 | MS | | |
| 5 | Memo (including advert) | 1 original | AT | | |
| 6 | Crime Prevention | 1 original | AT | | |
| 7 | Card | 1 original | MS | | |
| | | | | **TOTAL TYPING TIME** | |

TYPIST—please complete:
Typist's name:       Date received:       Date completed:
                     Time received:       Time completed:

> If the typed documents cannot be returned within 24 hours, the office services supervisor should inform the originator. Any item that is urgent should be marked with an asterisk (*).

¶T = Typescript    AT = Amended Typescript    MS = Manuscript    SD = Shorthand Dictation    AD = Audio Dictation
¥ to be charged to the originator's department    AP = Amended Print.

*Typist's Log Sheet—No 6*

# PRODUCTION DEVELOPMENT

*See page 183*

## Financial statements

1  Type the following Income and Expenditure Account on A4 paper.

THE BROADWELL HOUSE SOCIETY

Income and Expenditure Account for the financial year ended 31 March 1994

| Expenditure | £ | Income | £ |
|---|---|---|---|
| Printer | 156.40 | Balance in hand on 1 April 1993 | 108.84 |
| Hon Secretary's expenses | 37.20 | Subscriptions | 111.90 |
| Reunion - |  | Reunion - |  |
| Hire of hall | 127.50 | Fees | 470.00 |
| Food, etc | 249.59 | Sale of wine | 14.00 |
| Refund | 29.00 | Raffle | 10.50 |
| Balance of Income over Expenditure | 186.35 | Grant | 50.00 |
|  |  | Interest on bank account | 20.80 |
|  | 786.04 |  | 786.04 |

## Figures in columns and double underscore

*See page 216*

2  Type the following Balance Sheet on A5 landscape paper.

CONNINGTON CHORAL SOCIETY

Balance Sheet - 31st March 1994

| Capital and Liabilities | £ | Assets | £ |
|---|---|---|---|
| Emergency Benefit Fund | 131.63 | Cash at bank | 242.62 |
| May Fleet Fund | 17.82 | Investments | 375.18 |
| Subscriptions | 282.20 |  |  |
| Balance in hand | 186.15 |  |  |
|  | 617.80 |  | 617.80 |

**13**  Key in document 2 (filename FINAN) for 10-pitch print-out. Use the automatic underline feature, the vertical line key and the decimal tab key. When you have completed this task, save under filename FINAN and print out original. Recall the document and follow the instructions for text editing on page 162.

UNIT 11   See Practical Typing Exercises, Book Two, page 41, for further exercises on
**Income and Expenditure Account, Balance Sheet, Figures in columns and double underscore**

7 – (20 mins)

*As Treasurer of our local operatic society, I have prepared the financial statement for the end of this month. Would you type it for me, please, with 2 carbon copies. Mark the top copy for ELAINE STRINGER & the first carbon copy for MARK RIMMINGTON*

CLIFTON OPERATIC SOCIETY

Receipts & Payments A/c

for the yr ended (insert the last day of this month)

| RECEIPTS | £ | PAYMENTS | £ |
|---|---|---|---|
| Balance in hand & at bank | 295.55 | Printing, postage & stationery | 45.67 |
| Receipts from | | Costumes | 74.05 |
| Subscriptions | 172.20 | Press cuttings | 7.25 |
| Shows | 102.50 | Sundries | 9.04 |
| Sundry receipts | 6.80 | Repairs to stage | 110.30 |
| | | 'After Show' party | |
| | | Food & wine | 62.20 |
| | | Taxis | 22.40 |
| | | Balance of income over expenditure | 246.14 |

*Would you please enter the totals in both columns. They should, of course, be the same.*

## Vertical Balance Sheet

**3** Type a copy of the following Balance Sheet from page 4 of the Directors' Report and Accounts.

THE INTERNATIONAL HOTEL GROUP

BALANCE SHEET AT 31 MARCH 1994

|  | Notes | 1993 | 1992 |
|---|---|---|---|
|  |  | £000 | £000 |
| FIXED ASSETS |  |  |  |
| Investment properties | 6 | 37 010 | 54 055 |
| Investment | 7 | — | — |
|  |  | 37 010 | 54 055 |
| CURRENT ASSETS |  |  |  |
| Debtors | 8 | 3 940 | 9 957 |
| Cash |  | 4 694 | 9 |
|  |  | 8634 | 9966 |
| CREDITORS: Amounts falling due within one year | 9 | (5799) | (1838) |
| NET CURRENT ASSETS |  | 2 835 | 8 578 |
| TOTAL ASSETS LESS CURRENT LIABILITIES |  | 39 845 | 62 633 |
| CREDITORS: Amounts falling due after more than one year | 10 | (12 877) | (13 911) |
|  |  | £26 986 | £48 722 |

These a/cs were approved by the board** of directors on 18 Feb '95.

P L Travers  
F Holloway  } Directors

** TYPIST - Leave 2 blank lines here

6 — (20 mins)

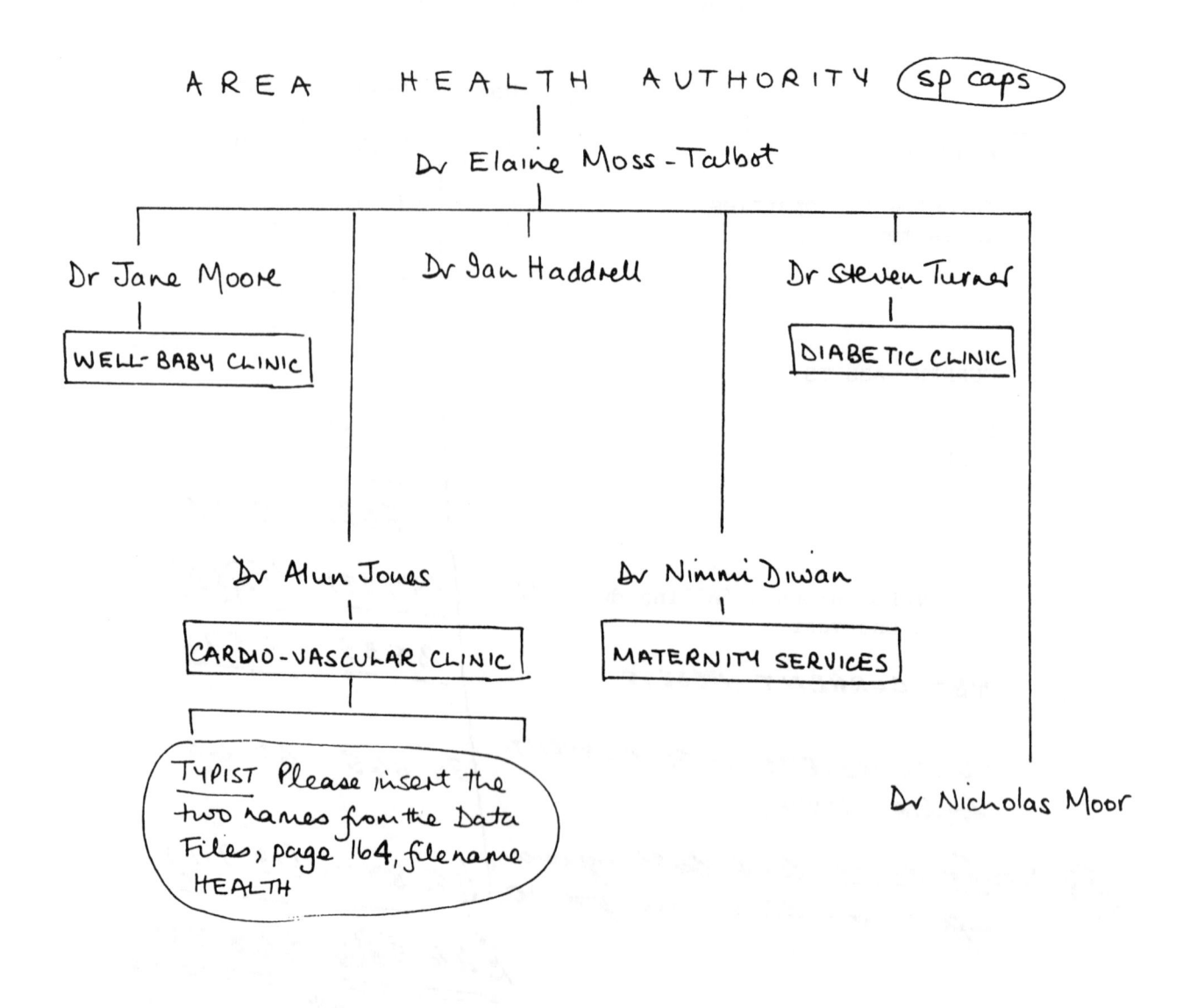

# A R E A   H E A L T H   A U T H O R I T Y  (sp caps)

Dr Elaine Moss-Talbot

- Dr Jane Moore → **WELL-BABY CLINIC**
- Dr Ian Haddrell
- Dr Steven Turner → **DIABETIC CLINIC**
- Dr Alun Jones → **CARDIO-VASCULAR CLINIC**
- Dr Nimmi Diwan → **MATERNITY SERVICES**
- Dr Nicholas Moor

(TYPIST Please insert the two names from the Data Files, page 164, filename HEALTH)

(Letterhead paper, please. Could you also type a label to Dr Turner.)

## Financial statements — Leader dots

**4** Type the following financial statement on A4 landscape paper and insert leader dots as shown.

*See pages 183, 211*

T K FELLOWS PLC

*Please follow suggested layout & insert leader dots in style shown.*

Source and Application of Funds for the year ended 31 December 1994 *(Emphasise this line)*

|  | £000 | £000 |
|---|---|---|
| Source of Funds |  |  |
| Surplus before taxation |  | 2 680 |
| Extraordinary items .. |  | — |
|  |  | 2 680 |
| Depreciation .. .. .. |  | <u>1 597</u> |
|  |  | 4277 |
| Application of Funds |  |  |
| Taxation paid .. .. | 1 459 |  |
| Purchase of fixed assets | <u>5471</u> |  |
|  |  | 6930 |
|  |  | <u>2653</u> |

*Leave 5 clear spaces between the 2 sections.*

|  | £000 | £000 |
|---|---|---|
| Net decrease/increase in working capital |  |  |
| Stock .. .. .. |  | (22) |
| Debtors .. .. |  | 319 |
| Creditors " " |  | <u>194</u> |
|  |  | 491 |
| <u>Net liquid funds</u> |  |  |
| Bank balances " | 856 |  |
| Short term deposits | <u>(4000)</u> | <u>(3144)</u> |
| Net decrease/increase |  | <u>2653</u> |

*Type this section side by side w. the one above. Subtotals & totals shd be typed opposite ea. other*

UNIT 11 — Financial statements — Leader dots — 73

## 5 — Cont'd

margarine labelled "high in poliunsaturates". (TYPIST - please check this spelling with the article on Blood Pressure para III (iii); ~~use skimmed milk, cottage cheese + plenty of low fat yoghurt.~~

~~It is better to grill than to fry.~~

When you come for yr blood test in 3 months time, please bring a stamped addressed envelope with you so tt the results can be sent on to you.

~~Please contact me if you have any questions.~~

I will write in the complimentary close — just type my name, leaving about 38mm (1½") before you do so. Thank you.

# SKILL BUILDING

Type each line three times and, if time permits, complete your practice by typing each group once as it appears.

Margins:
12 pitch 22–82
10 pitch 12–72

### A  Keyboarding skills

1  Speed       It will be necessary for you to inspect the food on arrival.
2  Accuracy    The five bottles of liquid antifreeze are in the yellow box.
3  Figures     Car 14 – £8,785.50; Car 20 – £9,643.75; Car 31 – £12,897.00.
4  Symbols     Position is Longitude 21° 12' 15" E – Latitude 15° 5' 20" N.

### B  Improve control of third and fourth fingers

5  saw paw law wax axes aqua plop swap pool plaza spool squalls
6  oxo sow awl zoo soap poll axle slap dose spawn polka possess
7  A squall of wind swept water from the pool on to my azaleas.
8  I possessed a polar bear which was in the zoological garden.

### C  Language arts—use of apostrophe
—see explanation on page 161

9   We don't know at what time it's possible to visit her today.
10  James said, 'Do write and let me know your time of arrival.'
11  The desks measured 5' 11" × 2' 10" × 2' 6" and 6' × 3' × 3'.
12  I am certain that the word 'embarrass' has 2 r's and 2 s's.

### Skill measurement

Two-minute timing          Not more than two errors

S/M14  Once upon a time people got up early in the morning in order      12
       to complete intricate work while the light was good.  Also,      24
       a great many folk went to bed early because they had no          35
       light to see with after dark.  They did have pine knots,         46
       wicks floating in smoky grease, and the tallow candle.  In       58
       the days of the Greeks, the theatres were open between sun-      70
       rise and sunset, as it was not possible to light places of       81
       amusement.                                                       83

       The Persians always met at daylight in order to pursue their     95
       studies and while the Arabians knew of petroleum and used       107
       it, they could not adapt the crude smoking oil for use          118
       indoors.                                                        119

       In this technological age, a great many people work at night    131
       in offices and factories, and they will tell you that they      143
       are more alert at night.                          (SI 1.33)    148

   1 | 2 | 3 | 4 | 5 | 6 | 7 | 8 | 9 | 10 | 11 | 12 |

UNIT 12                    *Skill building*                          74

5 — (15 mins) *TYPIST – Please type the following circular letter on headed paper. There is no need to leave a space for the name & address of the addressee, but insert a subject heading BLOOD TEST*

EM-T/Yr initials                                                Today's date

*Leave 25mm (1") here please. I will then write in the salutation.*

Yr recent blood test showed th yr blood cholesterol level is higher than desirable. There is no cause for concern because, if you follow the suggestions listed below abt diet & other habits, the level are likely to **considerably fall**. [To check th this has happened, please book another **early morning appt** with the nurse for a further blood test 3 months after starting the diet.

You should not hv anything to eat or drink (except water) for fourteen hrs before the test.

1. If you smoke cigarettes, it is very important that you stop or, if this is impossible, th you cut down the no th you smoke. I can help you if you find this difficult to do, & a pamphlet on stopping this dangerous habit is available from my surgery.

2. Try to eat plenty of the following foods:

*TYPIST: Inset the section marked ‖ 13mm (½") from the above numbered matter*

‖ green vegetables, beans, lentils, **fruit**, **cereals**, boiled rice, fish & lean meats such as veal, chicken, turkey, rabbit or game are partic suitable; for frying or salad dressings use corn or sunflower oil; & for spread or for baking choose a soft

---
*Integrated Production Typing Project – No 5*

# PRODUCTION DEVELOPMENT

*See page 202*

## Open and full punctuation

**1** Type the following in double spacing using open punctuation.

    C H A R I T Y   A U C T I O N

    Prof William G Mayers, who is Hon Sec of our local charities committee, will be holding an auction at his home -

    Maple Lodge
    Gildersome
    Leeds
    LS27 7TW

    on Thursday 21 July 1994 at 2.0 pm.  The items for sale are many and varied, eg,

    oil and watercolour paintings (including one oil painting in an attractive gilt frame - 1.5 m x 1.2 m); objets d'art, a grandfather clock, gold and silver jewellery, etc.  The main feature will be a 1940s car, still roadworthy, with a top speed of 60 mph - definitely a collector's item.

    To view, prior to the auction, contact -

    Prof W G Mayers DSc JP, or his wife, Mrs F Mayers MEP.
    Tel (0532) 468121.

**2** Type the following in double spacing using full punctuation. When you have completed this task, compare it with task 1, and notice the differences between open and full punctuation.

    C H A R I T Y   A U C T I O N

    Prof. William G. Mayers, who is Hon. Sec. of our local charities committee, will be holding an auction at his home -

    Maple Lodge,
    Gildersome,
    Leeds.
    LS27 7TW

    on Thursday 21 July 1994 at 2.0 p.m.  The items for sale are many and varied, e.g.,

    oil and watercolour paintings (including one oil painting in an attractive gilt frame - 1.5 m x 1.2 m); objets d'art, a grandfather clock, gold and silver jewellery, etc.  The main feature will be a 1940s car, still roadworthy, with a top speed of 60 m.p.h. - definitely a collector's item.

    To view, prior to the auction, contact -

    Prof. W. G. Mayers, D.Sc., J.P., or his wife, Mrs. F. Mayers, M.E.P.  Tel. (0532) 468121.

BLOOD PRESSURE

The heart is a strong, muscular pump. It's main purpose is to keep blood flowing around the body. Just as water in a tap needs to be under pressure to flow properly, so blood needs to be under pressure so that it can circulate effectively throughout the body's arteries. This pressure is supplied by the pumping action of the heart, and controlled by the amount by which the small arteries constrict the blood flow. In some people this constricting action gets too strong. This means that the heart has to pump much harder to overcome the resistance and force enough blood through the arteries. This condition is known as high blood pressure.

I CHECKING FOR HIGH BLOOD PRESSURE

It is most important that blood pressure is checked, and if it is high, that it is controlled, otherwise it could lead to a heart attack, a stroke, kidney or eye disease.

The check is quick, simple, and painless. The doctor or nurse winds an inflatable cuff around the patient's arm, pumps air into the cuff, and takes a 'reading' from a pressure gauge attached to the cuff.

Once high blood pressure has been diagnosed, it can be treated very effectively.

II AVOIDING HIGH BLOOD PRESSURE

(i) It is important to reduce weight if you are fatter than you should be, as it can not only cause high blood pressure, but other problems may arise.

(ii) Don't eat too much salt.

(a) Avoid obviously salty foods, eg, crisps, salted nuts.

(b) Never add salt to prepared food.

(c) Use less salt when cooking.

(iii) There is evidence that cutting down on hard 'saturated' fats and partially replacing them by foods 'high in polyunsaturates' can help to reduce blood pressure.

(iv) One of the many harmful effects of smoking is raised blood pressure. The answer is DON'T SMOKE!

III TREATMENT

The doctor may decide that all the patient needs to do is to lose weight, stop smoking and go on a less fatty diet. In more severe cases drugs can be given, which effectively reduce blood pressure without any side effects.

# Telephone index

See page **214**

**3** Type the following list of names and addresses. Put the names in alphabetical order according to the surname (if a personal name) or the first word of the name (if an impersonal name). Leave double spacing between each name. Use margins of 13 mm ($\frac{1}{2}$ inch) on either side and align (block) right margin. Type with full punctuation and insert leader dots.

An example of **full punctuation:**
RONALDSON, H., Ltd., 9 Park Lane, CROYDON, Surrey.   CRP 1TP   0667 437865

INTERNAL TELEPHONE LIST (UK ONLY) - ADDITIONS          List 4   05.09.89

J. D. Charteris, 12 Market Street, Glasgow.   G41 1QS ......  041-672 3443

S. Rana & Sons, 9 North Street, Leith, Edinburgh.   EH6 5TR   031-882 4489

S. Carter Plc, 23 Western Way, St. Andrews, Fife.   KY16 1AA   0334 77358

C. R. Clarke Ltd., 4 Blackburn Road, Manchester.   M20 8UF    061-432 4567

E. Clark PLC, 20 Paisley Road, BIRMINGHAM.   B34 2RG          021-444 2993

Gladstone & Parker, 45 Bath Road, BRISTOL.   BS4 2QE          0272 598841

J. T. Shera & Sons, Bristol Road, Cardiff.   CF3 7BL          0222 697741

*[handwritten]* J Clarke & Co Ltd., 70 London Rd, Luton LU1 5RD  598732
*[handwritten]* John Coleman & Co., Camp Hill, Leeds LS6 1RT  843555

*[margin annotation: Find area codes fr. Tel. Directory — AREA]*

**4(a)** Type the following list of names and addresses. Put the names in alphabetical order. Use open punctuation and align (block) right margin. Insert leader dots.

Example of **open punctuation:**
RONALDSON H Ltd   9 Park Lane   CROYDON   Surrey   CR9 1TP .....  0667 437865

INTERNAL TELEPHONE LIST (INTERNATIONAL) - ADDITIONS    List 2   05.09.89

Trade Corporation   59 Nanjing Road   Beijing   China      010-86 1 31 6551

Lee Custis Jnr   Jersey Stores Inc   188 Jersey Way
New York   NY 10038                                        010-212 440 79986

Manfred Hilgeland   Grüneburgweg 106   D-6000
Frankfurt 1                                                010-49 69 597 1567

Petroleum Corporation   PO Box 15466   Safat Kuwait        010-965 2455354

Chembase SpA   Strada 2 Palazzo F7   20094   Milan   Italy  010-39 2 5201

Asia Bank Ltd   50 Raffles Place   Singapore 0104          010-65 224 8739

Cayman Trust Ltd   PO Box 1877   Grand Cayman
Cayman Islands                                             010-1 809 94 97502

Anglo Bank Co Ltd   Tödistrasse 36   9002   Zurich         010-41 202167

*[handwritten]* The Cable Co  4 Jalan Landa PO Box 1344 Jakarta  010-62 216 7211

**(b)** Address labels to each of the above named. Where appropriate mark AIRMAIL and also insert country of destination where this has been omitted. Mark the label to Lee Custis REGISTERED MAIL.

UNIT 12                    *Telephone index*                             76

③ — 30 mins

**TYPIST** — From the information given below list the foods under their appropriate headings, & indicate the percentage of fat by inserting a capital X in the appropriate column

eg  PERCENTAGE OF FAT IN DIFFERENT FOODS

| FOODS | 50% - 100% | 30% - 49% | 10% - 29% | Under 10% |
|---|---|---|---|---|
| MEAT<br>Fried streaky bacon ----- |  | X |  |  |

MEAT

| | |
|---|---|
| Fried streaky bacon | 45% |
| Grilled streaky bacon | 36% |
| *Grilled lamb chops | 29% |
| Pork pie | 27% |
| Luncheon meat | 27% |
| *Liver sausage | 27% |
| Roast lamb (shoulder) | 26% |
| Fried pork sausages | 25% |
| *Roast leg of pork | 20% |
| Fried beefburgers | 17% |
| Grilled rump steak | 12% |
| *Casseroled pig's liver | 8% |
| Stewed steak | 7% |
| *Casseroled chicken | 7% |
| *Fried lamb's kidneys | 6% |
| Tinned ham | 5% |

MILK, BUTTER, OILS

| | |
|---|---|
| Oil (all kinds) | 100% |
| *Lard | 99% |
| *Butter | 82% |
| Margarine (all kinds) | 80% |
| *Double cream | 50% |
| Dairy ice-cream | 7% |
| *Gold top milk | 5% |
| Silver top milk | 4% |
| *Yoghurt | 1% |
| Skimmed milk | Less than 1% |

CHEESE

| | |
|---|---|
| Cream cheeses | 50% |
| *Stilton | 40% |
| Cheddar | 34% |
| *Parmesan | 30% |
| *Processed cheese | 25% |
| *Camembert | 23% |
| Edam | 23% |
| Cheese spread | 23% |
| Cottage cheese | 4% |

FISH

| | |
|---|---|
| Smoked mackerel | 16% |
| *Fried fish fingers | 13% |
| *Grilled kippers | 12% |
| Cod fried in batter | 10% |
| *Steamed plaice | 2% |
| Steamed haddock | 1% |

**TYPIST** — Do NOT enter those foods marked *. There are some others that I do not want entered. I will let you have these shortly.

**Integrated Production Typing Project — No 5**

# Distribution/circulation lists, Hanging paragraphs

See pages **179** **197**

5  Type the following memo from Inspector P Gosswing, Community Safety Department to Chief Superintendent Thruster, Divisional Headquarters. The reference will consist of Inspector Gosswing's initials and your own, and the subject heading is 'TEA TIME CRIME'.

*Insert today's date & use full punctuation*

As discussed at the recent Management Support Group Forum on (insert last Wed's date here) I have carried out a crime analysis of burglaries in this area. My findings confirm that the recent spate of house burglaries are mostly confined to mid-week evenings, Tuesdays, Thurs, & Fri they are predominately between the hrs of 4.0 pm & 8.0 pm.

NP  In that respect, therefore, I have prepared the self-explanatory advice guidelines. I am enclosing copies of these guidelines to be forwarded to the Unit Commander, in order that suitable distribution can be arranged. Further copies can be obtained by contacting me at the Community Safety Department, & a covering letter for distribution to householders in the vulnerable area, &, I wd suggest, the adjacent housing developments.

DISTRIBUTION LIST

*alpha order*
- P.C. K. Jones
- P.C. A. C. Jones
- P.C. F. W. Birch
- Sgt. J. Smith
- Sgt. J. Latimer
- Inspector A. Ryland-Wills

6  Type a copy of the following using hanging paragraphs for the numbered items.

TEA TIME CRIME  ← *sp caps*

With the arrival of the dark, winter nights many of us leave our homes unattended during those first hours of darkness around tea time.

Almost 80% of domestic housebreakings committed at this time of the year occur between 4.00 p.m. and 8.00 p.m. On a number of these occasions the householder was away for an hour or less. If you are often out at this time of the day, consider taking the following precautions before leaving your home.

*change to arabic figures*

(i)  Secure all doors and vulnerable windows with good-quality locks and get into the habit of checking that all are properly secured before leaving the house.

(ii)  A thief may pass you by if he thinks someone is at home. Leave a light on in the house. Consider fitting time switches to control the lights.

(iii)  Don't leave notes on the door or doorstep th wd indicate to a passing thief th you are out.

(iv)  Draw curtains & close blinds if you are going out for the evening.

(v)  Be vigilant with regard to strangers in yr area, or if you see a stranger calling at an unoccupied house. Note registration nos of any strange vehicles. If in doubt, contact the police.

(vi)  If you are leaving the house for long periods of time, inform a neighbour & ask them to keep a watch on yr home.

UNIT 12  See Practical Typing Exercises, Book Two, page 43, for further exercises on **Distribution/circulation lists, Hanging paragraphs**

# 1 - cont'd

## 1. APPOINTMENTS

We run an appointments system for all surgeries, the hrs of which are as follows:

| | |
|---|---|
| Sat (emergencies only) | 0930 - 1100 |
| Mon to Fri | 0900 - 1800 |

## 2. HEALTH VISITORS

The health visitors can be contacted by telephoning (insert tel no from front cover) between 0900 and 1000 hrs from Mon to Fri.

## 3. MATERNITY SERVICES

We operate a 'shared care' system with the local hospital. There is a community midwife for the practise.

---

# 2 - (10 mins)

MEMO to All doctors          FROM Elaine M—T—

PERCENTAGE OF FAT IN VARIOUS FOODS

I am enclosing a table which gives the percentage fat levels in various foods.

I think it would be useful to give to patients who have a high cholesterol level.

Most of those with raised cholesterol levels have been able to reduce the risk of heart disease by a simple diet, so I think the attached should prove useful.

Did you realize that we have tested well over 1,000 patients so far this year for blood cholesterol level? I think it is most encouraging that so many are coming forward for a check-up.

CIRCULATION — Dr Nimmi Diwan
                    etc     TYPIST — (Please copy names as on the front cover of the leaflet.)

EMT/Yr initials

## Centred display

*See page 179*

**7** Centre the following information horizontally and vertically on a card measuring 152 mm × 101 mm (6 inches × 4 inches) using full punctuation. Use any form of emphasis at your disposal.

> The Curator of the Rylands Town Museum
> Dr. Frederick Martingdale, C.B.E., F.S.A.
> requests the pleasure of the company of
>
> *Mr & Mrs Jaswa Singh*
>
> at a private view of the exhibition
>
> Local Country Pursuits
>
> Saturday 30th July 1994 at 12.30 p.m.
>
> Finger buffet and wine
>
> Please bring this card with you.      R.S.V.P.
>                                        Ms Joanna Findlay,
>                                             High Street,
>                                     Nantwich.  CW3 2RE

*[Handwritten note: Please type an envelope. You will find the address on p.17]*

## Invitations

*See page 191*

**8** Type the following invitation on a card measuring 152 mm × 101 mm (6 inches × 4 inches) using the centred style of display and open punctuation.

> You are invited to the
>
> Violet Cooper Memorial Lecture which will be delivered by
>
> Dr Emmanuel Phillips
>
> on
>
> Thursday 4 August 1994 at 1900 hours
>
> in the
>
> Main Hall of the University
>
> Subject:
> "Europe: Many Legacies, One Future"
>
> No tickets required for admission

UNIT 12 — See Practical Typing Exercises, Book Two, page 44, for further exercises on **Centred display, Invitations**

① – (25 mins)

*Use the centred style of display for the following leaflet.*

Abbey Health Centre*
Trinity Lane
BRISTOL BS8 1QC
Telephone – 0272 289228
- - - -oooo O oooo - - - -

Dr Jane Moore
Dr Alun Jones
Dr Ian Haddrell
Dr Nimmi Diwan
Dr Elaine Moss-Talbot
Dr Steven Turner
Dr Nicholas Moor

(Emphasize words marked *)

(Doctors' names in alphabetical order, please)

Your* doctor* is*: Dr E M_____ T_____

TYPIST – Items 1-3 that follow on the inside left; items 4-6 on inside right. Do not type the figures.

⑤ HOME VISITS
If you are too ill to come to the surgery + need a home visit, please try to telephone the Health Centre before 1000 hrs.

⑥ DISTRICT NURSES
The district nurses has an office in the Health Centre, + they may be contacted there at 1130 hrs Mon to Fri. Alternatively, a message may be left at reception.

③ Emergencies (CAPS)
If you need a doctor, in an emergency, when the Health Centre is open, telephone (insert tel no from front cover)

(TOP MARGIN – 51mm (2"))

# Semi-blocked letters (open punctuation) — Special marks, Display, Enclosure, Postscript

See pages 170, 171, 172

**9** Type the following semi-blocked letter on A4 paper, with open punctuation. Take one copy and type an envelope. Margins: 12 pitch 22–82, 10 pitch 12–72.

CF/BMP                                                                    2 September 1994

FOR THE ATTENTION OF VERA YOUNG

New Era Business Systems Ltd
Kempton House
Harrow Road
WEMBLEY
Middlesex        HA7 4CM

Dear Sirs

BUSINESS SHOW — OCTOBER 1994 *(Centre + u/score)*

Backed by more than 50 years' experience, Europack specialize in marketing innovative products for offices and businesses throughout Europe. If you come to the Business Show in Leicester during October, you will be able to see many of our products being demonstrated and meet our staff who will be able to answer any questions you may have.

DISCOUNT  You will also be able to obtain a discount of 33⅓% on all items being demonstrated at the show. Examples of the savings are:

*(Centre)*

| Value | Discount | Discount | Value |
|-------|----------|----------|-------|
| £ | £ | £ | £ |
| 1 000.00 | 335.00 | 33.50 | 100.00 |
| 900.00 | 301.50 | 30.15 | 90.00 |
| 800.00 | 268.00 | 26.80 | 80.00 |

Come and see us at the show on stand 42 and take advantage of our special exhibition promotion.

                                         Yours faithfully
                                         EUROPACK Co Ltd



                                         CARL FITCH
                                         Group Product Manager

PS   Also on show will be the latest and most up-to-date software package.

---

**15** Key in document 9 (filename EURO) for 12-pitch print-out. When you have completed this task, save under filename EURO, and print out original and one copy. Recall the document and follow the instructions for text editing on page 162.

UNIT 12   See Practical Typing Exercises, Book Two, page 45, for further exercises on
*Semi-blocked letters — Special marks, Display, Enclosure, Postscript*                    79

# INTEGRATED PRODUCTION TYPING

**ABBEY HEALTH CENTRE**

OFFICE SERVICES—REQUEST FORM

This sheet contains instructions that must be complied with when typing the documents. Read the information carefully before starting, and refer back to it frequently.

*Typist's Log Sheet*

Originator: Dr Elaine Moss-Talbot    Designation: —    Date: Today's    Ext No: 23

Typists operating a word processor, or electronic typewriter with appropriate function keys, should apply the following automatic facilities: top margin; carrier return; line-end hyphenation; underline OR bold print (embolden); error correction; centring; any other relevant applications.

Remember to (a) complete the details required at the bottom of the form; (b) enter typing time per document in the appropriate column; and (c) before submitting this **Log Sheet** and your completed work, enter TOTAL TYPING TIME in the last column so that the typist's time may be charged to the originator.

| Document No | Type of document and instructions | Copies – Original plus | Input form¶ | Typing time per document | Total typing time ¥ |
|---|---|---|---|---|---|
| 1 | Folded leaflet | 1 orig | MS | | |
| 2 | Memo | 1 orig | MS | | |
| 3 | Table giving percentage of fat in foods | 1 orig | MS + printed copy | | |
| *4 | Article on blood pressure | 1 + 1 | AT | | |
| 5 | Circular letter | 1 orig | MS | | |
| 6 | Organization chart + label | 1 orig | MS | | |
| 7 | Financial Statement | 1 + 2 | MS | | |

Could you please put the above on my desk in 2½ hrs with the exception of the article on blood pressure which I would like as soon as possible.

TOTAL TYPING TIME

TYPIST—please complete:
Typist's name:    Date received:    Date completed:
                 Time received:    Time completed:

If the typed documents cannot be returned within 24 hours, the office services supervisor should inform the originator. Any item that is urgent should be marked with an asterisk (*).

¶T = Typescript    AT = Amended Typescript    MS = Manuscript    SD = Shorthand Dictation    AD = Audio Dictation
¥ to be charged to the originator's department    AP = Amended Print.

*Typist's Log Sheet—No 5*

## Personal letters—Semi-blocked

*See page 197*

**10** Type the following semi-blocked business letter on A5 portrait paper.
Margins: 12 pitch 11–66, 10 pitch 6–56. Take one copy and type a label.

                    Cartref
                 Mountain Road
                    PENBERY
           Dyfed      SA16 3PJ


                                15 September 1994

Mrs Emma Foord
4 Range Lane
PENBERY
Dyfed      SA14 1FY

Dear Emma

     I am sorry I will not be able to be present at the
committee meeting at Arthur's house on Friday as I shall
be away on business.

     Please keep me in the picture.  I am still very
interested in being identified with the project. *I have been reading abt it in the local papers.*

     Best wishes

                              Yours sincerely



                              MARTIN HUMPHREY

## Name and address of addressee at foot of page

*See page 171*

**11** Type the following semi-blocked personal letter on A5 portrait paper.
Take one copy and type an envelope.

                              68 Manor Road,
                              Kempston Hardwick,
                              BEDFORD.      MK43 7OT

                              27th September 1994

     Dear Sir/Madam,

          I should be glad if you would send me details of your
     Autumn Breaks *(/c. 5-day)* as advertised in the national press last week.

                         *(Leave 5 spaces clear)* →
                              Yours faithfully,

                              Clarissa Longworth (Mrs.)

     The Manager,
     Cheddington House Hotel,
     TREENANT,
     Clwyd.      LL13 6UT

UNIT 12           *Personal letters—Semi-blocked,*           80
          *Name and address of addressee at foot of page*

## Press releases

8  Type an original and take one copy. Do not type in two columns. Follow this example.

> Should you be concerned with public relations work, you may be called upon to type or compile press or news releases.

*See pages 199, 200*

### 18.8 Press releases*

Should you be concerned with public relations work you may be called upon to type or compile press or news releases. These are announcements to the press or other media of imminent events—e.g., the opening of new showrooms, the appointment of a new managing director, or the launching of a new product. Because they are regarded as news and not advertisements, no charge is made for their insertion. However, as an editor may receive many demands on the space he has available, he will insert only those that are 'newsworthy' for his particular readership, succinctly and factually written (avoiding any tendency to advertise in glowing terms) and presented in an acceptable way. *It is therefore important to approach only the newspapers ... to know their publication dates & deadlines for submitting copy. Stale news is of no interest & wl not be printed. Occasionally an embargo is placed on a release prohibiting its publication until a specified date. This ensures the max impact.*

Acceptable display involves giving a short, factual heading in capitals, perhaps followed by a subtitle in upper and lower case. The body of the release should be typed in double spacing, with wide margins and indented paragraphs (except the first, which may be blocked).

The body of the release should be divided into short paragraphs on clearly discernible topics. If possible, the first paragraph—or sentence—should sum up the essence of the whole announcement, in case the editor has space only for this. As he will cut from the end upwards, make sure that you arrange the paragraphs in descending order of importance. Short sentences also make it easier for him to cut with the least risk of distorting the sense.

*If it carries over to another sheet or sheets, repeat ... avoid extensive use of capital letters & underscore. Give the date of issue &, if appropriate, a ref number.*

*Finally, give the name & tele number of the staff member responsible, so th the editor knows whom to contact for further info or for a photograph of the product (if one has not been sent w the release).*

* From *Modern Secretarial Procedures* by Kathleen M Trotman published by McGraw-Hill Book Company (UK) Limited.

## Speeches

*See page 207*

9  Display the following notes on a postcard 152 mm × 101 mm (6 inches × 4 inches).

*Chief Executive Committee — 10 Dec 1994* ← (Emphasize this line)

*Chairman  MR GEORGE GALBRAITH*

*Lecture Time      10.30 am — 11.30 am*

*Title  INFORMATION TECHNOLOGY TODAY*
*1 Office Automation*
*2 Integrating Data Processing Equipment*
*3 Choosing a Supplier*
*4 Problems During Installation     5 The Future*

---

UNIT 19 — Press releases, Speeches — 137

# Semi-blocked business letters—Continuation sheets, Blind carbon copies, Catchwords

See pages 170, 172, 173, 175

12 Type the following semi-blocked letter on A4 paper, with full punctuation. Take two blind carbon copies—one for Mrs. Esme Bacon and the other for David F. Cheetham. Address labels to Mrs. Bacon and Mr. Cheetham and an envelope for Ms Isobel Binnie.

Ref. Acc./48007032B                          24th August 1994

Ms Isobel Binnie,
Garden Flat,
24 Elm Hill,
LINCOLN.
LN5 8AQ

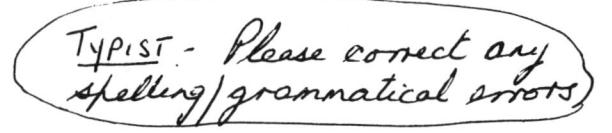

*TYPIST - Please correct any spelling/grammatical errors*

Dear Ms Binnie,

GOLD ACCOUNT NO. 48007032B

I am writing to advise you that your account will mature on 20th September 1994. From the day after this date the conditions and terms of your account will change as follows:-

*Replace bullet sign with an *, if nec*

* The guaranteed interest differential will cease and the rate of interest applicable will be the same as the nominal rate on our high interest instant access account. As from 1st August 1994 these are:

| Balance | Gross p.a. | Net Equivalent p.a. |
|---|---|---|
| £1 - £999 | 2.20% | 1.65% |
| £1,000 - £9,999 | 6.85% | 5.14% |
| £10,000+ | 7.85% | 5.89% |

*Retain abbreviations*

For currant rates you should cheque with your local branch.

*Insert "A"*

* Withdrawals and additions can be made at any time.

X. SPECIAL INVESTMENT OPPORTUNITIES (lc & u/sc)

We have two investment accounts offering very good rates of interest:

* MAXIMUM 6 is a limited issue one year bond, exclu-  H
  sively available to clients such as yourself. The terms of the account are the same as you are getting now, except that you can choose whether to have interest on maturity, or paid out monthly to provide you with a regular income from your investment.

* MAXIM 9 is a limited issue 12-month notice account ~~which~~ that gives you emergency access to your money

/should you need

UNIT 12 — Semi-blocked business letters—Continuation sheets, Blind carbon copies, Catchwords — 81

# Ditto marks
# Bring forward reminders

*See pages 179, 169*

**6** Type the following letter, use semi-blocked style and take two copies. On both copies type in the top right corner: 'BRING FORWARD on 19 December 1994'. On the second copy only, beneath the bring forward reminder, type the word FILE.

Ref HG/PR

Mrs Jill Haydon-Browne   2 Batchelors Cottage   Kirkcaldy   Fife   KY1 7UC

Dear Mrs Haydon-Browne

*Please type a label*
**MENACING PHONE CALLS** *(centre)*

I am so sorry to hear that you have been having disturbing phone calls. The following pointers may help you in future.

DON'T   answer the phone with your name and number; just say "Hello".
  "     engage in conversation before callers have identified themselves.
  "     record your name and telephone number in the opening message if you have an answering machine.
  "     give your marital status in the telephone directory; use the initial of your first name instead.

DO      hang up immediately if the call is disturbing, indecent or simply annoying.
  "     remember that the telephone is for your use; you have control.
  "     contact the police if the problems persist.

I do hope you do not have any further ~~trouble~~ *more*, but I will contact you again shortly in case there is anything further I can do.

Yours sincerely

# Signing letters on behalf of another person

*See page 173*

**7** Please type the following letter in blocked style with full punctuation.

JRT/OY
12.12.94

Dear Mr & Mrs Nash,

*Please type a heading:*
**BREAK-INS**

With the onset of winter the dark evenings are once more upon us. It is, however, just such evenings which create cover for a particular type of criminal activity. I refer to break-ins to houses in estates such as your own. Already this winter there have been a number of such incidents in the area.

// *In order, therefore, to reduce the likelihood of yr becoming a victim of such a crime, I hv prepared the enclosed doc. containing info. & advice to help you protect yr property.*

Yours sincerely

Dictated by James W Unwin,
Chief Superintendent and signed in his absence
*(Leave at least 4 clear spaces here)*

Mr Cyril & Mrs Amy Nash
Cherry Cottage
Yarrington Drive, CAMBRIDGE   CB4 8YE

Ms Isobel Binnie          2          24th August 1994

should you need it.  Interest is paid monthly or ~~paid out~~ annually, whilst allowing you to make additions as & when you wish.

[Insert "B"]

For further details of these accounts, please see the brochures enclosed with this letter.

[caps] As Maximum 6 and Maxim 9 [is] limited issues you must invest before the end of November to ensure you do not miss out.

                    Yours sincerely,



                    BABIR RASHID
                    Investment Adviser


"A" You may decide to keep yr Gold A/c open under the new terms. In wh case you need take no further action. However, to make the best of yr investment after maturity, there are a no of other options for you to choose from:

"B" If you wish to transfer part, or all, of yr Gold A/c to one of these a/cs, you may do so at yr local branch. Alternatively, please complete the enclosed application form & withdrawal/transfer authority & return them, with yr certs asap.

---

13  Please write to Kathy Grosvenor offering her the post of WP operator in our Personnel Dept. You'll find her name & address on p.60 Exl. Don't forget to insert my initials followed by yr own as a ref, date the letter for tomorrow, & head the letter WORD PROCESSOR OPERATOR.

- - - - oOo - - - -

EDUCATIONAL SERVICES INCORPORATED [centre]

(Type our address here - centred [see p 61]) Say th I am writing to inform her th she was successful in her interview for the above position, & wish her to commence duties as from 1st of next month (insert actual date here, please). The hrs wl be Mon-Fri 0900-1700 with 5 wks' pd holiday ea yr plus bank hols. Salary £10 000 pa. Ask her to contact AMELIA GREENE in the Personnel Dept asap. Say th I wish to take this opp of welcoming Mrs Grosvenor to E___ S___ I___ & wish her many happy yrs with us.

                                        M J SINGH

UNIT 12  See Practical Typing Exercises, Book Two, pages 46–47, for further exercises on    82
**Semi-blocked business letters—
Continuation sheets, Blind carbon copies, Catchwords**

## Cards

*See page 175*

3  Using a card measuring approximately 152 mm × 101 mm (6 inches × 4 inches), prepare an alphabetic file card for

> EUROPACK Co Ltd
>
> Fifth Floor   Enterprise House   56/60 Lonsdale Road
> CATERHAM   Surrey   CR3 8SY
>
> Telephone No   0883 46412
> Fax No         0883 13025
> Telex No       39076
>
> Customer Reference No BH/pqr/30975D

4  Type the following on two separate cards measuring approximately 101 mm × 152 mm (4 inches × 6 inches).

> BELLINGTONS
>
> S H O R T   L E T S
>
> A great variety of properties
> Country houses - thatched cottages
> Minimum of 2 weeks
>
> **From: £300 per week**
>
> East Devon area
> Call us on
> 04865 5661

> WANTED
>
> On behalf of clients, property co. urgently seeks:
> 2-bedroomed luxury flat;
> house w. garden;
> 3-bedroomed apartment w. balcony;
> cottage w. approx 3 acres;
> for occupation next month -
> tel (04865) 5661

## Symbol K equals a thousand

*See pages 195, 196*

5  Please display the following information attractively. Use the capital K exactly as it is shown.

> EUROPACK Co Ltd
> Fifth Floor   Enterprise House   56/60 Lonsdale Road
> Caterham   Surrey   CR3 8SY   Telephone: (0883) 46412
>
> ─────────────────────────────────────
>
> New appointments with in autonomous operating subsidiary of leading plc.  Major challenges to rejuvenate the manufacturing process.
>
> **OPERATIONS DIRECTOR** - £45K + car and benefits
>
> **CHIEF EXECUTIVE** - £40K + benefits
>
> **TREASURY PROJECT MANAGER** ⎫
> **EQUITIES PROJECT MANAGER** ⎬ Packages from £45K to £80K
> **PROJECT MANAGERS** ⎭
>
> Please reply in writing, enclosing full CV.  Ref M426

UNIT 19   See Practical Typing Exercises, Book Two, page 62, for further exercises on
*Cards, Symbol K equals a thousand*

# SKILL BUILDING

Type each line three times and, if time permits, complete your practice by typing each group once as it appears.

Margins:
12 pitch 22–82
10 pitch 12–72

### A  Keyboarding skills

1 Speed     We hope you will be able to call and see us in about a week.
2 Accuracy  Their extra-special prize was a cruise in the Caribbean Sea.
3 Figures   Jack paid £93,500 for his new house and £14,786 for his car.
4 Symbols   Cole & Co want 4 desks @ £130 each; discount of 8% for cash.

### B  Improve control of first and fourth fingers

5 far tame gape pave stab jamb quart amaze frame habit grafted
6 art game gram past tram jump razor staff plump barns varnish
7 He is travelling to Berlin on the 1100 hours train tomorrow.
8 Hamish asked Queeny for a good supply of food for my voyage.

### C  Language arts—non-use of apostrophe
—see explanation on page 161

9  He took a bus to catch the plane which was leaving at 10 am.
10 Kate asked, "Is that new car hers or yours or is it theirs?"
11 In the early 1960s Joe Brown was one of 2 MPs for this area.
12 The Works Manager was a member of the Engineers Association.

13 To develop your proofreading skills, turn to page 159, exercise 6.

### Skill measurement          Three-minute timing          Not more than three errors

S/M15  The interview is a 2-way process.  The interviewer should      11
       find out if you have the desired qualifications and suitable   23
       personality.  You must try to size up the job to see if it     35
       is what you are looking for.                                   41

       Before the interview, the interviewer will have studied your   53
       Application Form and Job Sheet to find out what the job is     65
       about — what has to be done, where it has to be done, and      76
       how it has to be done.  He will then be ready to ask you a     88
       number of questions, designed to confirm statements made on   100
       your Application Form and to discover other facts about you.  112

       When the most suitable person has been chosen, references     123
       will be checked.  This may be done by mail or by telephone.   135
       If they are in order, the chosen person will be offered the   147
       job.                                                          148

       When you receive a letter offering you a post, see that you   160
       write back straight away, thanking the writer for the offer   172
       and giving your decision.                                     177

       In the new job there are many things to learn.  No matter     188
       how well you have been trained, your new employer is sure to  200
       ask you to do one or 2 tasks in a different way.  When he     211
       does so, carry out all instructions he gives.  If, later on,  223
       you feel your way is better, there is usually no harm in      234
       saying that you think so.                        (SI 1.33)   239

       1 | 2 | 3 | 4 | 5 | 6 | 7 | 8 | 9 | 10 | 11 | 12 |

UNIT 13                    Skill building                          83

being banged into the first desk on entering unless a small wooden wedge are used to limit the doors arc of movement. The office cleaners often forget to replace this wedge after they hv done their early morning clean up.

2.4 Other hazards
Through frequent use .... (see accident report form filed 9 Feb 1994).

3.0 CONCLUSIONS

3.1 Electrical hazards in the office area are easily ... in advance of the next scheduled one.

3.2 Furnishing hazards wd seem to indicate a need for repair in some instances + purchase of new equipment in others.

3.3 Organizational hazards cld be rectified ... into the office.

3.4 Other hazards are limited to the state of the carpet + replacement of this wd seem to be of some urgency. The danger from a worn carpet in close proximity to a somewhat makeshift repair of the letter rack makes this a particularly hazardous area.

REF: TC/JT

2  Please send a memo to Tony Ashraf Safety Officer from me T—— C—— & say th further to his memo of 1/6/94, I hv looked into the safety hazards in the central office area, + attach my ~~précis~~ report.
Shd he require any further elucidation of the points made, I wd be pleased to explain them further.
Use the heading as given for the report, and the same date.

# PRODUCTION DEVELOPMENT

*Tabulation—Centred*

See page **209**

1  Type the following table using the centred style of display.

BT - OPTION 15

| Calls per quarter at basic rate of 4.935p* | Calls per quarter with Option 15 (inc £4.00 charge)* | The difference per quarter with Option 15 over the basic rate* |
|---|---|---|
| £75.00 | £71.50 | £3.50 |
| £100.00 | £94.00 | £6.00 |
| £150.00 | £139.00 | £11.00 |
| £200.00 | £184.00 | £16.00 |
| £250.00 | £229.00 | £21.00 |
| £300.00 | £274.00 | £26.00 |

* All figures are approximate and inclusive of VAT.

2  Type the following table using the centred style of display and full punctuation.

*(Retain abbreviations)*

TRAVEL BETWEEN MADRID AND LISBON BY AIR

| Tues., Thurs. & Sat. | Timings | Tues., Thurs. & Sat. |
|---|---|---|
| 0800 | Dep.   Madrid   Arr. | 0905 |
| 1105 | Arr.   Lisbon   Dep. | 1000 |

*(Leave 3 spaces)*

3  Type the following table using the centred style of display and open punctuation.

CRUISES - PRICES (PER PERSON)

| Departure on or between | 9 nights || 12 nights ||
|---|---|---|---|---|
| | Twin | Single | Twin | Single |
| 16 Oct 94 | - | - | 945 | 1 230 |
| 22 Oct 94 - 19 Nov 94 | 870 | 1 000 | 1 025 | 1 355 |
| 11 Dec 94 | 815 | 1 005 | 910 | 1 165 |
| 03 Jan 95 - 22 Jan 95 | 830 | 1 025 | 965 | 1 250 |
| 27 Jan 95 | 850 | 1 055 | - | - |

*(Please type dates as shown)*

UNIT 13   See Practical Typing Exercises, Book Two, page 48, for further exercises on
*Tabulation—Centred*

# PRODUCTION DEVELOPMENT

## Report

See page 203

**1** Type the following report on A4 paper.

SAFETY HAZARDS IN CENTRAL OFFICE AREA*

FOR Tony Ashraf - Safety Officer

FROM Tony Carr - Personal Assistant

16 July 1994

1.0 INTRODUCTION

I was asked on 4 July to prepare a brief report for yourself on potential and actual hazards in the central office area. I was asked to present my initial findings to you by 22 July.

2.0 INFORMATION

2.1 Electrical Hazards

The starter to one of the fluorescent tubes in the ceiling lighting is faulty & secs regularly stand on a chair to twist the starter to get the tube working.

Although inspected only 6 months ago, the power plugs to 2 of the electric typewriters in the clerical section of the office are cracked across their backs.

The main power input to the office photocopier is worn by constant contact with a filing cabinet. The worn area has been mended by being bound with insulation tape.

2.2 Furnishing hazards

Two of the filing cabinets are over 20 yrs old & often jam shut. They are only capable of being opened by tilting the cabinet backwards & holding the cabinet at an angle while being supported by the foot. The letter racks for the distribution of incoming mail are secured to the wall by masonry hooks with the exception of the lower left-hand corner where a large dictionary has bn placed to support the weight.

2.3 Organizational hazards

In order to maximize use of floor space, the secs' desks hv bn arranged so th the door into the office cannot avoid

* Extract from Communication & the World of Work by Christopher Beddows published by McGraw Hill-Book Company Europe.

UNIT 19     Report     133

## Tabulation—Vertical headings (*to be read downwards*)

See pages 212, 213

**4** Set out the following tabulation with vertical headings which should be typed as in the copy so that they can be read downwards.

PRINTER - List of fonts

| FONT | REGULAR | ITALICS | BOLD | PITCH |
|---|---|---|---|---|
| Gothic | * |  |  | 15 |
| AvantGarde | * | * | * | 8+ |
| Bookman | * | * | * | 6+ |
| Modern |  |  | * | 8+ |
| Palatino | * | * | * | 8+ |
| Courier | * | * | * | 6+ |

**5** Type the following table with vertical headings which are to be read downwards. Centre vertically and horizontally on A5 portrait paper.

ATTENDANCE

| SUBJECT | BUILDER | AUDANDRIEELYS | JULYIES T | MARILEETT |
|---|---|---|---|---|
| Word Processing | 26 | 30 | 28 | 29 |
| Shorthand | 24 | 29 | 29 | 23 |
| Financial Record Keeping | 22 | 27 | 30 | 27 |
| Office Procedures | 25 | 28 | 28 | 26 |

*TYPIST: Leave one clear space between words.*

UNIT 13 — See Practical Typing Exercises, Book Two, page 49, for further exercises on
**Tabulation—Vertical headings (*to be read downwards*)**

# SKILL BUILDING

Margins:
12 pitch 22–82
10 pitch 12–72

*Skill measurement*  Six-minute timing  Not more than six errors

S/M21 If you were asked to list all activities you do just for pleasure of doing them, how many different items would there be in your list? The chances are that the list most of us could compile would contain very few things. Even if we could make a rather lengthy list, it seems likely that most of the activities would be those in which we engage on an irregular basis, if indeed there is sufficient repetition of any one activity to indicate any sort of schedule at all. At first glance, it might seem that such a question has very little significance at all; yet, in a sense, it does seem to be important in the opinion of many employers.

Every job application form that I can ever remember filling in or studying always had the same question: what do you do with your spare time; how much time do you devote to each activity? Regardless of how the question was worded, the main point of the question seems to be that it is important for a person not to devote too much time to work, the idea being that all work and no play makes you extremely dull.

I feel it must be true that spending several hours a week on activities that are in no way connected with your job, and deriving sheer pleasure and relaxation from doing so, must make a person a less dull individual; however, when I have discussed the subject with other people, it does seem that a great many individuals did not engage in any activity solely for the purpose of deriving pleasure from it. Four persons, who gave me their views on the subject, said that they would be more than happy to take up a hobby of some kind if they could only find the time to research the various pastimes available, and then choose one that they thought might be something that would indeed provide complete relaxation.

The number of working wives and the number of husbands who work at two jobs, one of which is performed on a regular full-time basis and the other on a regular part-time basis, seems to be ample testimony to the fact that a great many people do not have the time for engaging in hobbies at all, to say nothing of doing so for whatever pleasure they may derive from them. Not that the wives and husbands with whom I have spoken feel that they are martyrs of some kind, but they usually point out the economic necessity of having two breadwinners in the family. It seems to me that it is not what a person does that causes dullness but the attitude of the person to what he does.

There is just one more point I must mention, and that is to remind you of how difficult it can be for older people to settle down when they retire, and this is especially so if they do not have a hobby.
(SI 1.33)

| 1 | 2 | 3 | 4 | 5 | 6 | 7 | 8 | 9 | 10 | 11 | 12 |

UNIT 19  *Skill building*  132

## Tabulation—Vertical column headings

See page 212

6 Type the following table with vertical column headings as shown.

A COMPARISON OF INTEREST RATES

| Investment | Minimum investment | Net return after basic rate tax | Withdrawal notice |
|---|---|---|---|
| | £ | % | |
| Building Societies | | | |
| Instant access | 500 | 5.75 | None |
| | 2,000 | 6.00 | None |
| | 5,000 | 6.50 | None |
| | 10,000 | 6.75 | None |
| Notice accounts | 500 | 6.75 | 90 days* |
| | 10,000 | 7.00 | 90 days |
| | 25,000 | 7.25 | 90 days |
| Banks | | | |
| Deposit accounts | None | 3.00 | 7 days |
| High interest cheque accounts | 2,000 | 6.00 | None |
| | 10,000 | 6.20 | None |
| National Savings | | | |
| Investment account | 5 | 7.30 | 1 month |
| Deposit bonds | 100 | 7.66 | 3 months |
| Income bonds | 2,000 | 7.66 | 3 months |
| National savings certificates‡ | 25 | 7.00 | 5-year term |

\* Variable.

‡ Fixed rate for the term, all other rates variable.

**16** Key in document 6 (filename RATES) for 10-pitch print-out. Use the save function for the first horizontal ruled line and copy this where necessary. Also, use the vertical line key and the decimal tab key. When you have completed this task, save under filename RATES, and print out original. Recall the document and follow the instructions for text editing on page 163.

**UNIT 13** See Practical Typing Exercises, Book Two, page 50, for further exercises on
*Tabulation—Vertical column headings*

(7)

TAKABREAK — 15 mins — *TYPIST - Display the following attractively as a folded 3-page leaflet.*

**Front cover:**

HOLIDAY MONEY

All major currencies on demand
International money transfer service
Travel insurance

EXPERT ADVICE

**Inside left:**

HOW MUCH MONEY WILL YOU NEED?

Are you travelling around or staying in one ~~location~~ ~~destination~~? ✓

Are you catering for yourself or getting full board?

How many excursions will you be taking?

Are you going to more than one country? Will you be purchasing and/or presents *souvenirs* for friends or family?

CASH OR TRAVELLERS CHEQUES

**Inside right:**

Remember! It is much safer to carry travellers cheques than cash, but you will need to take some cash for your first day or two. You may need to take a taxi or a local bus from the airport, and you may want a snack on your arrival.

If yr travellers cheques are lost or stolen, a prompt refund service is provided by our world-wide network of branches. // If you don't use all yr traveller cheques during yr holiday, you can bring them back to us & we wl encash them w'out any charge. // All major currencies + travellers cheques are instantly available @ Takabreak. *caps*

7 Type the following table with vertical headings as shown using the centred style of display.

<u>NO-CLAIM DISCOUNT</u>

| No-claim discount at last renewal | No-claim discount at next renewal in the event of |||
| --- | --- | --- | --- |
| | 1 claim | 2 claims | 2 or more claims |
| 30 per cent ..... | Nil | Nil | Nil |
| 40 per cent ..... | Nil | Nil | Nil |
| 50 per cent ..... | 30% | Nil | Nil |
| 60 per cent ..... | 40% | Nil | Nil |
| 65 per cent ..... | 50% | 30% | Nil |

8 Type the following table with vertical headings using the blocked style of display and A5 portrait paper.

SUBSCRIPTION RATES

| | Inland Mail | Europe Surface Mail | Europe Airmail |
| --- | --- | --- | --- |
| | £ | £ | £ |
| 3 months | 35.88 | 47.58 | 54.60 |
| 6 months | 71.76 | 95.16 | 109.20 |
| 9 months | 94.20 | 120.14 | 178.40 |
| 12 months | 143.62 | 190.32 | 218.40 |

**UNIT 13**     *Tabulation — Vertical column headings*     **87**

to be dealt w 2-3 mnths in advance of yr hol. date.

*TYPIST - No. ea. item w a small roman numeral, please.*

- Does yr passport or credit card need to be renewed?
- Will you require vaccinations or other medication?
- Have you taken out an appropriate insurance policy?
- Are there any currency restrictions in the country you are visiting?
- Order yr currency & travellers cheques in good time.
- Make a list of the following items & keep in a safe place away fr the items listed:

*[Indent & list items one under the other]* Passport No; Travellers cheques serial nos; credit card details; Emergency telephone no. in case of loss of passport or travellers cheques; copy of holiday ins. policy.

- Take confirmation of any hotel or car reservation.
- Make arrangements for any pets & mail.
- Cancel the milk & the papers.

---

6  **Going on Holiday?** *(caps)*   (10 mins)

u.c. The caravan in Cornwall, the Boarding House /l.c. in Blackpool or the *beach in Florida*; *sunny* wherever you choose, don't forget what you *have left behind* — I am referring to yr house, *not just the cold & rain* —

REMEMBER **&**

- cut the lawn before you go;
- hide valuables out of site or deposit them in a bank;
- arrange for a friend *or neighbour* to check yr house *regularly* & (a) close & open curtains; (b) remove mail or *circulars*.

By taking a few simple precautions like those mentioned here & in the check-list, there shd be no problems on yr return.

ENJOY YOUR HOLIDAY!

**Integrated Production Typing Project—No 4**

## Tabulation—Oblique column headings

9 Type the following with oblique column headings.

SALMON'S SUPERSTORES

There's one near you!

|  | BIRMINGHAM | BRISTOL | CARDIFF | EDINBURGH | NORTHAMPTON | SWANSEA |
|---|---|---|---|---|---|---|
| Car park for over 250 cars ......... | X | X | X | X | X | X |
| Open 7 days a week | X |  | X |  | X |  |
| Late opening on Fridays* ......... | X | X | X | X | X | X |
| No quibble guarantee ......... | X | X | X | X | X | X |
| Low, low prices‡ | X | X | X | X | X | X |
| Garden Centre & DIY shop |  | X | X |  |  | X |
| Petrol at discount prices | X |  | X | X | X |  |
| Self-service bar snacks | X | X |  | X |  | X |

*  9.0 pm
‡  Compare our prices w those of other superstores

10 Please send a letter to Mr Dave Clements & his wife thanking them for their enquiry regarding a 2-bedroomed flat at our Beechgate development. Send them our Information Brochure & price-list & tell them th if they hv any further queries to call in to the show flat @ Beechgate any day between 10.00 & 12.00 or 2.00 & 4.00. This letter is rather urgent as I was away from the office last wk. Take a copy & type an envelope. Don't forget to type my name & designation ready for signature & use our ref MV/Prop 42651A/ &, of course, yr initials. By the way, Mr & Mrs Clements' address is in the Data Files (filename PROP) on page 164.

Melissa Vyner    Marketing Manager

UNIT 13

| | |
|---|---|
| Vaccinations are required in the following countries - | |
| **MALARIA** | China, Egypt, Gambia, India, Malaysia, Mexico, Thailand, Turkey, Venezuela, Zimbabwe |
| **CHOLERA** | Egypt, Gambia, India, Malaysia, Singapore, Thailand, Tunisia, Turkey, Zimbabwe |
| **TYPHOID** | Bahamas, Barbados, China, Carribean, Egypt, Gambia, Hong Kong, India, Israel, Malaysia, Mexico, Singapore, Thailand, Tunisia, Turkey, Venezuela, Zimbabwe |
| **POLIO** | Bahamas, Barbados, China, Carribean, Egypt, Gambia, Hong Kong, India, Israel, Malaysia, Mexico, Singapore, Thailand, Tunisia, Turkey, Venezuela, Zimbabwe |

insurance is an absolute must. Most travell insurance policies include unlimited medical cover, plus cover against loss of luggage, cancellation charges, personal accident & various benefits.

### Theft & loss abroad

**TYPIST - Shoulder hdg.**

There are certain steps you can follow to minimize problems shd theft or loss occur.

(i) Keep a note of yr passport no. Report loss or theft w'out delay, to the police & the nearest British Consul, ideally within 24 hrs.

(ii) Avoid taking valuables on holiday w. you, but, if you must, keep them in the hotel's safe.

(iii) Use travellers cheques and/or credit cards rather than cash. Make a note of the serial nos printed on the travellers cheques, & keep them seperate fr the cheques themselves.

(iv) If you are taking yr own car, keep the registration documents separate fr the vehicle. If the car is stolen, yr insurance co wl need to know the engine & chassis nos.

### Check-list

This check-list shd be used as a reminder to make sure th yr holiday wl be a success. Some of the items is a useful precaution. a money belt may need

to be/

# SKILL BUILDING

Type each line three times and, if time permits, complete your practice by typing each group once as it appears.

Margins:
12 pitch 22–82
10 pitch 12–72

### A  Keyboarding skills

1 Speed     At this stage we are not able to quote you a definite price.
2 Accuracy  Has Jacques told you about his experiments with frozen zinc?
3 Figures   They travelled 10,145 miles in 32 days and visited 9 cities.
4 Symbols   £0.34 (34p) + £0.16 (16p) - £0.10 (10p) × 2 = £0.80 (80p).

### B  Language arts—agreement of subject and verb
—see explanation on page 161

5  A daisywheel <u>is</u> a fast spinning disk that prints characters.
6  Floppy disks <u>are</u> used for recording and storing information.
7  You <u>were</u> our <u>first</u> customer when we opened our shop in town.
8  He <u>agrees</u> with me, I agree with you, and they agree with us.
9  Neither William nor Brian <u>was</u> at the meeting on Monday last.
10 A new diary and a phone <u>index</u> <u>are</u> necessary for your office.

### Skill measurement            Four-minute timing            Not more than four errors

S/M16 Before leaving for your holidays, give your car a good wash,  12
and waxing can be important if you plan to stay by the sea.  24
Salt air is highly corrosive and can damage the finish on an  36
unprotected car.  Keeping the outside of your car in good  47
condition will help when you want to sell.  Also, when driv-  59
ing on a motorway, do not stay too close to the car in front  71
as, apart from being dangerous, its tyres will throw up  82
stones and other debris that can chip the paint on your car.  94

If a breakdown should occur, the first rule is to remain  105
calm and report to the police or a motoring association.  On  117
motorways, there are emergency telephones at regular inter-  128
vals.  In addition, the motorways are well patrolled by the  140
police.  When something goes wrong on a country road,  151
determine your location, then try to find a phone and call  163
a garage or a motoring association.  170

Do not give your car a lengthy warm-up.  When the engine  182
starts to run smoothly, pull away from the kerb.  Contrary  194
to popular belief, a lengthy warm-up wastes fuel and causes  206
excessive wear.  Avoid fast stops and starts.  Whenever  217
possible, stop gently and start slowly.  Fast acceleration  229
wastes fuel.  Before moving away from the kerb, check to  240
see that it is safe to move off, and when pulling into the  252
kerb, give a timely and clear indication that you are doing  264
so.  265

If you are involved in an accident, remember to write down  277
the name and address of a witness, if there is one, and also  289
to record the name and address of the other driver, owner of  301
the vehicle, if different, and name and address of the other  313
driver's insurance company.                         (SI 1.39)  318

    1  |  2  |  3  |  4  |  5  |  6  |  7  |  8  |  9  |  10  |  11  |  12  |

**UNIT 14**                    *Skill building*

(5) (35 mins)

TAKABREAK

*TYPIST – Insert address here for task 4, please.*

### HOLIDAY TIPS (sp caps & centre)

Takabreak has produced this leaflet to help ensure th there are no nasty surprises when you go on holiday – financial or otherwise. We hope th the tips & info wl help you on yr way to a trouble-free holiday.

#### Innoculations (at least 2 mnths before departure)

Although inoculations are not often req'd for the more popular & established holiday destinations, you shd always double check exact requirements w. yr GP or w. us. The following is a guide for some of those destinations wh are becomeing more popular w. our clients:

| COUNTRY | MALARIA | CHOLERA | TYPHOID | POLIO |
|---|---|---|---|---|
| Australia | * | * | * | * |
| Bahamas | * | * | ** | ** |

** Vaccination req'd
* No vaccination req'd

*TYPIST – Type this table as shown above, using the info. over the page. Include only – Australia, Bahamas, China, Cyprus, Carribean, Hong Kong, USA.*

#### Insurance

Even if you are going on a very short holiday, insurance/

# PRODUCTION DEVELOPMENT

See page **186**

## Form letters

**1 (a)** Type an original and take two copies of the following skeleton letter on the A5 headed paper (EUROPACK Co Ltd) provided in the *Solutions and Resource Material*.

```
Ref

12 October 1994


Dear

Thank you for your application for the post of

NP [ I should be glad if you would attend for an interview,
     at this address on                      at
     Please go to the                              and ask for


Yours sincerely




Personnel Department
```

(b) On the original insert:

**Ref** PBA/FT  **Addressee** Ms Abiola Rashad  10 The Leys  Grafton Way  Caterham  Surrey CR7 9XF  **Salutation** Dear Ms Rashad  **Post** Shorthand-typist  **Date of interview** Tuesday 25 October at 0930 hours  **Go to the** 6th Floor, Room 612  **Ask for** Julian Rochester.

(c) On the first copy insert:

**Ref** PBA/FT  **Addressee** Mr Robin Cobb  87 Fleet Way  Caterham  Surrey CR4 0PT  **Salutation** Dear Mr Cobb  **Post** Operations Planning Manager  **Date of interview** Wednesday 26 October at 1030 hours  **Go to the** 1st Floor, Room 12  **Ask for** Melanie Pierce-Jones.

(d) On the second copy insert:

**Ref** PBA/FT  **Address** Mrs Isabel Hemming  1 Glebe Crescent, off Forest Road  Caterham  Surrey CR9 3UM  **Salutation** Dear Mrs Hemming  **Post** Marketing Co-ordinator  **Date of interview** Thursday 27 October at 1330 hours  **Go to the** 2nd Floor, Room 25  **Ask for** Jonathan Franklyn.

(4)     *20 mins*

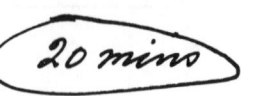

# TAKABREAK

**Greenfield Place Camber Rye East Sussex TN31 4XY**

Telephone: 0797 43876     Fax: 0797 30915

## TRAVEL RECEIPT

b.o. Departure Date [ ]     Code [ ]

Name _____ Balance due £[ ]

Address _____

_____ Postcode _____

b.c. Telephone No _____ Destination [ ]

Departure point [ ]

**HOLIDAY DETAILS**

Date of departure     No of nights     Flight no

Date of return     Flight no

Insurance no [ ]

Deposit paid £[ ]

Total cost of holiday less deposit £[ ]

*TYPIST — Please display the above attractively on plain paper. Rule boxes of appropriate size where indicated.*

# Circular letters

See pages 175, 176

2  Type the following circular letter on A4 paper. Use margins of 38 mm (1½ inches) and 25 mm (1 inch) with 12 pitch, and 25 mm (1 inch) and 13 mm (½ inch) with 10 pitch.

In reply please quote   FDW/op

4 October 1994

*[Please leave sufficient space for name & address of addressee]*

Dear Member

Branch Opening  *[centre & emphasize]*

I am pleased to write ~~and~~ to let you know that the Society has extended its service to members in your area with the opening of two branch-type agencies.

*[Leave 5 spaces]*

*[Inset 5 spaces]*

Bland Business Consultants          Bland Business Consultants
13 Fore Street                      58 Rose Drive
Eynsham                             Bampton
Oxfordshire                         Oxfordshire
OX8 2IJ                             OX18 7FR
 (Telephone: 0865 330977)            (Telephone: 0993 837654)

Full facilities for payments and withdraw[a]ls on investment accounts are available.  The agency will also be pleased to provide you with details of the Society's large range of investment, savings and mortgage lending schemes.  The new offices will be open:

    Monday to Friday - 9.00 am - 5.00 pm
    Saturday -        9.00 am - 12.00 noon

Should you require any further information, please do not hesitate to contact either our Agents on the above mentioned numbers or Alan O'Dwyer, our Manager, telephone 0865 207856.

*[These services are in addition to any existing agencies or professional advisers you may presently use.]*

Yours sincerely

Anna Brookes-Clements
Agency Administration Manager

*[give you all the help & advice you need concerning yr a/c(s) &]*

UNIT 14   See Practical Typing Exercises, Book Two, page 53, for further exercises on *Circular letters*   91

(2) 20 mins

(a) Complete the copies of the Holiday Confirmation letter you hv just typed. Send one to Dr & Mrs Raymond Morley & the other to Charity Colton. Their details are in the Data Files (filename TAKA) p. 164, but I hv got to confirm the balance th Dr & Mrs Morley owe. I wl give it to you shortly. Type an envelope to both clients.

(b) Enclose a short letter to Mrs Colton saying th I was sorry to hear th she had been unwell & th I hope she is now fully recovered after her operation & wl benefit fr her hol. in Italy. Give her my very best wishes. Don't forget the ref on both letters (my initials followed by yr own).

(3) 15 mins

I must send a memo to Janet at our Hastings Branch. ~~She is the senior travel consultant there.~~ She has asked me to let her hv details of the bookings we hv organized to Hong Kong so far this season. Apparently H.O. are undertaking some sort of survey. Tell her th so far we hv 12 clients who hv bn / are going to Hong Kong. Apologize to her for the delay in replying (pressure of work) & say th I am looking forward to seeing her @ the conference next month. Just type my first name & Rye Branch after it, as well as our ref, & the date, of course.

(Will you type this FIRST please)

## Circular letters—Tear-off portion

See page **176**

**3 (a)** Type an original and take one copy of the following circular letter with tear-off portion. Use blocked style of display with full punctuation.

Date as postmark

*Please insert a subject heading: TECHNICAL SEMINARS*

Dear Sir/Madam

Our new seminars are designed to help you discover the power and capabilities of your latest software. As a member of our previous seminars you will know how much you can learn in one day from our experts on the spot. ~~and the Technical Resource Kits which are available free — worth £50 each.~~

*Display clearly & neatly.*

Programme  8.30 - 11.00 Registration; customizing and optimizing your system for maximum performance; demonstrations.  11.00 - 11.30 Break for coffee.  11.30 - 12.30 Hands-on.  12.30-1.00 Question-and-answer session.

The afternoon seminar is similar to the morning session but of a more advanced nature, and will include file and printer sharing, networking, electronic mail, scheduling, etc.

Our Technical Seminars are popular events.  Make sure you reserve a place by completing and despatching the Priority Registration Form at the end of this letter.

Our Hotline is open from 9.0 am to 5.0 pm, Monday to Friday, *for all general enquiries. We look forward to seeing you.*

Yours faithfully

*TYPIST — please use 24-hr clock throughout.*

N J TONG (Mrs)
Conference Organizer

*Leave 4 clear spaces*

--------------------------------------------------------------

PRIORITY REGISTRATION

Yes, I would like to attend the Technical Seminar(s).  Please register me as follows:

Morning Session  ☐

Afternoon Session  ☐

*make boxes approx. 6mm (¼") square*

(Please tick as appropriate)

Title _____  Initials ____  Surname _____
Position _____  Tel. _____
*Organization* _____
*Address* _____  Postcode ____

*Display clearly using double spacing.*

**(b)** On the original only, cross out the word **Madam** and on the tear-off portion type: Simon F. Bullivant, Bridge Cottage, Hunters Close, South Chard, Somerset. TA20 2QL. Mr. Bullivant is Office Manager for Aspel Machines plc in Chard. He wishes to attend the afternoon session only. His telephone number is (0460) 411772.

UNIT 14   See Practical Typing Exercises, Book Two, page 54, for a further exercise on
*Circular letters—Tear-off portion*

① (20 mins) TYPIST – Would you set out the following letter on our headed paper w 2 extra copies, please. The date + name + address of individual clients wl be inserted later, as well as our ref + other details.

*Leave approx 2 in (51 mm) above the salutation*

Dear

Thank you for booking yr holiday at TAKABREAK. I am pleased to enclose yr holiday confirmation a/c.

N.P. [The balance of payment, £ _____, is due by _____. I can accept payment by cheque payable to TAKABREAK or by credit card.]

For yr convenience, you can also deal w yr a/c over the tel. if you are paying by credit card.

I shd point out th no further letter wl be sent, & ask you th make a careful note of the payment date.

Arrangements can be made for –
- Airport Hotel Reservations
- Car Hire
- Airport Parking.

*No. These items in some way*

Please make sure th yr passport(s) are is current & valid for the destination(s) you are visiting, including visas where nec, & th you hv had any vaccinations th may be req'd. [If you are at all uncertain abt this, or hv any queries concerning yr travel arrangements, please call in or tel. me on the above no.

Also, we hold all major currencies + hv a wide range of travellers cheques in stock. We wl be pleased to take yr order over the tel. so th yr money is ready to collect / when yr tickets arrive.

Yrs sinc

Alun Edward Cheetham
Senior Travel Consultant

*TYPIST – Insert a heading to the letter, in caps – Holiday Confirmation*

**Integrated Production Typing Project – No 4**

## Standard paragraphs (Document assembly)

*See pages 179, 207*

**4** Type the following letters from Peter Black, Supervisor, HS (ELECTRICAL) LIMITED.

(a) Ref PB/yr initials
6/7/94
Birkett & Sons 16 Commercial Str
Sheringham Norfolk NR26 8AB
Dear Sirs
Standard para SP1 Order No. 127/94
dated 3/7/94
out of stock of CAVALIER 8 fridges
delivery on 14/7/94
Standard para SP4
Yrs ffy

*(Take standard paras fr. the Data files, p. 164; filename STAN.)*

(b) Ref & date as in (a)
Richard Braintree Ltd 11 Market Place
Cromer Norfolk NR27 8BB
SP3 - letter dated 4/7/94 cheque for £2500
up to 31 May 94
still owes £3 476.82 pay by 14/7/94
SP5 - Order No. CM/119/Pur was
despatched on 5/7/94  Yrs ffy

(c) Ref & date as in (a)
Jean Robôt PLC          [ROBÔT]
1 Brook Street
Ipswich IP4 2DF
SP7 balance of £7 396.41
a/c for May '94    SP6
Yrs ffy

**UNIT 14** See Practical Typing Exercises, Book Two, page 55, for further exercises on **Standard paragraphs**

93

# INTEGRATED PRODUCTION TYPING

## TAKABREAK—TRAVEL AGENTS

## OFFICE SERVICES—REQUEST FORM

This sheet contains instructions that must be complied with when typing the documents. Read the information carefully before starting, and refer back to it frequently.

*Typist's Log Sheet*

Originator: ALUN EDWARD CHEETHAM    Designation: Senior Travel Consultant    Date: Tomorrow's    Ext No: 4

> Typists operating a word processor, or electronic typewriter with appropriate function keys, should apply the following automatic facilities: top margin; carrier return; line-end hyphenation; underline OR bold print (embolden); error correction; centring; any other relevant applications.

Remember to (a) complete the details required at the bottom of the form; (b) enter typing time per document in the appropriate column; and (c) before submitting this **Log Sheet** and your completed work, enter TOTAL TYPING TIME in the last column so that the typist's time may be charged to the originator.

| Document No | Type of document and instructions | Copies— Original plus | Input form ¶ | Typing time per document | Total typing time ¥ |
|---|---|---|---|---|---|
| 1 | Letter | 1 + 2 | MS | | |
| 2 | Details‡ to be inserted in copies of letter typed above together w. another short letter. | 1 + 2 envelopes | MS | | |
| *3 | Memo | 1 original | MS | | |
| 4 | Travel Receipt Form | 1 original | MS | | |
| 5 | Holiday Tips | 1 " | MS + print | | |
| 6 | Going on Holiday | 1 " | MS | | |
| 7 | Holiday Money (3-page leaflet) | 1 " | AT | | |
| | ‡ Some of these details are in the Data Files. I will give you the others shortly. | | | **TOTAL TYPING TIME** | |

TYPIST—please complete:
Typist's name:           Date received:           Date completed:
                         Time received:           Time completed:

> If the typed documents cannot be returned within 24 hours, the office services supervisor should inform the originator. Any item that is urgent should be marked with an asterisk (*).

¶ T = Typescript    AT = Amended Typescript    MS = Manuscript    SD = Shorthand Dictation    AD = Audio Dictation
¥ to be charged to the originator's department    AP = Amended Print.

*Typist's Log Sheet—No 4*

# SKILL BUILDING

Type each line three times and, if time permits, complete your practice by typing each group once as it appears.

Margins:
12 pitch 22–82
10 pitch 12–72

### A  Keyboarding skills

1  Speed      I trust that you will be willing to join me for lunch today.
2  Accuracy   The earthquake was extremely severe and set the town ablaze.
3  Figures    tie 583 row 492 you 697 eye 363 wit 285 your 6974 tire 5843.
4  Symbols    Invoice No 87/2/9/A for lengths of wood 12' 9" × 1' 3" × 2".

5  To develop your proofreading skills, turn to page 160, exercise 7.

### Skill measurement        Five-minute timing        Not more than five errors

S/M17  A visit to India is a unique experience because this vast          12
nation is a blend of races, religions and cultures; it is                 22
one of the most fascinating places in the world.  It is a                 33
country rich in tradition and legend, covering more than                  44
5,000 years of history.  It is a land of great variety and                56
contrast with tranquil temples and exciting bazaars, always               67
a vivid mixture of colour and sounds.                                     74

We start at Delhi where we arrive at 6 am and go straight                 86
to our hotel, the Kanishka.  Today we are free to relax and               97
wander at our leisure round the city, and after a good                   108
night's sleep we join our coach for a tour of New Delhi and              120
Old Delhi.  We visit the Red Fort, India's largest mosque,               132
the Jama Masjid, and the site where Gandhi was cremated.  We             144
also have time to see the Raj Ghat, in Old Delhi, and the                155
Qutab Minas and India Gate in New Delhi.                                 163

Next day, after breakfast, we leave by coach for Jaipur, the             175
Pink City, where we arrive in the early afternoon.  We stay              187
at the Hotel Ashok and, after checking in, go by coach to                198
the Palace of the Winds, and the grand eighteenth-century                209
observatory.  The following morning we will visit nearby                 220
Amber, a large hilltop palace-fortress which we enter in                 231
style on the back of an elephant.  The afternoon is free.                242

After breakfast we leave by coach for a visit to the Ghana               254
Bird Sanctuary, one of the world's finest bird reserves                  265
and also call at the deserted city of Fatehpur Sikri, one-               277
time capital of Emperor Akbar.  In the afternoon we go on                288
to Agra, city of the magnificent Taj Mahal, which we visit               300
in the evening when it is said to be at its most beautiful.              312
Our hotel is the Galaxy Ashok.                                           318

We leave Agra after breakfast and stop at Sikandra to see                329
the great mausoleum of Emperor Akbar.  The afternoon will                341
be free in Delhi for any last-minute shopping, and we will               352
have dinner before leaving for the airport.  This will be                364
a holiday to remember and we are sure you will wish to go                375
back and enjoy the beauty of Kashmir, the very tempting                  386
shops of Bombay, and laze on the tropical beaches of Goa.                397

(SI 1.43)

  1 | 2 | 3 | 4 | 5 | 6 | 7 | 8 | 9 | 10 | 11 | 12 |

# Bibliography

See page **168**

**4** Type the following bibliography.

TYPIST - Please type in alph order according to the author's last name.

| | |
|---|---|
| OUTHWAITE, Barbara | *Using Word Processing Effectively* pub by McGraw-Hill 1992 |
| ODDY, Jo and DUCKHAM, Rita | *Key into Europe* pub by McGraw-Hill 1991 |
| DANDO, Sylvia | *Word Processing Dictionary* pub by McGraw-Hill 1987 |
| STANANOUGHT, Joyce & Derek | *Advanced Word Processing & the Electronic Office* pub by McGraw-Hill 1986 |
| GREENFIELD, Peter | *Introduction to Computing* pub by Mc—H— '92 |
| ATTWOOD, Gaynor | *Using Spreadsheets Effectively* pub by Mc—H— '92 |
| DRUMMOND, Archie and COLES-MOGFORD, Anne | *First Course, Sixth Edition; Keyboard & Document Processing* pub by Mc—H— '93 |

## Justified right margin

See page **191**

**5** Set margins at 12 pitch 22–82, 10 pitch 12–72, and type the following on A5 landscape paper. Take the paper out of the machine and, on the typescript, mark where an extra space(s) should be inserted to justify the right margin. Insert another sheet of A5 landscape paper into the machine and type the same passage with a justified right margin.

THE ELECTRONIC ORGANIZER

Today the essential executive tool is said to be the electronic organizer. These hand-held devices range from simple machines for storing names and telephone numbers to highly complex machines one step down from lap-top computers. Common features include an address or telephone book function, a diary, a calculator, a place to store birthday lists, a world clock, etc. **N.P.** [Some machines, costing ~~approximately~~ btwn £350, will bleep to remind you of appointments, others have a touch-screen facility which can be activated with a pen. (£250 and) simply tap the pen on the screen & a command is carried out. The pen can also be used to draw pictures, such as maps & diagrams as well as write notes & tel. numbers.

UNIT 18 See Practical Typing Exercises, Book Two, page 59, for further exercises on *Justified right margin*

# PRODUCTION DEVELOPMENT

See page **196**

## Organization charts

**1** Type the following vertical organization chart on a sheet of A5 portrait paper. Set the left margin at 13(11). Turn up once before and twice after the horizontal line, and leave three spaces after the longest line in each column.

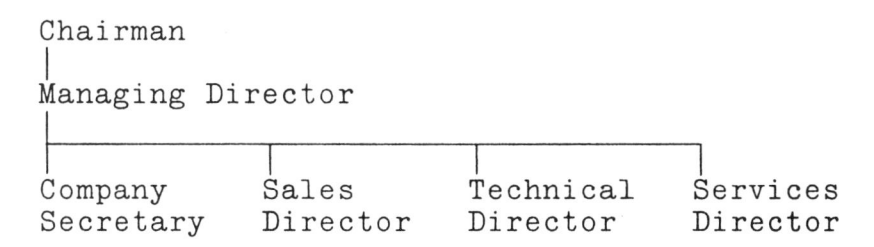

```
            Chairman
            |
            Managing Director
            |
    _____|_____
    |           |            |           |
    Company    Sales        Technical   Services
    Secretary  Director     Director    Director
```

**2** Type the following vertical organization chart on a sheet of A5 landscape paper.

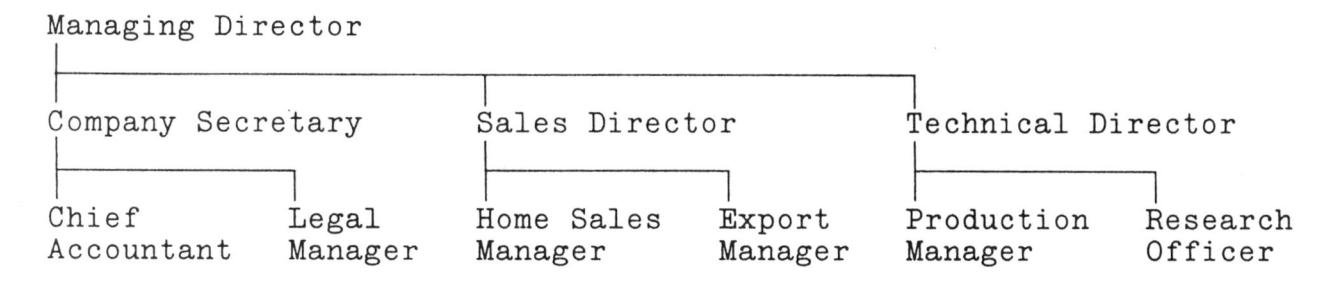

```
Managing Director
|
|_____
|                          |                           |
Company Secretary          Sales Director              Technical Director
|                          |                           |
|_____                |_____                 |_____
|         |                |         |                 |         |
Chief     Legal            Home Sales Export           Production Research
Accountant Manager         Manager    Manager          Manager    Officer
```

**3** Type the following vertical organization chart on a sheet of A5 landscape paper.

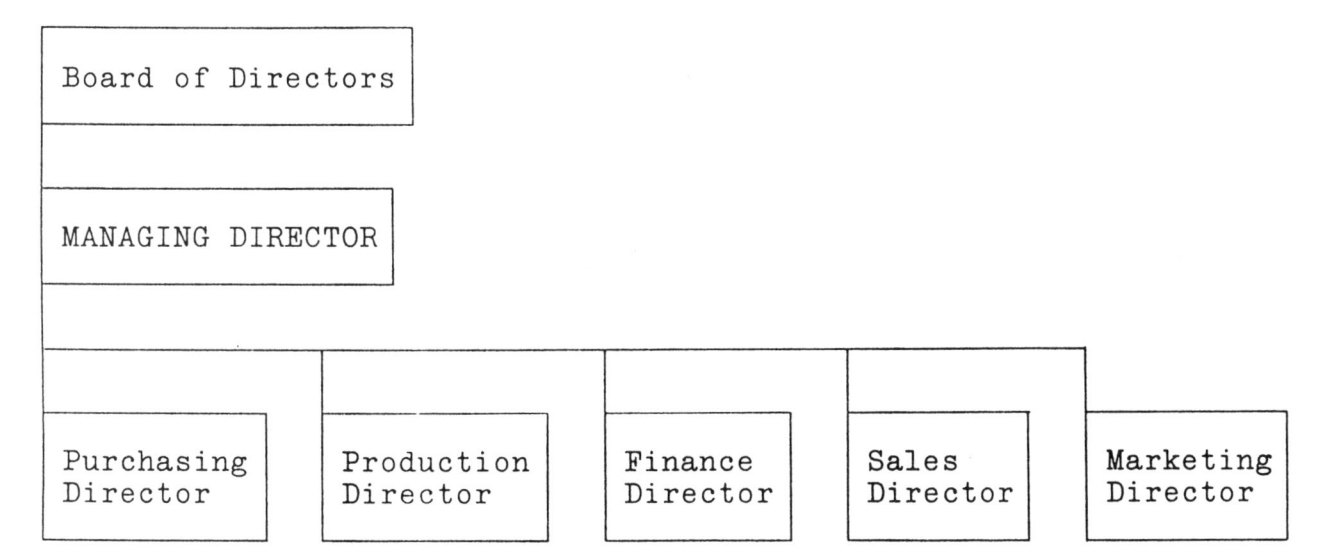

```
┌──────────────────┐
│ Board of Directors│
└──────────────────┘
         │
┌──────────────────┐
│ MANAGING DIRECTOR │
└──────────────────┘
         │
   ┌─────┬─────────┬─────────┬─────────┬─────────┐
┌──────────┐ ┌──────────┐ ┌──────────┐ ┌──────────┐ ┌──────────┐
│Purchasing│ │Production│ │ Finance  │ │  Sales   │ │Marketing │
│ Director │ │ Director │ │ Director │ │ Director │ │ Director │
└──────────┘ └──────────┘ └──────────┘ └──────────┘ └──────────┘
```

UNIT 15     *Organization charts*     95

3  Type the following on A4 paper. List the terms in alphabetical order.

# GLOSSARY OF TERMS USED IN OFFICE TECHNOLOGY*

| | |
|---|---|
| Satstream | The BT satellite telecommunications service |
| Voice commands | A means of providing instructions to a computer or word processor using a range of spoken words |
| Microwriter | A small hand-held key pad used for recording text |
| Mouse | An input device for a computer. By moving the mouse around the desk top, it is possible to move the cursor around the VDU screen. |
| Teleconferencing | A term used to cover audio or video communication among several people in remote locations |
| User-friendly | A term used to describe hardware or software which is easy for the inexperienced typist to understand and use |
| Videostream | BT's portable video conferencing system. This means that conferencing can take place in the normal office environment rather than using a special Confravision studio. |
| Identification code | A personal code made up of numbers and/or letters which indicates the identity of the operator |
| MICR (magnetic ink character reader) | A means of recognizing characters which are printed with special magnetic ink. |
| Light pen | A pen-shaped device for a computer, used to select options displayed on the screen of a VDU or for drawing shapes directly on to the screen |
| Intelpost | A service provided by the Post Office using FAX as a means of communicating information |
| Gateway | A means of allowing viewdata users access to other computers and databases |
| Data link | A telecommunications link for transmitting numbers and letters, eg, Datel |
| Compact disk | A small audio- or videodisk. It is used as an input device for a computer. |

* Extracts from **THE PRACTICAL SECRETARY** by Bea Holmes and Jan Whitehead, published by McGraw-Hill Book Company Europe.

TYPIST: - It is not necessary to justify the right margin.

**4** Type the following horizontal organization chart on a sheet of A4 portrait paper.

## G R O U P   O R G A N I Z A T I O N

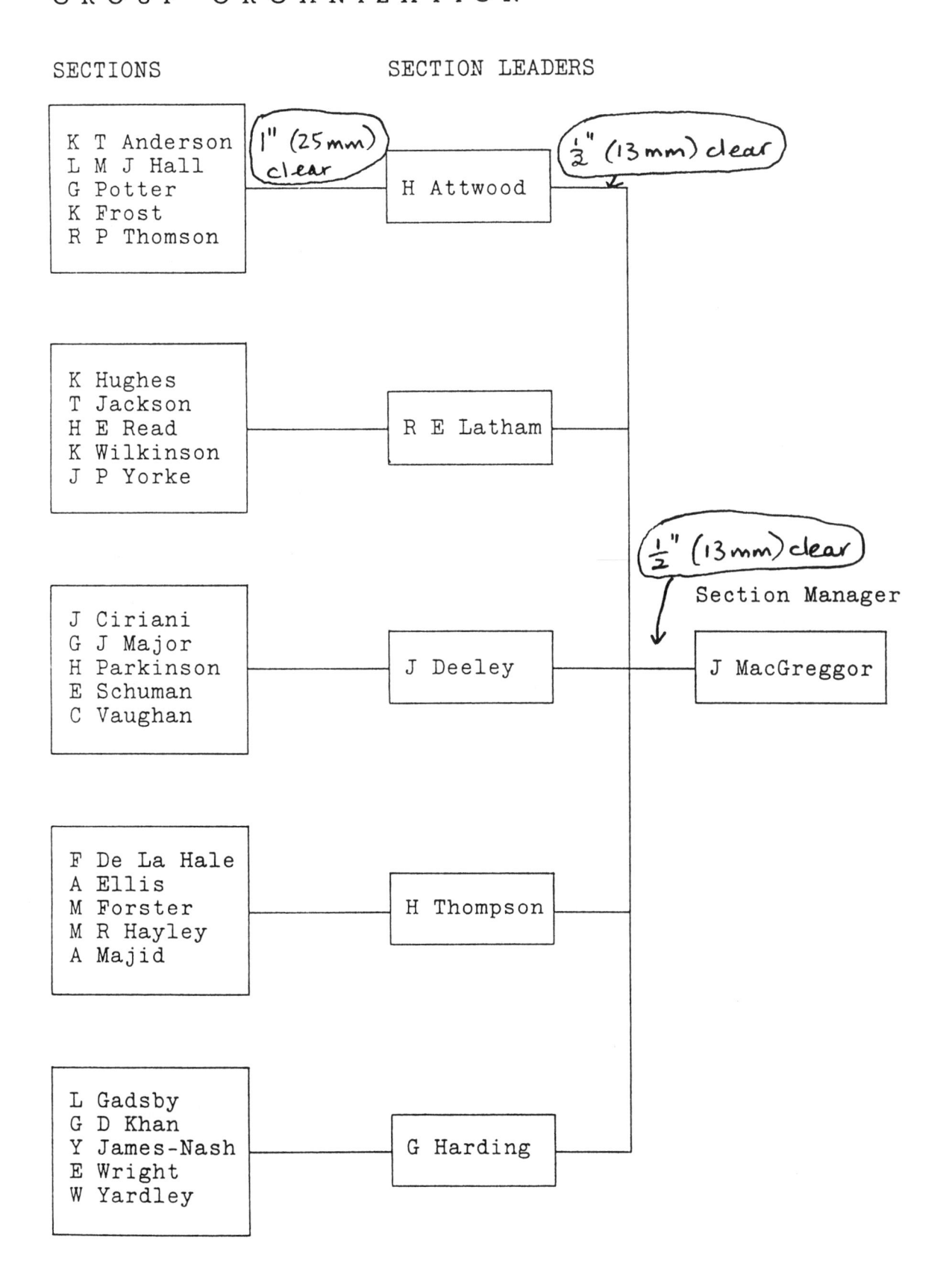

SECTIONS               SECTION LEADERS

```
┌──────────────┐
│ K T Anderson │        1" (25mm) clear           ½" (13mm) clear
│ L M J Hall   │      ┌───────────┐
│ G Potter     │──────│ H Attwood │────────────────┐
│ K Frost      │      └───────────┘                │
│ R P Thomson  │                                   │
└──────────────┘                                   │
                                                   │
┌──────────────┐                                   │
│ K Hughes     │                                   │
│ T Jackson    │      ┌───────────┐                │
│ H E Read     │──────│ R E Latham│────────────────┤
│ K Wilkinson  │      └───────────┘                │
│ J P Yorke    │                                   │
└──────────────┘                                   │
                                          ½" (13mm) clear
                                                   │
                                              Section Manager
┌──────────────┐                                   │
│ J Ciriani    │                                   │       ┌──────────────┐
│ G J Major    │      ┌───────────┐                │       │ J MacGreggor │
│ H Parkinson  │──────│ J Deeley  │────────────────┼───────│              │
│ E Schuman    │      └───────────┘                │       └──────────────┘
│ C Vaughan    │                                   │
└──────────────┘                                   │
                                                   │
┌──────────────┐                                   │
│ F De La Hale │                                   │
│ A Ellis      │      ┌───────────┐                │
│ M Forster    │──────│ H Thompson│────────────────┤
│ M R Hayley   │      └───────────┘                │
│ A Majid      │                                   │
└──────────────┘                                   │
                                                   │
┌──────────────┐                                   │
│ L Gadsby     │                                   │
│ G D Khan     │      ┌───────────┐                │
│ Y James-Nash │──────│ G Harding │────────────────┘
│ E Wright     │      └───────────┘
│ W Yardley    │
└──────────────┘
```

UNIT 15                 *Organization charts*                96

**2** Type the following in *draft* form please.

### HOW DOES THE EC WORK?

*The idea behind the commission is to have a people's Europe.*

[TYPIST - I think the printer has made a no. of errors - spelling, punctuation, etc. You watch out for them & correct them, please.]

#### 1 Your influence

As we have closer links with Europe, vital consumer protection measures originate not at Whitehall but in Brussels, the headquarters of the European Commission. However, only after it has passed through a complex system involving the European Parliament and the member state governments can a proposal become law. Can *you* have any influence on it? Perhaps you can. Anyone can lobby the Commission while proposals are formulating - individuals, consumer bodies, pressure groups, etc. They might do so because legislation is being written wh/ affects their interests, or because they feel they hv bn a victim of a breach of EC law.

#### 2 Put your views

The first stage in lobbying will usually be a letter giving your points of view or your grievance. Make sure this is short, clear and to the point. If you feel an issue needs a face-to-face meeting then contact your local *Euro-MP*. Lobbying the Parliament is made easier by the fact that most MEPs keep a staffed office in their constituencies - but it is usually better to send a letter first. If you explain your problem clearly, your *Euro-MP* will be able to advise you as to whether s/he can help.

#### 3 Your Euro-MP

As well as knowing your *Euro-MP*, it is worth finding out which members sit on which committees. Most of the Parliaments real work is done in one of a number of committees covering a particular area of legislation.

#### 4 Influences

If you feel these rights are being transgressed, then tell the commission or yr MEP.

Neither the commission nor the Parliament makes laws. This is still done by the governments of the member states whose ministers meet regularly in one of a series of *Councils*. The EC is as much concerned with the spirit of the law as the letter - indeed, its declared policy is far more about empowering the consumer than about the creation of rigid regulations. As a Community citizen you have the right to protection of your health and safety and economic interests, and to be correctly informed and represented at all levels of government.

[TYPIST - Separate sheet for the following. Rule is a single, not double line.]

### HOW EC LAW IS MADE

*The Directive* is the most common form of EC legislation. After being drafted and proposed by the Commission, it must be debated by the Parliament, which gives its opinion and may suggest amendments, and by the Council, which decides whether it will be adopted. After a Directive has been adopted, each member state must, if necessary, pass it into national law.

*The Regulation* is much less common. Available only in certain narrowly-defined legislative areas. It becomes law immediately it is adopted and does not need to be written into national laws. Recommendations go through similar procedures to the Directives, but are non-binding.

The Commission may also, from time to time, issue an *Opinion*, which is a document with no necessary legislative implications.

**5** Display the following chart on a sheet of A5 landscape paper. Leave 51 mm (2 inches) clear at the top of the page, and centre each line horizontally on the paper.

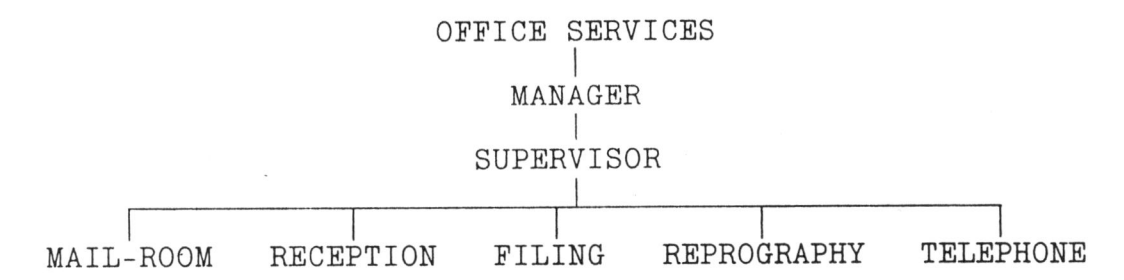

```
                          OFFICE SERVICES
                                 |
                              MANAGER
                                 |
                            SUPERVISOR
        ┌────────────┬────────────┼────────────┬────────────┐
    MAIL-ROOM    RECEPTION     FILING     REPROGRAPHY   TELEPHONE
```

**6** Type the following chart on a sheet of A5 landscape paper. Centre each line horizontally.

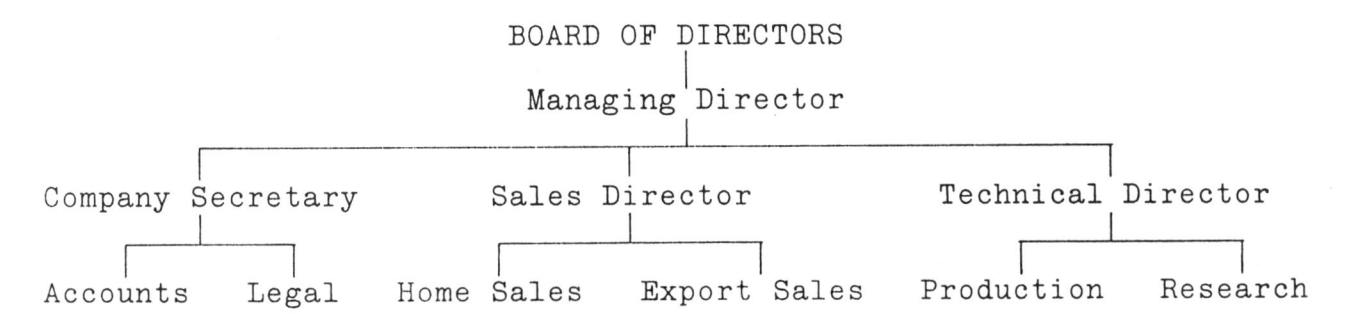

```
                          BOARD OF DIRECTORS
                                  |
                          Managing Director
        ┌─────────────────────────┼─────────────────────────┐
  Company Secretary          Sales Director           Technical Director
      ┌───┴───┐              ┌─────┴─────┐             ┌──────┴──────┐
  Accounts  Legal      Home Sales   Export Sales   Production    Research
```

**7** Type the following chart on a sheet of A4 landscape paper. Centre each line horizontally.

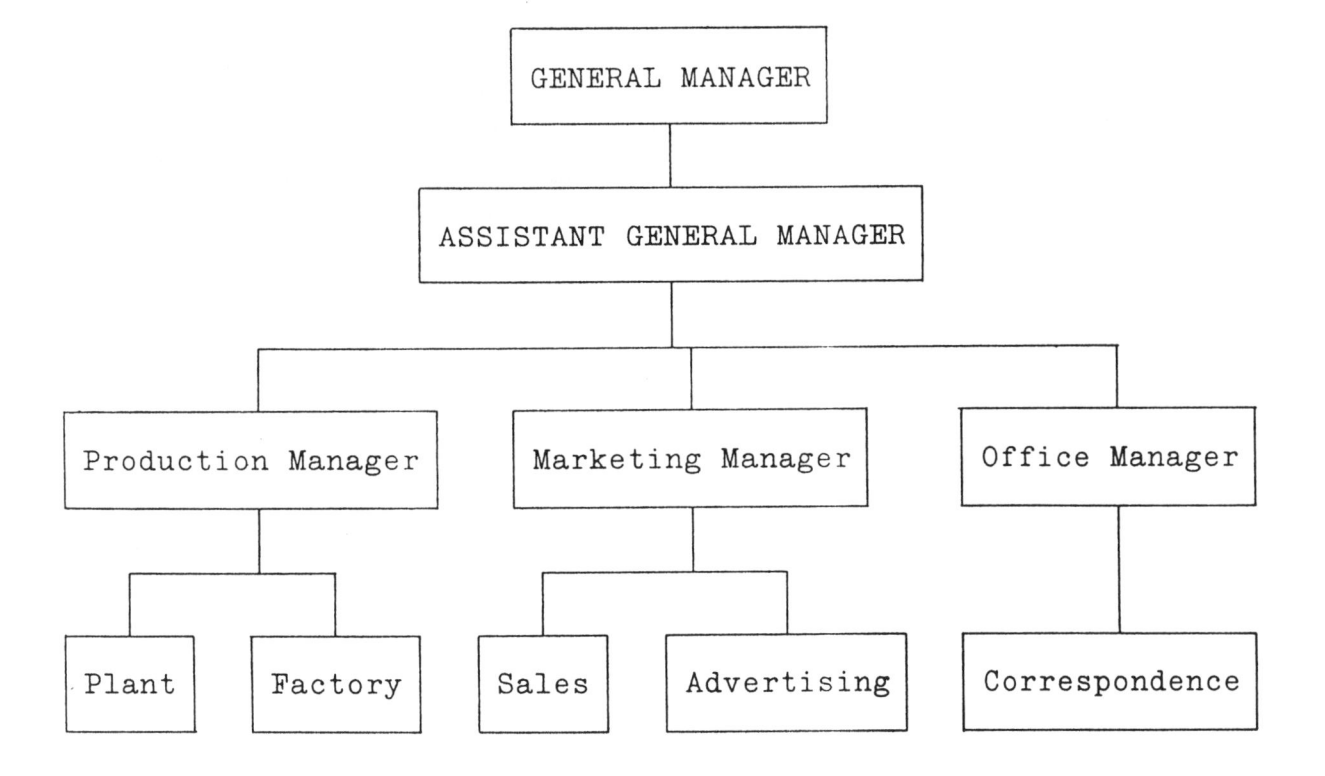

```
                    ┌─────────────────────────┐
                    │     GENERAL MANAGER     │
                    └────────────┬────────────┘
                    ┌────────────┴────────────┐
                    │ ASSISTANT GENERAL MANAGER│
                    └────────────┬────────────┘
        ┌────────────────────────┼────────────────────────┐
┌───────┴────────┐      ┌────────┴────────┐      ┌────────┴───────┐
│Production Manager│    │Marketing Manager│      │ Office Manager │
└───────┬────────┘      └────────┬────────┘      └────────┬───────┘
    ┌───┴───┐              ┌─────┴─────┐                  │
┌───┴──┐ ┌──┴────┐     ┌───┴──┐ ┌──────┴────┐       ┌─────┴──────┐
│Plant │ │Factory│     │Sales │ │Advertising│       │Correspondence│
└──────┘ └───────┘     └──────┘ └───────────┘       └────────────┘
```

UNIT 15 — *Organization charts* — 97

3 the seat height should be adjustable** and between 406 and 533 mm (16-21 inches) from the floor (necessary to meet the needs of short and tall operators and the height of the desk);

4 seat and back padding should be firm (not hard or soft) and about 25 mm (1 inch) thick;

5 seat width should be at least 457 mm (18 inches) - the thighs should not overlap the side edges;

6 seat depth (back to front) should be between 381 and 432 mm (15-17 inches);

7 the front lip of the seat should fall away slightly to reduce pressure underneath the knees and avoid circulatory problems;

8 allow btwn 200 & 300 mm (8-12") btwn seat & work surface;

9 covering shd be easy-to-clean (fabric);

10 armrests (palm rests) can give added comfort; however, great care is needed when choosing them - they must be adjustable & not restrict arm movement, e.g. too high or too low, at an angle & height similar to th of the keyboard.

Suggestions to help the operator feel more comfortable when the ideal is not available:

1 if there is not a back support, use a cushion;
2 if the seat is too low, sit on a cushion;
3 if feet do not reach the floor, use a small box or a telephone directory; better still, use a specially designed footrest placed at 60-90° angle to the lower legs;
4 stretch, twist, flex and perform any other unobtrusive exercises while sitting at the desk;
5 whenever convenient, walk around.

### Lighting

Adequate lighting can reduce glare on display screens and help avoid operator eyestrain and fatigue. Eyestrain will tire the operator more easily and, when the eyes are tired and strained, there will be more mistakes.

Many repetitive strain injuries have been linked to the poor posture of the operator because of the unsuitability of the chair, desk, and poor typing techniques.

### Helpful measures

1 adjust brightness and contrast whenever the machine is switched on;
2 have a timing device on the machine to remind the operator when to take a break;
3 if possible, do not use the screen for more than four hours a day;
4 never sit with ankles or legs crossed;
5 move screens away from the sunlight (to prevent glare) or exclude the brightness by curtains or blinds.

Ideally, to be as readable as possible, the screen should be 3 to 4 times brighter than the lighting in the room. A difficulty arises when one needs to illuminate the paper copy and, at the same time, avoid screen glare. Where possible the ceiling lights should be dim and replaced by a desk lamp with a bowl-shaped reflector.

Some vendors recommend that a screen shield (a mesh or glass device with a special coating of conductive material) should be placed in front of the screen to reduce glare and/or radiation from the VDU. At present there seems to be no absolute proof that eye problems are a result of radiation levels.

### Noise

Noise can cause stress and fatigue and noise can be a problem when using electronic office systems: the sound of printers and other automated equipment located in an open space with freestanding partitions can create a difficult situation - so much noise that operators can neither concentrate well nor communicate effectively with one another.

** Many operators prefer gas-lift height adjustment chairs.

8  Type the following chart on a sheet of A5 landscape paper.

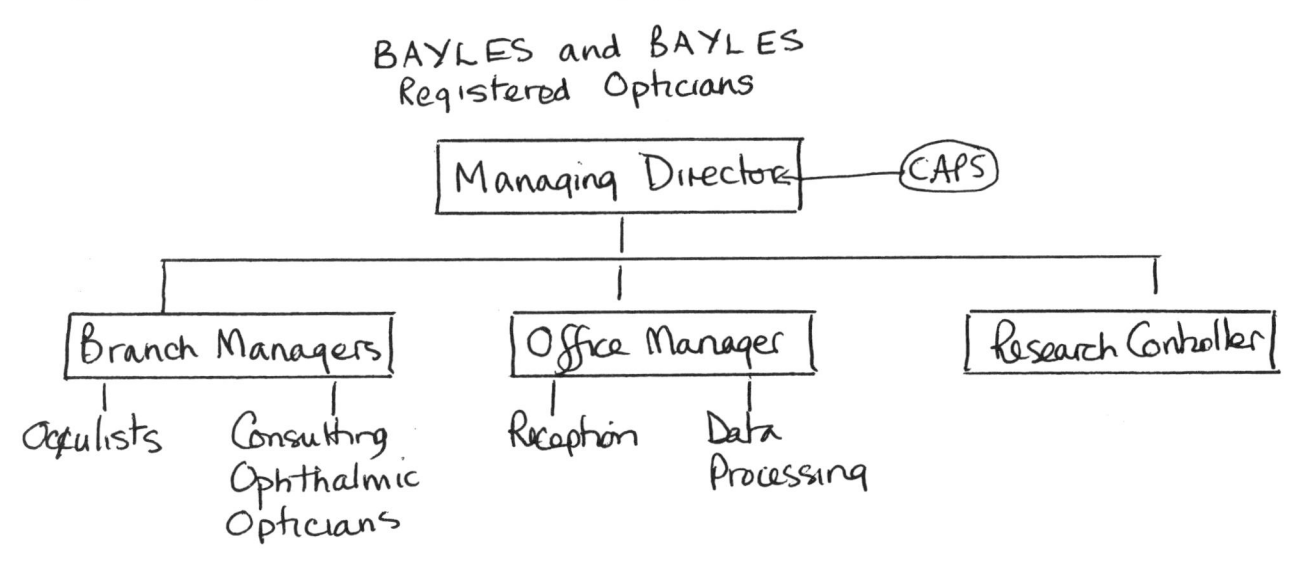

BAYLES and BAYLES
Registered Opticians

```
                    ┌───────────────────┐
                    │ Managing Director │──── (CAPS)
                    └───────────────────┘
                              │
        ┌─────────────────────┼─────────────────────┐
┌─────────────────┐  ┌─────────────────┐  ┌─────────────────────┐
│ Branch Managers │  │ Office Manager  │  │ Research Controller │
└─────────────────┘  └─────────────────┘  └─────────────────────┘
    │        │            │        │
 Oculists  Consulting   Reception  Data
           Ophthalmic              Processing
           Opticians
```

9  Type the following chart on A4 portrait paper.

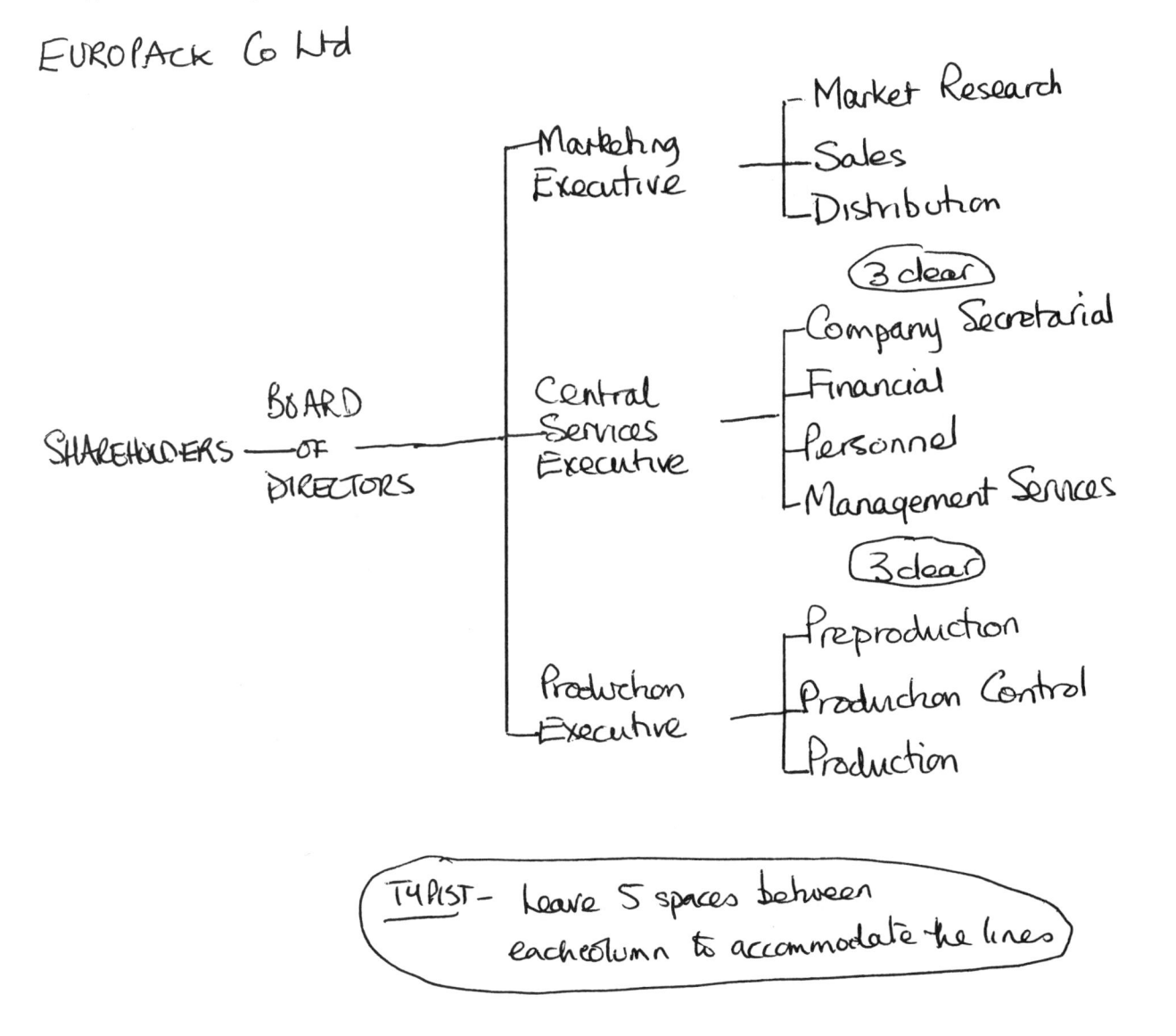

EUROPACK Co Ltd

```
                                              ┌─ Market Research
                              Marketing ──────┼─ Sales
                              Executive       └─ Distribution

                                              (3 clear)
                                              ┌─ Company Secretarial
                              Central   ──────┼─ Financial
SHAREHOLDERS ── BOARD ────────Services        ├─ Personnel
                OF            Executive       └─ Management Services
                DIRECTORS
                                              (3 clear)
                                              ┌─ Preproduction
                              Production ─────┼─ Production Control
                              Executive       └─ Production
```

(TYPIST — Leave 5 spaces between each column to accommodate the lines)

## Typing from amended print

See page 216

1 Type a correct copy on A4 paper in single spacing. The first page is number 12 and subsequent pages should follow in numerical order.

Type across the page, NOT in 2 columns. Use single spacing w. double btwn numbered items. Emphasize emboldened words in some way.

# THE OFFICE ENVIRONMENT*

## Ergonomics and repetitive strain injury

Adapting the working conditions, environment, and equipment design to suit the workers is called **ergonomics.** The psychological and physical well-being of workers is the most important consideration in planning an ergonomically designed office, because any piece of equipment or furniture will fail in its ultimate function if a person does not feel comfortable when using it.

Legislation such as the **Offices, Shops and Railway Premises Act 1936** [1963] and the **Health and Safety at Work Act 1975** were forerunners of a number of official regulations safeguarding employees' rights.

[There are a no. of factors that have led to better office furniture + equipment design:]

1 technology has changed the office workers' way of life;
2 more people are working in offices than in any other kind of work environment;
3 because of the immediate availability of information from modern electronic systems, there is less need for office personnel to move about;
4. Office productivity levels must be raised to compete effectively in world markets;
4 many health complaints from keyboard operators relate to back pain, repetitive strain injury (RSI) and fatigue;
5 legal issues are receiving the attention of employers who want to reduce the possibility of liability claims;
6 there will be office inspections to see that legislation has been complied with.

[Renumber accordingly]

A new European Community Directive (Directive 90/270/EEC May 1990) making the employer legally responsible for the safety, health and comfort of office workers came into force in December 1992 but will not be fully implemented until late 1996.

Some of the recommendations for keyboard operators are:

1 the height of the desk should suit the operator;
2 the desk surface should not reflect light;
3 VDU screens should be separate from the keyboard;
VDU screens should be adjustable;
keyboards should be adjustable for slope and height;
height of chairs should be adjustable;
the employer should arrange, and pay for, eye tests and spectacles (where required);
staff using VDUs should be given regular breaks away from the screen;
noise, temperature and humidity should be regulated.

[Number ea. new point]

A great deal of research has taken place in an endeavour to find the most suitable designs for office furniture and equipment and there are variations in what is thought to be the 'best'; therefore, most authorities define their specifications within top and lower limits.

**The chair** - a suitable chair is essential - not only for work, but also for health. A posture chair is best because it can be adjusted so that the operator can maintain correct posture when seated at the keyoard.

1 a swivel type with 5 or more castors (with only four castors the chair topples over more easily);

2 the angle, height, and tension of the back support should be adjustable and give support to the lower and middle part of the back;

* Taken from: FIRST COURSE, Sixth Edition, HANDBOOK, SOLUTIONS and RESOURCE MATERIAL by Archie Drummond + Anne Coles-Mogford

# Flow charts

See page 184

**10** Type the following simple flow chart on A5 landscape paper.

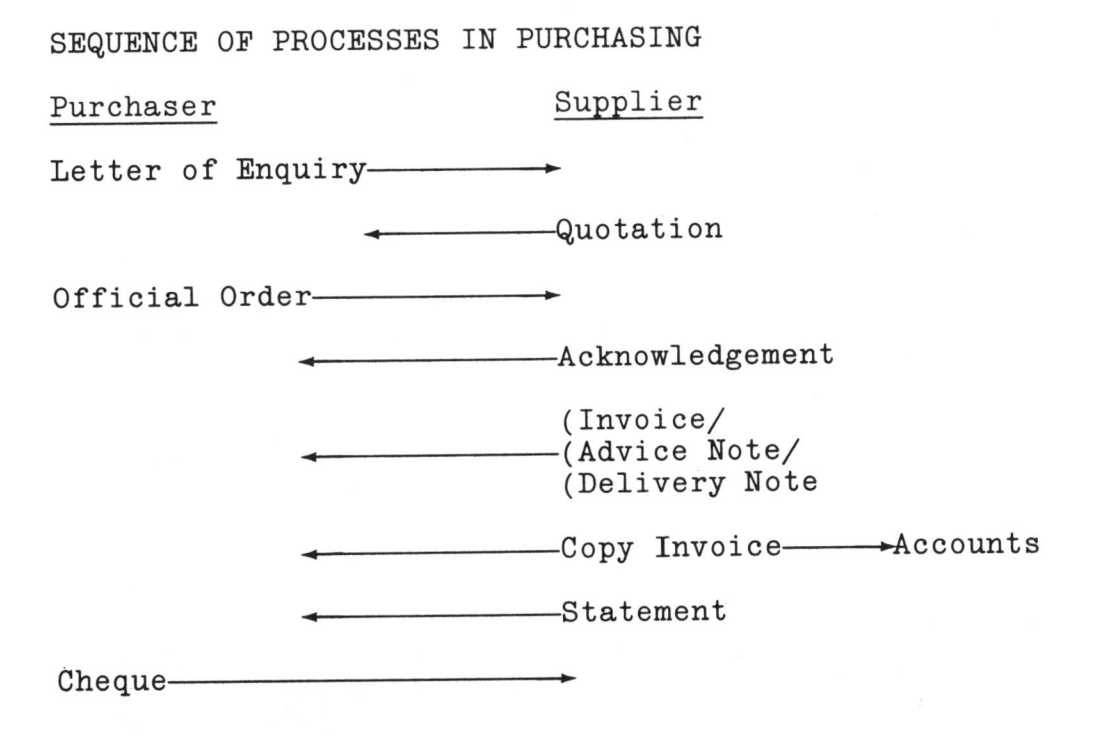

```
        SEQUENCE OF PROCESSES IN PURCHASING

        Purchaser                        Supplier

        Letter of Enquiry ─────────►

                            ◄───────── Quotation

        Official Order ──────────►

                            ◄───────── Acknowledgement

                                       (Invoice/
                            ◄───────── (Advice Note/
                                       (Delivery Note

                            ◄───────── Copy Invoice ─────► Accounts

                            ◄───────── Statement

        Cheque ──────────────────►
```

**11** Type the following flow chart on A5 landscape paper.

INFORMATION PROCESSING

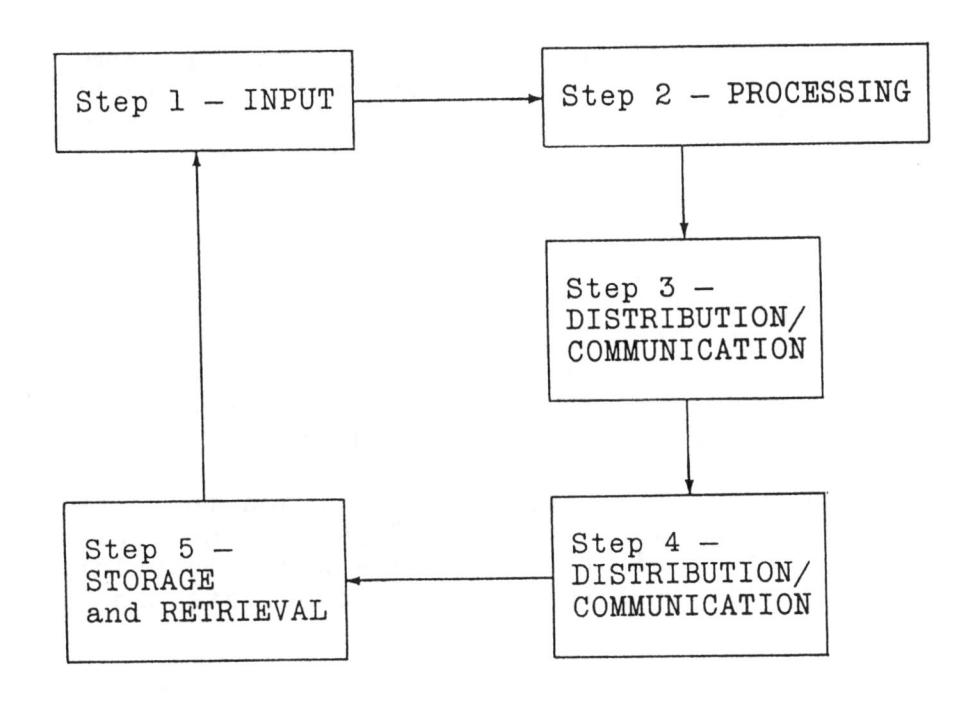

```
    ┌──────────────────┐         ┌──────────────────────┐
    │ Step 1 – INPUT   │────────►│ Step 2 – PROCESSING  │
    └──────────────────┘         └──────────────────────┘
             ▲                              │
             │                              ▼
             │                   ┌──────────────────────┐
             │                   │ Step 3 –             │
             │                   │ DISTRIBUTION/        │
             │                   │ COMMUNICATION        │
             │                   └──────────────────────┘
             │                              │
             │                              ▼
    ┌──────────────────┐         ┌──────────────────────┐
    │ Step 5 –         │◄────────│ Step 4 –             │
    │ STORAGE          │         │ DISTRIBUTION/        │
    │ and RETRIEVAL    │         │ COMMUNICATION        │
    └──────────────────┘         └──────────────────────┘
```

UNIT 15 — Flow charts

# SKILL BUILDING

Type each line three times and, if time permits, complete your practice by typing each group once as it appears.

Margins:
12 pitch 22–82
10 pitch 12–72

### A  Keyboarding skills

1 Speed     Please sign this letter before forwarding it to your banker.
2 Accuracy  The exquisite artwork was ruined by the over-zealous guards.
3 Figures   your 6974 were 2343 pert 0345 ripe 4803 wore 2943 port 0945.
4 Symbols   Now!  Order 10 sq m (107.64 sq ft) for £42 less 2% discount.

### Skill measurement

Five-minute timing                                Not more than five errors

S/M20  Shorthand writers should always be ready to take dictation.    12
       A notebook should be easily available at all times to take     24
       instant dictation.  If you place a rubber band around the      35
       used pages, the first blank sheet will be found quickly.       47
       A pen or pencil can be slotted through the rubber band, and    60
       the book placed by the side of your typewriter ready for use   72
       as soon as you are asked to take dictation.                    81

       When you are taking dictation, concentrate on the content of   93
       the matter being dictated.  For easy reference, date each     105
       page of your shorthand notebook at the bottom.  Always have   117
       a wide margin so that you can mark very clearly any special   129
       instructions such as the urgency of a particular document,    141
       items to be verified, etc.  If the dictator is accustomed     152
       to giving additional instructions during or after dictating,  164
       it may be a good plan to have an extra shorthand notebook     176
       specifically for the purpose of making notes.  Never rely on  188
       your memory.                                                  190

       If additions have to be made to your shorthand notes, each    202
       one should be numbered and a numbered caret sign inserted in  214
       your notes at the appropriate point.                          221

       If the dictator pauses in the dictation to find some notes    233
       or to consider a point, use the time beneficially by reading  245
       through the shorthand already taken down — do not yawn, tap   257
       the desk with your pen or stare at the dictator.              266

       If you feel at all unsure about being able to transcribe the  278
       notes accurately, clear up any queries immediately.  It is    290
       just possible that the dictator may be leaving the office    301
       for the remainder of the day and the finished documents may  313
       be urgent.  If you cannot read your notes immediately after  325
       the dictation, it is unlikely that you will be able to do so 337
       later on in the day.  Ask if you may read through any part   348
       of your notes about which you feel unsure.                   356

       Shorthand, like typewriting, is a skill and the clarity with 368
       which you write and the accuracy of your transcript will be  379
       dependent on dedicated practice and a wide vocabulary.  In   391
       addition, you must be able to spell, punctuate and use words 403
       correctly.                                          (SI 1.44) 405

       1  |  2  |  3  |  4  |  5  |  6  |  7  |  8  |  9  |  10  |  11  |  12  |

**12** Type the following chart on A4 paper.

STEPS IN SECURELY WRAPPING A PARCEL

* String, cellulose tape and scissors.
  Wrapping paper of suitable size.

↓

[Position parcel on wrapping paper.]

↓

Wrap lengthwise. ─────→ Secure with tape.
Edges should over-
lap about an inch.

↓

Tuck in ends and ←───── Make neat folds at
secure with tape.        corners.

↓

Loop string around ────→ Pull tight and
one end of parcel,       knot.
then lengthwise.

↓

Pull tight and ←───── Loop string around
knot.                 the other end of
                      parcel, then
                      lengthwise.

↓

Weigh and affix
correct postage.

───────────────────────────────

* Today, few people use string — just the
  sealing tape; however, a strong string
  makes a heavy parcel easier to carry.


**13** Type the following chart on A5 landscape paper.

ROUTEING OF A LETTER AND COPIES

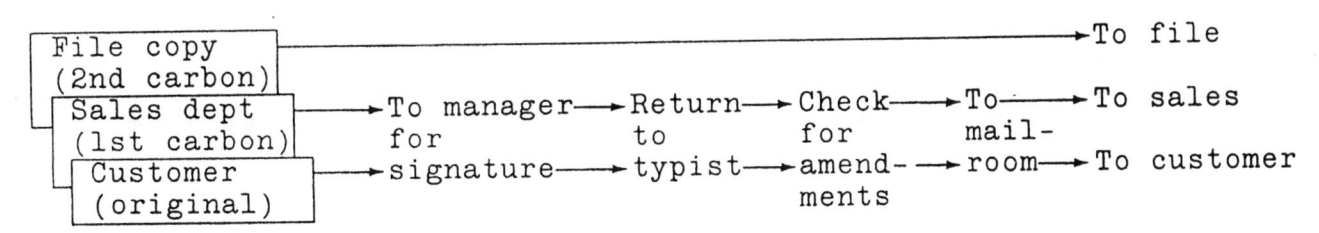

[File copy (2nd carbon)] ──────────────────────────────────────→ To file
[Sales dept (1st carbon)] ──→ To manager ──→ Return ──→ Check ──→ To ──────→ To sales
[Customer (original)]          for            to         for       mail-
                          ──→ signature ──→ typist ──→ amend- ──→ room ──→ To customer
                                                       ments

---

UNIT 15                    *Flow charts*                    100

3  Type an original and two copies of the following on A4 paper. Use double spacing for the main part.

## ELIZABETH BARRETT (BROWNING)

<u>England's greatest female poet</u>

Elizabeth Barrett was born in London abt 1806. She had an extraordinary education & studied Greek, Latin, philosophy & the sciences.

Her name became famous for various important translations she undertook. In 1823 she became ill & moved to Torquay so tt she wd benefit from the milder climate. Here a terrible calamity took place; her favourite brother & two of his friends were drowned when their boat sank. This event so shocked Miss Barrett th, for some yrs afterwards, she lived a very quiet life reading & writing poetry.

In 1846 she married Robert Browning, also a poet, & together they retired to Italy where she lived until her death in 1861.

### FLUSH, MY DOG*

"Yet, my little sportive friend,
Little is't to such an end
That I should praise thy rareness!
Other dogs may be thy peers
Haply in these drooping ears,
And in this glossy fairness.

But of <u>thee</u> it shall be said,
This dog watched beside a bed
Day and night unweary —
Watched within a curtained room,
Where no sunbeam brake the gloom
Round the sick & dreary..."

(TYPIST: Indent the 3rd & 6th lines in ea verse 2 spaces.)

---

* An extract from one of Elizabeth Barrett Browning's poems.

---

**17** Key in document 3 (filename POET) for 15-pitch print-out. When you have completed this task, save under filename POET, and print out original and two copies. Recall the document and follow the instructions for text editing on page 163.

**14** Type the following flow chart on A4 portrait paper.

## THE EC SYSTEM

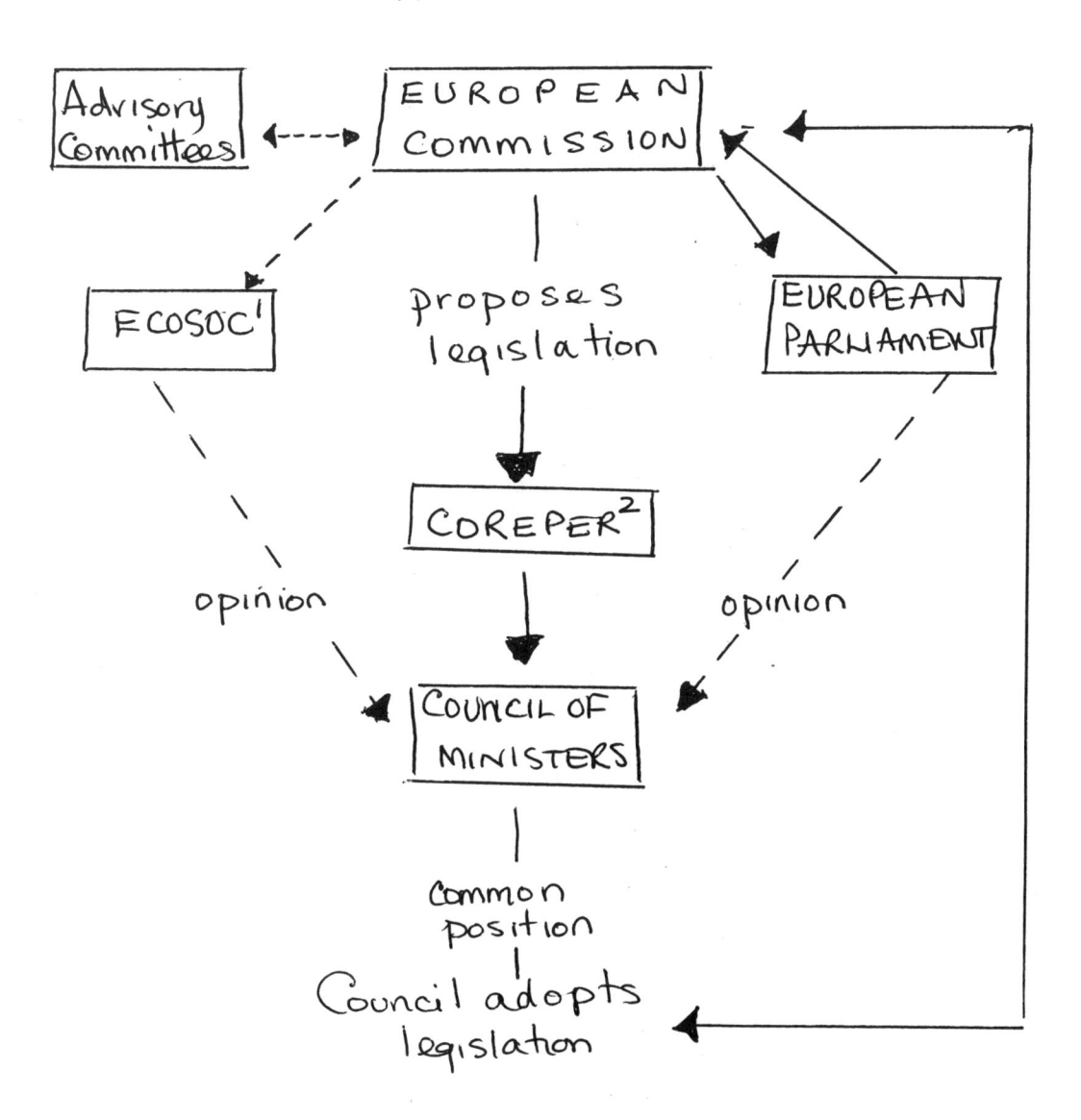

```
[Advisory Committees] <---> [EUROPEAN COMMISSION] <---> [EUROPEAN PARLIAMENT]
         |                         |                           |
         v                    proposes                          |
       [ECOSOC¹]              legislation                       |
          \                        |                           /
           \                       v                          /
    opinion \                 [COREPER²]                     / opinion
             \                     |                        /
              \                    v                       /
               `------>  [COUNCIL OF MINISTERS]  <--------'
                                   |
                                common
                                position
                                   |
                            Council adopts
                              legislation  <-----------------
```

1  The Economic & Social Cttee is an advisory body consisting mainly of reps of employers & trade unions.

2  The Cttee of Permanent reps of the Member States.

RODNEY    Actually the more you travel the less you see & understand. (He laughs.) Our writers, the Brontës, hardly travelled at all, & lived nearly all their lives in a remote Yorkshire village, yet they knew all abt human nature.
(Mikhail, the mysterious Russian, approaches the little group by the window, & they fall silent, because they are suspicious of him.)

MIKHAIL   I want to know all abt yr London... Is it near the Houses of Parliament where yr Prime Minister lives in his Downing St.? I want to see for myself.
(They all stare at him suspiciously.)

TANIA     How I wd love to see London. It is impossible for us here in Russia.

JAMES     You must come when you get yr freedom.

TANIA     Ah... but wl it ever be.

## Poetry

See pages 198 199

2  Type the following on A5 portrait paper.

```
              LIFE'S RICH FEAST

              I owe you more than I can say
              You arrived like a free spirit
              As from another world.

              Your beauty dazzled
              Your energy revived me
              Your love enfolded.

              I was alone and lonely
              Sick at heart
              And tired of mind.

              The world and everything therein
              Had gone wrong for me
              My emotions drained.

              You gave me back today
              And tomorrow
              - and life's rich feast.

                         J. W. D. DAVIES
```

UNIT 17                **Plays and Poetry**                116

# INTEGRATED PRODUCTION TYPING

## EURO INSURANCE PLC

### OFFICE SERVICES—REQUEST FORM

This sheet contains instructions that must be complied with when typing the documents. Read the information carefully before starting, and refer back to it frequently.

**Typist's Log Sheet**

Originator: *Tom R TEMPEST*   Designation: *Chief Underwriter*   Date: *Today's*   Ext No *401*

> Typists operating a word processor, or electronic typewriter with appropriate function keys, should apply the following automatic facilities: top margin; carrier return; line-end hyphenation; underline OR bold print (embolden); error correction; centring; any other relevant applications.

Remember to (a) complete the details required at the bottom of the form; (b) enter typing time per document in the appropriate column; and (c) before submitting this **Log Sheet** and your completed work, enter TOTAL TYPING TIME in the last column so that the typist's time may be charged to the originator.

| Document No | Type of document and instructions | Copies— Original plus | Input form ¶ | Typing time per document | Total typing time ¥ |
|---|---|---|---|---|---|
| ① | 2-page letter | 1+1 | MS | | |
| ② | Table of cost areas + an envelope | 1 original | MS & print | | |
| ③ | Article about Security Discount | 1 original | AT | | |
| ④ | Flow chart on Car Safety | 1 Original | MS | | |
| ⑤ | Postcard - Don't type this until I have checked the figures. | 1 Original | MS | | |
| *⑥ | Memo | 1+1 | MS | | |
| ⑦ | Circular Letter | 1 original | MS | | |
| | | | | TOTAL TYPING TIME | |

TYPIST—please complete:
Typist's name:                 Date received:                 Date completed:
                               Time received:                 Time completed:

> If the typed documents cannot be returned within 24 hours, the office services supervisor should inform the originator. Any item that is urgent should be marked with an asterisk (*).

¶T = Typescript     AT = Amended Typescript     MS = Manuscript     SD = Shorthand Dictation     AD = Audio Dictation
¥ to be charged to the originator's department     AP = Amended Print.

*Typist's Log Sheet—No 3*

# PRODUCTION DEVELOPMENT

## Plays

See page **198**

1 Display the following play on four separate sheets of A4 paper.

```
                T H E   F R E E D O M   T O   T R A V E L
```
⎫
⎬ (TITLE PAGE)
⎭

BY

JOHN W DOSSETT-DAVIES

*(2nd page)*

TIME: The 1970s

SCENE: An apartment in central Leningrad. The room is furnished with dark, heavy furniture, but there are bright, modern paintings on the walls. A cold buffet of cooked meats etc, is laid out on a table in the centre of the room. The vodka is flowing freely. There are 12 people in the room and the party has been in progress for about an hour.

*(3rd page)*

CHARACTERS: James (an Englishman, about 40)
Rodney (his friend of a similar age)
Tania (a Russian female engineer of about 25)
Olga (her friend, a poet, about 30)
Mikhail (a mysterious, middle-aged Russian)

⎫ *(Double)*

Act I - Scene 1  ← *(u/sc)*

THE FREEDOM TO TRAVEL

<u>It is a Tuesday evening about 10.00 pm. Tania approaches James. She is a well-built young woman, and she is clearly fascinated by this visitor from the West.</u>

TANIA        Are you also like the others, a social worker? <u>(James nods.)</u>

JAMES        And you?

TANIA        I am a lady engineer.

JAMES        A lady engineer!

TANIA        Yes. I design *electric* power stations.

JAMES        I've never met a lady engineer who designs power stations.

TANIA        You have been to many, many countries? Tell me about them. I want to know everything. <u>(She speaks earnestly.)</u>

*(James moves over to the window & gestures at the snowy scene outside.)*

JAMES        You tell me about Leningrad. This is one of the most ~~fascinating~~ ~~incredible~~ cities in the world.

TANIA        You have a saying 'travel broadens the mind'.

---

UNIT 17        *Plays*        115

(1) – 25 mins   Top + 1 on headed paper, please

In reply please quote TRT/PJG/46218
Date as postmark

TYPIST – The name & address of addressee wl be inserted here later.

Dear Policyholder

Home Protection Policy ← Emphasize

We are pleased to inform you th our new Home Protection Policy replaces yr existing Home Insurance Policy. This new Policy has bn designed to meet current market trends as well as the needs of Policyholders. As you wl see from the attached ~~accompanying~~ literature, this is a very attractive package with much more to offer than policies available thru other cos. Insert "A"

To enable you to compare the differences between the old & new policys, & we hope you wl find the enclosed Summary of Main Changes useful.

Rate Changes

In line with other cos, we have experienced a dramatic increase in the claims rec'd for subsidence, arson & theft.

Yr new Policy covers

Double please:
- Fire
- Lightning
- Explosion
- Earthquake
- Storm & Flood
- Subsidence
- Theft
- Escape of Water or Oil
- Falling trees, branches or aerials

We hv, therefore, bn forced to increase our rates & min premiums for /

Integrated Production Typing Project – No 3

# SKILL BUILDING

Type each line three times and, if time permits, complete your practice by typing each group once as it appears.

Margins:
12 pitch 22–82
10 pitch 12–72

### A  Keyboarding skills

1  Speed     They will try to agree on a time for the next board meeting.
2  Accuracy  That equipment is part of our integrated information system.
3  Figures   Invoice No 1234/89 is for £345.67 less £87.65 – 10 May 1989.
4  Symbols   King & Co give 2½% discount.  She said, "Call soon – today."

5  To develop your proofreading skills, turn to page 160, exercise 8.

### Skill measurement          Five-minute timing          Not more than five errors

S/M19  You will find Mexico surprising and exciting.  An exuberant    12
and fascinating country bridging 2 continents with a great          24
variety of scenery: a panoramic mixture of high mountains,          35
secluded valleys, deserts, sundrenched beaches and tropical         47
forests.  It is a land steeped in history and there are more        59
pyramids than there are in Egypt.  There are large ruins            70
with secrets yet to be unlocked and vast deserted cities            81
which were in being when Europe was still in the Dark Ages.         93
You will find the echoes of over 300 years of Spanish rule,        105
and enjoy a wealth of folklore.  There is a marvellous array      117
of handicrafts ranging from the brightly coloured, handwoven      129
textiles to gold and silver copies of ancient treasures.  On      141
your Mexican tour you can be sure that each and every day         153
will be filled with memorable sights.                             160

Mexico City lies in a mountain-ringed valley nearly a mile        172
and a half above sea level.  This, the oldest city in the         184
Americas, has something for everyone – Aztec ruins, baroque       196
churches, modern buildings, lively markets and several fine       208
museums.  You can explore the city's lovely old colonial          219
quarters and see the celebrated floating gardens.                 229

Taxco is one of the most delightful colonial towns full of        241
olde-worlde charm.  Its narrow cobbled streets and tranquil       253
little squares are set on a steep hillside, and the richly        264
decorated twin towers of the church rise high above the red-      276
roofed houses.  The town is still renowned for its silver-        288
smiths, and you will have the opportunity to visit many           298
shops which sell silver.                                          304

While in Mexico you may wish to visit Brazil which is a vast      316
country occupying about half the continent of South America       328
and which is so enormous that all of Western Europe could         339
fit into it and still leave room to spare.  There is a whole      351
world of contrast within its borders – scented orchids bloom      363
in the tropical heat of the Amazon jungle while Rio's famous      375
beach is a mecca for sun, sand and sea lovers.  You will          386
enjoy the different facets of this delightful country.            397

(SI 1.44)

1 | 2 | 3 | 4 | 5 | 6 | 7 | 8 | 9 | 10 | 11 | 12

premiums for certain areas where ~~we find~~ claims experience has bn adverse. (Insert "B") You wl note th even with our rate changes we remain more competitive than other major cos. [We wd like to take this opp to thank you for yr continued support. Please be assured ~~insured~~ of our endeavours to give you the best poss service.

Yrs sinc

Tom R T—
Chief Underwriter

PS   Euro Insurance offers you many valuable extras. Please see p3 of the enclosed booklet.

"A"  , and a wider range of cover than our existing contract.

"B"  The new rates also reflect an increase in premium to meet the extra cover given under the new Policy.

2 — (35 mins)
TYPIST — From the attached list please select the items marked # and type them, using the display given in the example below.

COST AREAS

| Postcode Area | Contents Area | Buildings Area |
|---|---|---|
| LEEDS | | |
| (Inset 2 spaces →) LS1 | F | Z |
| LS7 | H | Z |

Integrated Production Typing Project—No 3

# Last Will and testament

See pages 191, 192

2. Type the following Will on A4 paper in double spacing, except for the attestation clause which should be typed in single spacing. Fold a separate sheet of A4 paper once, left edge to right edge, and endorse.

THIS IS THE LAST WILL AND TESTAMENT of me HAROLD PIERRE LUÇON of The Old Priory Blackfriars Road Lichfield Staffordshire WS13 6NQ.---------

1. I HEREBY REVOKE all former Wills and testamentary dispositions whatsoever heretofore made by me and declare this to be my last Will and Testament.------------------------------------------------------

2. I HEREBY APPOINT my brother LOUIS LUÇON of 47 North Avenue Lichfield Staffordshire WS13 7BG and REES STUART MCINTYRE of Cavendish Buildings Lichfield Staffordshire WS13 9EA Solicitor to be Executors and Trustees of this my Will and I give to each of them if he shall prove my Will the sum of One thousand pounds.------------------------

3. I give to my cousin VALÉRIE LUÇON of 113 Fir Tree Avenue Tile Hill Coventry CV6 2FR all my personal chattels as defined by statute contained in my bungalow in Blackfriars Road aforesaid.---------------

4. SUBJECT thereto and to the payment of my debts and funeral and testamentary expenses I DEVISE AND BEQUEATH all my real and personal estate wheresoever and whatsoever not hereby otherwise disposed of unto my said Brother LOUIS LUÇON absolutely.-------------------------

5. I declare that the said REES STUART MCINTYRE shall be entitled to charge and be paid all professional or other charges for any business or act done by him or his firm in connection with this my Will and the trusts thereof including acts which an Executor could have done personally

IN WITNESS whereof I have hereunto set my hand this *sixth* day of *September* One thousand nine hundred and ninety-four.------

Signed by the said HAROLD PIERRE LUÇON )
as and for his last Will and Testament )
in the presence of us both present at )
the same time who in his presence at )
his request and in the presence of each )
other have hereunto subscribed our names )
as witnesses:- )

*TYPIST - You will need the Solicitor's address for the endorsement -
Rees Stuart McIntyre
Solicitor
89 Roman Way
LICHFIELD Staffs WS14 1AA*

UNIT 16 — Last Will and testament — 113

| Postcode Area | Contents Area | Buildings Area | Postcode Area | Contents Area | Buildings Area | Postcode Area | Contents Area | Buildings Area |
|---|---|---|---|---|---|---|---|---|
| **LINCOLN** | | | **MANCHESTER** | | | **LEEDS** | | |
| LN1 | C | 4 | M1 | J | 2 | LS10 | F | 2 |
| LN2 | A | 5 | M2 | J | 2 | LS11 | G | 2# |
| LN3 | B | 4 | M3 | J | 3 | LS12 | F | 2 |
| LN4 | B | 5 | M4 | J | 2 | LS13 | F | 2# |
| LN5 | B | 3 | M5 | J | 2 | LS14 | F | 2# |
| LN6 | A | 3 | M6 | J | 2 | LS15 | E | 2 |
| LN7 | A | 4 | M7 | J | 3 | LS16 | E | 2 |
| LN8 | A | 5 | M8 | J | 3 | LS17 | F | 2# |
| LN9 | A | 2 | | | | LS18 | E | 2 |
| LN10 | A | 3 | **OLDHAM** | | | LS19 | F | 2# |
| LN11 | A | 3 | OL1 | H | 2 | LS20 | E | 2 |
| LN12 | A | 3 | OL2 | F | 2 | LS21 | D | 2 |
| LN13 | A | 3 | OL3 | F | 2 | | | |
| | | | OL4 | H | 2 | **WAKEFIELD** | | |
| **LEEDS** | | | OL5 | E | 2# | WF4 | C | 2 |
| LS1 | F | 2# | OL6 | G | 2 | WF5 | C | 2# |
| LS2 | F | 2 | OL7 | F | 2 | WF6 | C | 2# |
| LS3 | G | 2 | OL8 | H | 2 | WF7 | C | 2 |
| LS4 | G | 2 | OL9 | G | 3# | WF8 | C | 3# |
| LS5 | F | 2 | | | | WF9 | D | 2 |
| LS6 | H | 2 | **WAKEFIELD** | | | WF10 | D | 2 |
| LS7 | H | 2# | WF1 | D | 2# | WF11 | D | 2 |
| LS8 | H | 2 | WF2 | D | 2 | WF12 | C | 2 |
| LS9 | F | 2 | WF3 | C | 2 | WF13 | C | 2# |

TYPIST — When you have typed the selected items from the above table, wd you please send them to Mr & Mrs F Rollinson, together with a copy of the letter you hv just typed. You w/ need to type Mr & Mrs Rollinson's name & address on the letter as well as the envelope. You w/ find it in the Data Files (filename EURO) on page 163.

**Integrated Production Typing Project — No 3**

9. The Trustees agree that the Tenant may bring to and keep at the said property personal possessions including items of furniture carpets and household effects and the Tenant hereby acknowledges that he will be solely responsible for their upkeep and insurance

10. The Trustees hereby agree to keep the said property comprehensively insured to its full replacement value and further to keep insured against loss or damage by fire and other risks usually insured against all the items enumerated in the Schedule attached hereto

11. The Tenant hereby agrees to re-imburse the Trustees the amount of the annual premium paid by them for keeping the said property and contents insured

AS WITNESS the hands of the parties hereto the day and year first before written

SIGNED BY CALUM ST ANDREW-GREGORY

in the presence of:-




SIGNED BY KARIN ELIZABETH HENDERSON

in the presence of:-




SIGNED BY ALEXANDER BRUCE MCKAY

in the presence of:-

                    EURO INSURANCE PLC

                    SECURITY DISCOUNT

Euro Insurance PLC offers you a 10% discount from your Contents and "All Risks" premium when your home is fitted with our required minimum level of security.  In order to qualify for this discount, the doors and accessible windows of your home must be fitted with the types of locks specified on pages 7 or 8.

If you live in Area J (see Postcode Table leaflet) your home must be fitted with, or you must agree to fit, this minimum level of protection in order for you to take out the Contents and "All Risks" section of this policy.

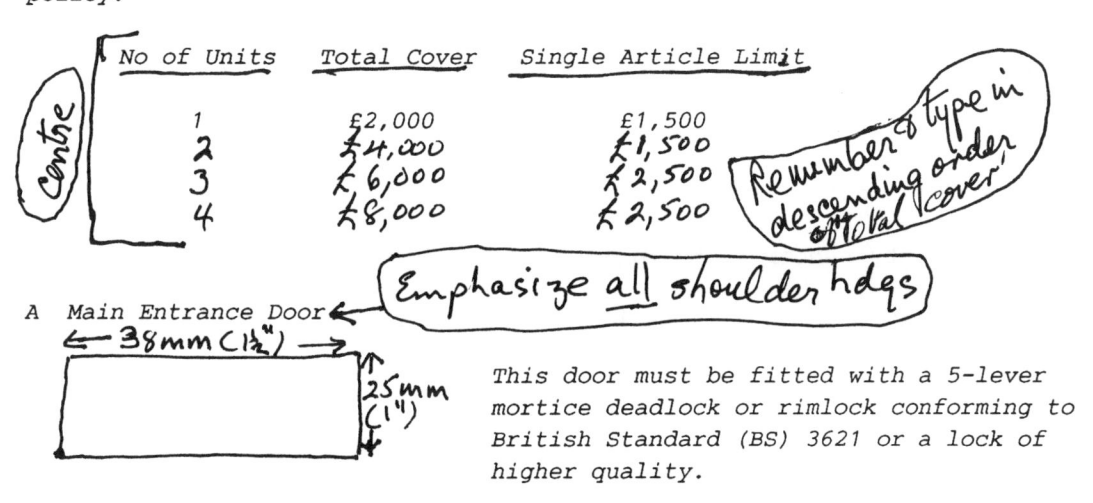

| No of Units | Total Cover | Single Article Limit |
|---|---|---|
| 4 | £8,000 | £2,500 |
| 3 | £6,000 | £2,500 |
| 2 | £4,000 | £1,500 |
| 1 | £2,000 | £1,500 |

**A   Main Entrance Door**

This door must be fitted with a 5-lever mortice deadlock or rimlock conforming to British Standard (BS) 3621 or a lock of higher quality.

**B   Other Single External Doors**

All of these doors must be fitted with either a mortice or rimlock as in A or with two key-operated mortice or rim-security bolts locking in to the door jamb and fitted one third from the top of the door and one third from the bottom of the door.  The keys must be removable.

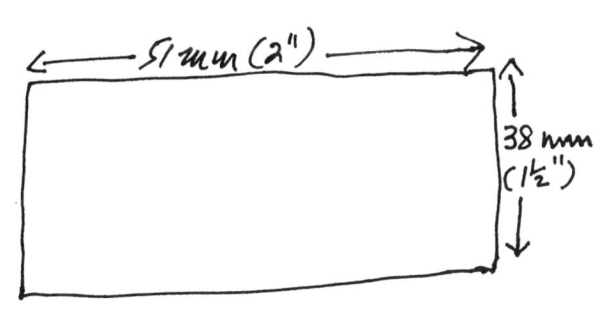

**C   French Doors or Windows**

All of these doors in your home must be fitted with the same type of key-operated mortice or rim-security bolts with removable keys.  If the discount on the security locks is allowed, the security devices must be used when the home is left unattended.

Family Legal Protection

Standard cover - £0.66 per month.
Super cover - £1.00 per month.

# PRODUCTION DEVELOPMENT

## Agreements

> See page **191**

**1** Type page 1 and page 4 of the following Agreement in double spacing. Take one copy.

THIS AGREEMENT is made the                     day of                     1994

BETWEEN CALUM ST ANDREW-GREGORY of 97 Highland Gateway Stirling FK8 4AA

KARIN ELIZABETH HENDERSON of 2 Falkland Road Stirling FK9 5LH aforesaid

(hereinafter called "the Trustees") of the one part and ALEXANDER BRUCE

MCKAY of The Higher Temple 14 Cyprus Road Stirling FK9 4EW (hereinafter

called "the Tenant") of the other part

W H E R E A S :-

(1)   The Trustees are the present trustees for the time being of the

Golden Citizens Association (hereinafter called "the Association")

(2)   By her Will dated 1 August 1993 Jean Grant Chisholm gave her

freehold property number 4 The Middles Stirling FK8 2RG (hereinafter

called "the said property") together with the furniture therein to the

Association for the sole use of Senior Citizens to live in the said

property free of rent

(3)   The said Jean Grant Chisholm died on the sixth day of January

1994

(4)   It has been agreed between the parties hereto that the Tenant

occupy the said property

NOW IT IS HEREBY AGREED as follows:-

1.   With effect from the sixth day of January 1995 the Tenant shall

occupy ALL THAT dwelling house garden and premises at Stirling in the

County of Stirlingshire and known as number 4 The Middles TOGETHER WITH

the carpets curtains furniture and household effects now in and about

the property upon the terms and conditions hereinafter mentioned

2.   The said carpets curtains furniture and household effects are

itemized in the schedule to this Agreement and the Trustees and the

Tenant hereby respectively testify that it is correct

- 1 -

**UNIT 16**                             ***Agreements***

4 — (15 mins)

Car Safety ← (Sp caps)

Park in well-lit areas at night & busy, public areas in day light- if poss.

↓

Before you leave the car unattended

↓

Close the windows ⟶ Close the sunroof

uc/ or hide them in the boot ← Remove valuables

↓

Remove ignition key

↓

Engage the steering lock

↓

Lock all doors ⟶ Lock the boot

Remember to retract the aerial. An extended aerial is an open invitation to vandals

# SKILL BUILDING

Type each line three times and, if time permits, complete your practice by typing each group once as it appears.

Margins:
12 pitch 22–82
10 pitch 12–72

### A  Keyboarding skills

1 Speed     John will write to you when he returns from a week in Spain.
2 Accuracy  Ask a knowledgeable consultant to explain computer software.
3 Figures   21 and 23 May 1987, 19 and 20 June 1988, 4 and 15 July 1969.
4 Symbols   4' 2" @ £9 (not £6).  I said, "Give Jones & Co 2% discount."

### Skill measurement                Five-minute timing                Not more than five errors

**S/M18** If you are not already in a full-time job, no doubt you are          12
thinking about your future career.  Like most of us who have                   24
gone through a similar stage of selecting and preparing for                    36
an occupation in business, you may be finding it difficult                     47
to make up your mind as to exactly what type of work you                       58
would like to do.  Whatever you decide, you can be certain                     70
that the method of using the skills required will change two                   82
or three times in your lifetime.                                               88

When I was a teenager forty years ago, the aim was to find                    100
a secure and permanent job, and if one even suggested a                       111
change of occupation from time to time, one would have been                   123
labelled a shiftless individual who would never be able to                    134
support himself/herself, to say nothing of supporting a                       145
family.  Now the general attitude of most people has changed                  157
completely, and it is not unusual for many people to change                   169
their minds about the kind of work they would like to do.                     180
Today, of course, there is a much greater variety of jobs                     192
from which to choose.                                                         196

The electronic office indicates that it would be unwise for                   208
workers to limit their thinking and not be able to adapt to                   220
the ever-changing technology.  The requirements of most jobs                  232
change rapidly and often, and people who are preparing for,                   244
or at present holding, one of these jobs, are expected to be                  256
willing and able to change their minds, adapt and prepare to                  268
use the new technology.                                                       273

Not much has changed about the kind of office tasks being                     285
carried out in offices today, but the kind of equipment                       296
that helps to make the job easier has changed tremendously.                   308
The improved equipment allows a business to streamline the                    320
flow of work and, at the same time, provides more efficient                   332
ways of completing the work.  The automated office of the                     343
future will bring a greater use of electronics — new and                      354
faster machines which, in most cases, will be easier to                       365
operate.  The majority of these machines will be designed to                  377
interact with each other and, therefore, bring much greater                   389
efficiency to all office work.                                                395
                                               (SI 1.41)

     1  |  2  |  3  |  4  |  5  |  6  |  7  |  8  |  9  |  10  |  11  |  12  |

5 — (10 mins) [TYPIST — Type the following info on a postcard & send it to Mr & Mrs Rollinson]

DID YOU KNOW?

- In the UK more than 1 million vehicles are stolen or broken into every yr.
- One in four cars that are reported missing is never recovered.
- The estimated annual loss to owners exceeds £260 m, & th is after ins claims hv bn settled.

[TYPIST. I have to check on this figure. Don't type it yet. I wl let you hv it shortly.]

6 (10 mins)

TYPIST — This memo is urgent. Could you type it quickly please with one copy, & let me hv it right away. It is to go to Rowland Towson. Tell him that I have noticed th our stock of the CONTENTS INSURANCE APPLICATION FORM (use as a hdg) is very depleted, so perhaps now is the time to think abt redesigning the form for the future. Ask him if he could give some thought to this matter — and then if he wld come & see me in my office at 1400 hrs on (I think 2 wks from today wd be suitable; check on the date and insert it ) — & bring any rough drafts he has made with him.
Just use my initials followed by your own for the ref; remember to type my name in full — & designation

(20 mins) (Headed paper)

Ref
(Turn up 2 single spaces here)                    Date as postmark

Dear (Leave blank)

INSURANCE ENQUIRY FORM

Before you complete the form below check that you comply with the following points:

(a) you require cover for the contents of yr home;
(b) the full replacement value of yr home contents is £35,000 or less;
(e) the home is NOT let, sub-let, by you;
(f) the home is yr permanent place of residence & not a holiday or weekend/weekday home.

(TYPIST (c) & (d) are in the Data Files (filename EURO) p 163. Please type them in the appropriate place.)

If you cannot confirm all of these points, our ins. is not suitable for yr requirements.

Yrs sinc


T R T ─────────

(TYPIST — Copy hdg here from letter & then display the following information clearly so th our prospective clients can complete it.)

Full Name ──────── Address ──────── Daytime tel no. ────

Occupation ──────── Age ──────── Full address of the property to be insured ──────── No of bedrooms in property to be insured ────

Signature ────────────        Date